FRANK H. UNDERHILL

Frank H. Underhill

Intellectual Provocateur

R. DOUGLAS FRANCIS

UNIVERSITY OF TORONTO PRESS

Toronto Buffalo London

ISBN 0-8020-2545-5

Printed on acid-free paper

Canadian Cataloguing in Publication Data

Francis, R. D. (R. Douglas), 1944–
Frank H. Underhill, intellectual provocateur
Bibliography: p.
Includes index.
ISBN 0-8020-2545-5
1. Underhill, Frank H., 1889–1971. 2. Historians –
Canada – Biography. 3. Socialists – Canada –
Biography. I. Title.
FC151.U53F73 1986 c.1 971'.007'2024   c86-093193-5
F1024.6.U53F73 1986

49,509

For my parents

Contents

Preface

Frank H. Underhill excelled in the role of intellectual provocateur, resisting the mainstream of popular thought, challenging a prevailing viewpoint, theory, or interpretation, and throwing out contentious ideas for debate. Believing that a professor had a responsibility to make a direct contribution to society, he became involved in controversial public affairs. He founded, along with Frank Scott, the League for Social Reconstruction, a 'brain trust' for the new CCF party in the 1930s; he actively participated in the CCF at a time when professorial involvement in politics was suspect, helped keep alive the *Canadian Forum* during the years of the Depression, and gave innumerable public speeches on an array of controversial subjects in an effort to reach an audience beyond the confines of the university. This 'reaching out' got Underhill into considerable controversy and dangerously close to losing his academic position in an age before academic freedom had become an established right.

Yet there was far more to the man than the public controversialist. For over half a century – from 1914 to 1971 – he carried on an active life of essay writing, public speaking, and university teaching in which he presented a novel view of Canadian history and politics. As a university history professor, he inspired a generation of young historians to rewrite their history; as a polemicist, he aroused public debate on issues that he believed should be of concern to Canadians; and as a man of ideas, he offered insight into the enigmas of Canadian politics, and an understanding of Canadian liberal, socialist, and conservative thought. This biography reviews the life and ideas of one of English Canada's most important thinkers and writers in the mid-twentieth century.

This book has been a long time in the making, and during that time I have benefited from the assistance and encouragement of a number of people. While all have assisted in some way, none can be held responsible for the final product. I would like to thank the archivists at the various archives listed in the

bibliographical note for their assistance, in particular, the Public Archives of
Canada, and the many people who consented to be interviewed about their
recollections and impressions of Frank Underhill. Blair Neatby gave permission
for me to examine the Underhill Papers and shared his views of Underhill with me.
The Underhill family – Frank, Ruth, and Betty (Harfenist) – were most
supportive, and I feel fortunate to have had the opportunity to interview Frank
Underhill once before his death. Duncan Meikle shared with me his research
material on Frank Underhill's early life. A number of people read parts or all of the
manuscript and provided me with constructive criticism: Jack Granatstein,
Michiel Horn, Paul Stevens, Barry Ferguson, and Donald Smith. Brayton Polka of
York University aroused my interest in intellectual history, while Jack Granatstein
suggested a study of Underhill's ideas for a doctoral dissertation. I am especially
indebted to Ramsay Cook, who directed my dissertation on Underhill, commented
on an early draft of the manuscript, and at all times offered support and
encouragement. Gila Wertheimer and Carol Gerein gave editorial assistance at an
early stage of the work, while Ramsay Derry made valuable structural changes to
the final draft. Florence Smith, and the secretarial staff at York University under
the direction of Doris Rippington, typed an earlier version of the manuscript
during a sabbatical year I spent at York University. The staff at McLaughlin
College, York University, provided me with office space and a pleasant
atmosphere during that year, and Douglas Baldwin offered his cottage one summer
while I worked on Underhill. At the University of Calgary I benefited from the
moral support of my colleagues in the history department, and from the cheerful
assistance of the secretarial staff who typed parts of the manuscript. Doreen
Nordquist typed the final version.

I wish to acknowledge the financial support of the Grants Committee of the
University of Calgary and of the Social Sciences and Humanities Research
Council to help cover the cost of research. This book has been published with the
help of a grant from the Social Science Federation of Canada, using funds provided
by the Social Sciences and Humanities Research Council of Canada, and a grant to
University of Toronto Press from the Andrew W. Mellon Foundation. At the
University of Toronto Press I wish to thank R.I.K. Davidson for his assistance in
guiding me through the various stages of publication, while Rosemary Shipton
provided her superb editorial expertise in bringing clarity to the final manuscript.

Above all, I owe an immeasurable debt of gratitude to my wife, Barbara, and to
our three children, Marc, Myla, and Michael, who have had to 'live with Frank
Underhill' for many years and who believed in me even when I doubted my ability
to finish the book. Finally, the dedication of this book to my parents is only a
partial expression of my deep affection for and gratitude to them.
RDF

The Underhill house,
82 O'Brien Street, Stouffville,
c 1891
Photo by W.D. Meikle
With one exception as noted, all illustrations are from the
F.H. Underhill Collection, Public Archives of Canada.

Richard and Sarah Underhill, with Frank and Isa, 1893
Photo by W.J. Mertens, Stouffville

Underhill at one year and, below, as a young boy

*Underhill (left), Carleton Stanley, and Charles Cochrane
on board the* ss Teutonic *bound for Oxford, September 1911*

Oxford scholar, 1914

In uniform, England 1916

Ruth Mary Carr around the time of her marriage
Courtesy Betty Harfenist

Underhill and his daughter Betty, Saskatoon, March 1927

*The Historical Association at the University of Saskatchewan, 1920–1
(Underhill, bottom left)*

*Executive of University College Literary and Athletic Society,
University of Toronto, c 1930 (Underhill, front centre)*

Frank and Ruth Underhill
at the Learned Societies meetings,
Quebec, June 1963

Curator of Laurier House, Ottawa, 1958
Photo by Newton, Ottawa

At Park Plaza, New York, 1961

FRANK H. UNDERHILL

1

A Gifted Child

On 26 November 1969 some hundred guests assembled at the Rideau Club in Ottawa to celebrate an eightieth birthday.[1] The most distinguished was Lester Pearson, recently retired as prime minister and now heading a commission for the World Bank. He came in his business suit (the invitation had said 'dress optional') and found himself surrounded, as he said, by 'socialists in dinner jackets': Frank Scott, King Gordon, Joseph Parkinson, Graham Spry, Escott Reid – all of whom had been involved in the League for Social Reconstruction in the 1930s. The other guests demonstrated the range of interests and friendships achieved by the guest of honour: politicians, journalists, businessmen, boyhood friends from Stouffville, professors and students from a number of Canadian universities.

The celebration had been organized by Blair Neatby, professor of history at Carleton University, who, together with Timothy Reid and Pauline Jewett, had selected the four guests who were to make speeches. The first was Hilda Neatby, who recalled her early years as a student of the guest of honour in his classes at the University of Saskatchewan. She chided him for being 'a stern critic' while praising him as an excellent teacher. 'No matter what a professor says, students know when they are respected.' The second speaker, Frank Scott, reminded the audience that they were 'celebrating the authenticity and vitality of a great mind,' especially on the subject of Canadian political life. Ramsay Cook followed Scott. Representing the younger generation of Canadian historians, Cook compared the guest of honour to the renowned American historian Frederick Jackson Turner in his ability to incite new ideas. 'The historical thinker is a fertile mind, evolving new interpretations and ideas. He delights in throwing off an abundance of suggestions. He hews to no one line.' The analogy was fitting; heads nodded in approval. Last to speak was Lester Pearson. He recalled the 'invective wit' that oozed from this writer's pen; he had helped to keep 'the Liberal Party on its toes for decades.'

The time had come for the guest of honour himself to speak. He needed no further introduction. The distinguished previous speakers had described his accomplishments, and they had alluded to his paradoxical nature. Long recognized as one of the finest and most influential university teachers of his era, he had several times been threatened with dismissal from his university. A leading historian and political scientist, he had completed no major work of scholarship. With a worthy army record in the First World War, he had later been reviled for expressing unpatriotic views. A founder of the CCF, he had subsequently become curator of the archives of the Liberal party. Despite these puzzling contradictions, no one at the dinner, and few members of the informed Canadian public, doubted the value of his contribution to Canadian intellectual and political life through his critical thinking, speaking, writing, and teaching over the past half century. The master of ceremonies simply rose and announced Frank Hawkins Underhill.

Amid the applause, there rose a slim and frail individual of short stature, bald-headed and round-faced with horn-rimmed glasses which revealed sparkling blue eyes. In customary fashion he took some brief notes from his vest pocket, shifted nervously, and embarked on a sketch of his life history: *Apologia Pro Vita Sua* or 'The Education of Frank Underhill.'

Eighty years earlier, 26 November 1889, in the apartment above their shoe store in Stouffville, Ontario, Richard and Sarah Underhill were celebrating the birth of their first child, a boy. They had decided to christen him Frank Hawkins Underhill. 'Frank' was the name of his godfather, a local lawyer friend of the family; 'Hawkins' the maiden name of his grandmother Underhill.

Frank's grandfather, Richard John Underhill, had been the first in his family to become a shoemaker. Born in December 1824, the son of a farm labourer in Dorset, England, he had apprenticed with a cobbler in Shebbear, a small town near Plymouth, and had become a master, which entitled him to set up his own business and to work for shoemaker's wages. In 1849 he married Susanna Hawking (later changed to Hawkins) who was a glover by trade. They subsequently moved to Plymouth where Richard John was in business for about fifteen years. The couple had six children. Richard junior, Frank's father, was the fourth, born in 1857. In 1867 Richard John and Susanna and their children emigrated to Canada and settled in Toronto. At first, Richard John worked for the Dack, Forsythe and Leslie Company, the eighth largest shoe-manufacturing firm in Toronto. Then in 1870 he moved to Brougham, a small town some twenty miles northeast of Toronto, and a decade later established an independent boot and shoe shop in nearby Markham.[2]

Two of his sons, Richard, junior, and Fred, carried on the family business.[3] In 1884, at the age of twenty-seven Richard, junior, established his own specialty boot and shoe shop on Main Street in Stouffville, a thriving Ontario village of some 900 people with a grist mill and harness factory, a tannery, a foundry, and a cabinet-making business, some thirty miles northeast of Toronto.[4]

Toronto dominated the economic and cultural life of Stouffville. It supplied the village with its manufactured good, its swelling population on market day, and its only major newspaper with national and international news coverage, the *Globe*. Some villagers resented this hinterland dependency and looked back with pride on the support that Stouffville had given William Lyon Mackenzie in the rebellion of 1837. Others, like Richard Underhill, appreciated the importance of the interrelationship for village trade.

Richard Underhill's shoe business was an immediate success. In the assessment roll of 1888 his store was valued at $900 and his personal property at an additional $500. A shrewd man of business, he had bought land in the surrounding area of Stouffville as well. By 1889, he was sufficiently secure financially to provide for a wife and a family. He married Sarah Monkhouse, the oldest daughter of Thomas and Isabella Monkhouse of Altona, a village three miles east of Stouffville.

Thomas Monkhouse, his brother, and, later, their parents, had immigrated from Carlisle in the north of England in 1849. The family's general store in Altona, which had opened in 1850, was noted 'not only for its large stock of drygoods and groceries, but especially because it carried the largest stock of delftware in the district. The whole of the upper flat of the large building was transformed into a veritable "China Hall."' Thomas's first wife was Isabella McFarlane from Uxbridge, Ontario, by whom he had six children, including Frank's mother, Sarah, who was the oldest. Isabella died in 1874 and two years later Thomas married her sister Jane McFarlane. The McFarlanes, from Aberdeen, Scotland, were staunch Presbyterians and the Underhill family's affiliation with the Presbyterian church came from the McFarlane branch of the family.[5] Sarah was born in Altona on 15 June 1864. She attended the local public school but her education was cut short by the sudden death of her mother. At the age of ten, she assumed motherly responsibility for her five brothers and sisters, the last child, Sophia, being born in the year of her mother's death. Two years later her father remarried, and there were three children by this marriage. Sarah's stepmother, Aunt Jane, relieved her of the responsibility of looking after the children alone, but Sarah never returned to school. She always felt grieved at this and was to project onto her children the importance of schooling that had been denied to her.

In 1890, a year after Frank was born, Richard had built a magnificent, three-story, brick, Victorian-style house with spacious rooms, a large ornately decorated verandah on the front, and a smaller one on the side. It provided evidence of middle-class affluence in a village that judged success in material terms. As a young child Frank enjoyed exploring the numerous nooks and crannies in the large house at 82 O'Brien Street and considered the third floor his domain, where he played with his sets of toy soldiers. As he grew older he was allowed to play with the boys on his street but was not to associate with the rough and boisterous boys along Main Street. Most of the time he preferrred his own company; he was an excessively shy boy. When he did venture into the community he gravitated to adults who would answer his numerous questions or listen to his ideas. He enjoyed train trips to Toronto with his mother to shop at Eatons's or Simpson's, and especially with his father when he went on business. Toronto was an exciting city that opened up a new world beyond the confines of a small Ontario village.

Most of his early life centred on Stouffville. His parents were hard-working people who took little time for pleasure. Six days a week were devoted to work and household chores, while Sundays were spent going to church and visiting nearby relatives – particularly the Monkhouses, whom Frank came to know better and to enjoy more than the Underhills. Frank acquired from his parents an appreciation for hard work and self-discipline; it would be other adult friends who would teach him the only sports he would learn: tennis and swimming. His parents were strict, particularly his mother, who was the disciplinarian in the family. Frank and his sister Isa, who was born in 1891, were expected to be well behaved, since their manners reflected their upbringing.[6]

In September 1895 Frank entered Stouffville Public School. From the beginning he was singled out as a precocious child. His teacher, Elsie Hawthorne, let him advance at his own pace and he finished six years in five. The greatest pleasure of public school was to learn to read. Reading opened up a new world of exotic places and exciting ideas. At first he read romance stories and the Henty novels, which told of daring feats and noble acts of courage by Anglo-Saxon heroes saving the empire in the distant corners of the world. Then he became interested in popular history books. An aunt gave him Charles Dicken's *A Child's History of England* as a graduation gift from public school, and Underhill claimed in later life that Dicken's history 'cured him of his romantic view of the monarchy.' Frank's public school graduation gift to himself was a membership in the Stouffville Public Library which provided a wider range of books.

Evenings and weekends found Frank absorbed in a book. Being smaller than the other boys his age and not particularly good in competitive sports, he avoided getting involved. He got the reputation of being a bookworm, and was conscious of being different and better intellectually than his peers by his greater perception, quickness of mind, and the depth and breadth of his knowledge. From an early age he stood apart.

His early religious upbringing reinforced this aloofness. His family was Presbyterian, and Frank inherited the Calvinist concept of the elect or chosen. He grew up believing that Presbyterians were superior because they displayed no outward show of emotion as did the Baptists and Methodists with their 'evangelical meetings.' Nor did they need to rely on social position for their feeling of self-importance, as the Anglicans did. Presbyterians had that instinctive sense of 'uncertain certainty,' that inherent belief in their own righteousness and self-worth.

In his formative years Frank's Presbyterian upbringing was pervasive. Religion was an integral part of his life. His mother was a regular church-goer, and Frank attended both church and Sunday school. He performed the expected tasks of reciting by heart the Presbyterian creed and memorizing the books of the Bible. But he was soon questioning his faith. He was troubled by his doubts about the historical accuracy of Genesis and was relieved when the minister told him to think of the creation story in terms of allegory. He was also impressed at an early age by the independent views of his father, James Hand, the school principal, and Walter Sangster, the local doctor. The three would walk out of church at communion time because they were not certain enough about Presbyterian beliefs to participate in this most holy of religious acts. Thus, at an early age, Underhill perceived religion as something to question and challenge like any other belief and not merely to accept as sacrosanct. Still, it was his Presbyterian faith with its puritanical strain and rigorous life-style – that 'perseverance of the saint' – that instilled in him the need to do something meaningful with his life. 'I was born,' he recalled, 'with this native feeling that if you don't keep a tight hold on yourself you'll never accomplish anything ... To waste your energy on what seems to be a dissolute life never attracted me.'

Religion was one important subject in young Frank's early life; politics was the other. He lived in a politically conscious household. His first impressions were of events rather than of people or ideas. There were, for example, the vivid recollections in later life of the picture of the first Laurier cabinet on the dining-room wall, next to the one of Wilfrid Laurier with his characteristic smile as he was being knighted at Queen Victoria's Diamond Jubilee; both pictures were gifts of the Toronto *Globe* to their subscribers. He remembered the numerous casual conversations between his parents at the dinner table about good or bad politicians; the discussions village politicians had over a glass of whisky in the back room of his father's store (drink was forbidden in the Underhill house); the town meetings with lists of grievances from tariffs to taxes, political patronage to local improvements; or his father's political speeches in support of local Grit candidates. Among Liberal organizers Richard Underhill had the reputation of a 'no-nonsense speaker who [could] hand it straight to a few chattering tories.'[7] He was also responsible for visiting recalcitrant Liberals in the region at election time. It mystified Frank how, in elections by secret ballot, his father was so uncannily accurate in picking out the 'dissenters' in the town. It was small-town politics in which the stakes were never high – nor were the political ideas. Underhill recalled that his father's chief worry during the great Liberal election celebration of 1896, when Wilfrid Laurier first came to office, was whether 'George Kemp, the village butcher and a Tory, might refuse to pound the big brass drum in the band in the Liberal victory parade' down Main Street in a candlelight procession to the village fairground.

It was the Toronto *Globe*, 'the Scotsman's Bible,' that opened up for young Frank a political world beyond Stouffville and even Canada. He read glowing accounts of Victoria's Diamond Jubilee in 1897 and eagerly collected the Canadian commemorative stamps. He knew about the American invasion of Cuba and the Philippines in 1898 and re-enacted the fighting in the street battles with his friends.[8] He watched local volunteers drill in the village square to become soldiers in the Queen's infantry for the Boer War, and he listened attentively to first-hand accounts of the fighting from a former Stouffville student, Chester McClelland, when he returned from South Africa. To Frank, the Victorian era seemed the best of all possible worlds with Britannia ruling the waves and the Laurier Liberals ruling Canada. He maintained in later life that 'he or she who was not born soon enough to grow up in that delectable quarter century before 1914 can never know what the sweetness of life is.'[9]

In 1901 Frank entered his first year at Markham High School. Markham was a short train trip from Stouffville and had the only high school for the rural communities from northern Toronto to Uxbridge and Aurora east to Pickering Township. Frank's public school principal, James Hand, had primed his prize student for the Markham High School entrance examinations by drilling him after school. Frank enjoyed the attention and the added challenge, and he had responded well. In the spring examinations of 1901, he had scored 967 marks out of a possible 1100, 'the highest honour ever given to a Markham High School pupil' – and this at the young age of eleven.[10] At high school Frank excelled in all his subjects, but he liked mathematics best because of the sheer enjoyment of working out abstract problems. His science teacher, Fletcher Calvert, desperately tried to turn him into a botanist. Calvert and he became close friends (a friendship that lasted a lifetime) and spent summer holidays together doing science experiments at a makeshift laboratory at Calvert's summer cottage at Pleasant Point on Lake Simcoe. But it would be the principal, George Reed, who would decide Frank's academic future. A graduate of the University of Toronto honour classics program, Reed maintained that Frank's 'future duty was to go to University College to take Greek with Maurice Hutton,' professor of classics and co-founder, along with George Wrong, of the Toronto honour classics program.

In 1905 Frank received first-class honours in the junior matriculation examinations and was awarded the McCaul Scholarship and the Moss Scholarship, both for classics at Toronto. He could have gone to university at this time, but Principal Reed advised him to stay on an extra year, since at the age of fifteen he was too young for university, to prepare for the senior matriculation examinations. Frank ended up spending two extra years. In the first year he received matriculation standing in Greek, adding to his previous firsts in Latin, French, and German, and also passed his senior teacher's examination. By the end of the second year he was ready to take the summer entrance examinations in July 1907.

He expanded his intellectual horizons during his high school years by reading widely, particularly on current events in the popular American magazines – *Saturday Evening Post* and *Harpers*. Though primarily yellow journalism, these magazines had occasional articles on the American progressive revolt led by the noted muckrakers Ida Tarbell, Lincoln Steffens, and Upton Sinclair, with their fight for social justice and humanitarian causes. He pictured them as the modern-day equivalent of the Puritans and Cavaliers of the English Civil War that he knew so well from J.R. Green's *A Short History of the English People*, a history textbook that he used for two consecutive years. At an early age he accepted without question that radicals were better than reactionaries and Liberals superior to the Tories – radicals and Liberals being synonymous in his mind. It was the Liberal view of progress in a world of unlimited possibilities.

Frank's father was certainly progressing in politics and in business in the Liberal heyday of prosperity at the turn of the century. He became a village councillor and then reeve in 1903. In the same year he helped arrange a visit to the village by Sir Wilfrid Laurier, as part of a tour of the region. Frank enjoyed the opportunity of seeing Laurier, who had become his political hero. Then in 1904 Richard sold his shoe shop in Stouffville to go into partnership with his brother, Fred, and Thomas Sisman, a Toronto superintendent of a shoe business who had moved to North York in the 1890s, in a shoe-manufacturing outfit in Aurora. The partnership was part of a large-scale expansion of the business which would increase its value to $40,000, its employees to 200 people, and its output from 600 pairs of shoes a day to 1500. Richard put up $20,000 and became secretary-treasurer of the company. The Underhill-Sisman Company remained in business for five years, at which time both Fred and Richard decided to sell their shares. Richard got $25,000 back, an increase of $5000 over five years – a substantial monetary return at the turn of the century.[11]

During his high school years Frank spent his time reading and taking the occasional short trip with school chums. His parents did not want him to work, so he had ample time for leisure activities. They encouraged him in intellectual pursuits in every way possible: discussing ideas with him, encouraging him in school, and exposing him to books. He set himself the ambitious task one summer of reading a set of books on world literature purchased by his father from an itinerant book salesman. He was impressed with *Hours in a Library* and *Studies of a Biographer*, both by Leslie Stephen, the British essayist and noted freethinker. Another summer he made a train trip to Buffalo and to the Thousand Islands, the farthest he had ever been from home. The remainder of his time was spent playing tennis or swimming and learning to play the piano, at which he received a pass in

his junior piano examination and then lost interest. In the final summer of his high
school years he studied with Fletcher Calvert at his cottage in preparation for those
all-important university entrance examinations.

Frank approached the examinations nervous but confident. He had studied hard
and had been encouraged by parents, friends, and teachers; their reputation was at
stake as much as his. In the end he came through as expected. The headline in the
Toronto *World*, 'Results of the Examinations and Awards – Underhill of Markham
in Forefront,' attested to his outstanding performance. He stood first in the
province. He was reawarded the McCaul Scholarship, which entitled him to 'free
tuition for four years and a cash prize of $75 so long as he registered in the Classics
Programme at University College.' He received, in addition, the Prince of Wales
Scholarship and the highest award granted at the University of Toronto – the
Edward Blake General Proficiency Scholarship for top grades in a variety of
subjects. He stood first in classics, modern languages, mathematics, Greek, Latin,
and English: ironically, he came only sixth in history. The gifted boy from
Stouffville, 'an unassuming chap ... [who] bears his honors with due humility,'[12]
already had made a mark in life.

2

Student Days at the
University of Toronto

Frank Underhill was a shy lad of seventeen when he entered University College at the University of Toronto in the fall of 1907. His knowledge of the institution came chiefly from George Reed, whose enthusiasm for the university and the honour classics program had intimidated as much as encouraged him. Despite his outstanding grades, Underhill wrote to Malcolm Wallace, the registrar, to enquire about enrolling only in the honour program of English and history with the classical option in his first year and then transferring the following year to honour classics. Wallace calmed his doubts: 'you will probably not find it a very difficult matter to carry both during the first year.'[1]

Other students had to struggle with the normal frustrations of figuring out timetables, getting acquainted with the layout of the campus, and taking the first nervous step of meeting professors, but not Frank. Principal Reed had introduced him to James Brebner, the registrar of the University of Toronto and the father of Bartlet Brebner, who in turn took him through the registration procedure, familiarized him with the campus, and personally introduced him to each of his professors.

Settling in the city was difficult. Boarding was a lonely experience, and Frank was homesick. On weekends he escaped to the security of Stouffville. His parents decided, as a result, to sell their house and move to Toronto so that Frank could continue his education in comfort. It was a major decision and a tremendous adjustment for the family. His father had to commute daily by radial car to Aurora, some fifteen miles north of Toronto; his mother had to adjust to city living and a new circle of friends; and his sister had to attend a strange school in her final year. But no sacrifice was too great for Frank's education.

The Underhills moved into a large three-storey brick house at 479 Palmerston Boulevard near the corner of Bathurst and Bloor streets, a substantial and respectable area of the city. It was a fifteen-minute walk to the campus, and Frank was able to come home for lunch. While living at home provided comfort, it restricted his socializing and retarded a feeling of independence. His parents, for example, forbade him to go to shows, theatre, or dances since they frowned on these frivolous and ungodly activities. His University of Toronto days greatly expanded his intellectual horizons but did less to develop his social skills.

The year 1907 inaugurated a new era in the history of the university.[2] In the previous year a university commission had brought in the University Act which ended a period of direct government control by placing the university under an appointed Board of Governors responsible for overseeing the financial and administrative well-being of the university and for uniting the affiliated colleges more intimately into the university as a whole. To launch the bold experiment a new president, the Reverend Robert Falconer, was appointed in 1907. His presidential regime would span a quarter of a century, and Underhill would come to know him from the perspective of both an undergraduate and much later a professor in the university. From both vantage-points he had the highest regard for Falconer's abilities as an intellectual and an administrator.

The university was also witnessing the first substantial increase in student enrolment. From 1906 to 1908 the number of students jumped by 40 per cent from 2500 to 3500. Prosperity and an increasing demand for better-educated students, particularly in the professions, put pressures on the university to take in more students than it could accommodate and to accept students who in the past would not qualify for entrance. As a good student, Underhill felt the negative repercussions of these changes. He resented the large classes in his first two years which prevented him from getting to know his professors. He complained too about poorer students who robbed a class of valuable time for dealing with challenging issues by having the professor go over straightforward material.

It had been predetermined by Reed that Underhill enter University College, but it was a wise and obvious choice. The largest of the colleges, it was associated in most people's minds as *the* University of Toronto. The name implied such an identity. It was the provincial college, and the only one without religious affiliation, a result of Egerton Ryerson's decision, as superintendent of education in the 1840s, to establish a non-sectarian form of education. Its long affiliation with the university, and its list of distinguished alumni – including Edward Blake, Stephen Leacock, and William Lyon Mackenzie King – gave the college a prominent academic position. University College students, including Underhill, considered their college the best, and looked down on students from other colleges.

Underhill was equally conscious of being among the elite as a student in the combined honour program: classics, and English and history with the classical option, the quintessence of liberal arts education at Toronto. Honour classics was chiefly the work of Maurice Hutton, professor of classics from 1880 to 1928. His aim was to make honour classics at Toronto the Canadian equivalent of Oxford 'Greats,' a program that Hutton knew and respected as one of its graduates.[3]

Hutton formed part of a long line of Canadian academics who saw the university as a haven from the materialism and vulgarity of life. His famous aphorism – 'Our annals are dull as ditch-water, and our politics are full of it' – captured his feeling precisely. Underhill would quote it throughout his life as an insightful comment. Hutton feared that the university would become a victim of modern society, and so emphasized in his speeches and writings that its only concerns should be scholarship and teaching.[4] He saw classics as a vital and alive subject which was still relevant in the modern world. Half a century later Underhill expressed the same opinion of classics: '[T]here has never been any university discipline that can be compared for its effect in awakening the mind of a young student with that which sets him to study the Classical Hellenic civilization and which introduces him to modern political ideas when they were still fresh, when they occurred for the first time in human history to the minds of the Greeks of the sixth and fifth centuries B.C., before they had been devitalized by all the jargon which historians and political scientists and sociologists have piled up around them since.'[5]

There were two principles underlying the classics program. One was the need to know the languages – Greek and Latin – thoroughly, before going on to the more rewarding task of discussing the ideas in the classical texts. To Underhill, this was a weakness of the program; so much time was spent on translation and style that professors never got around to discussing ideas. The other principle was to complement the study of texts by learning the historical context in which the texts were written through a study of ancient history. Underhill agreed. He would use the same approach when teaching British and Canadian history.

Underhill's other honour program, English and history with the classical option, was equally as revered as classics; it also had a similar approach: the study of great literary texts in conjunction with the history. It was the brain-child of William J. Alexander of the English department and George M. Wrong of the history department. Alexander, who had been appointed professor of English literature in University College in 1889, was one of Toronto's most respected professors. He had the ability to excite students, particularly gifted students, about the importance of literature as a creative art in which truth was presented in poetic form. For Alexander, the aim of honour English and history was to introduce students to good literature through an appreciation of the original texts, by showing the ideas in the texts to be an embodiment of the views of a particular era which itself was but part of a continuum of great English literature from ancient times to the present.[6] George Wrong decided the history component of the combined honours program. The son-in-law of Edward Blake, one-time chancellor of the university, he had come to history through theology. He was committed to making history a respectable and independent discipline by creating a separate department and by developing its own methodology and form of inquiry. Yet he also saw history as being closely allied to literature and classics, and so readily agreed to support the English and history honour program as long as it was modelled on Oxford 'Greats.'[7] Wrong drew inspiration and guidance from Oxford. The majority of his department members were selected from its halls of learning, and teaching was conducted on the Oxford style. Wrong proudly informed George Parkin, the administrator of the Rhodes Trust, in 1911 how far Toronto had advanced along Oxford lines: 'We are rapidly adopting the Oxford tutorial method. Slight stress is placed upon lectures and every week we meet all the Honour men in small group classes where essays are read, and criticism and discussion follow.'[8]

Wrong adhered to the British belief that scholars had a right to express opinions on current affairs in order to guide public opinion. To him, the role of university education was to produce an elite of educated and informed students prepared to assume positions of responsibility as public servants – a view Underhill also came to share. Wrong also wanted to cultivate friendships in high places, among members of the 'best classes' in Canadian society. He believed that a good intellectual should be a man of influence, holding a position to affect the decisions of politicians and businessmen. Wrong worked assiduously to widen his range of influential friends, and in so doing helped forge a link between the university and the public which made the concept of 'the ivory tower' meaningless. Many of Frank Underhill's early acquaintances with businessmen came through Wrong, particularly as a result of membership in the Historical Club in his third and fourth year.

In the first year of the combined honour program the emphasis in both options was on ancient history and classical texts. This was natural in honour classics, but it was equally true in honour English and history because the course took a chronological approach, beginning with ancient history in first year, medieval in second, early modern in third, and modern in fourth. Thus, in first year he was getting a thorough grounding in the languages, literature, and history of Greece and Rome. He was also being exposed to some of the great classics scholars at Toronto, people who would be instrumental in his intellectual development, such as William Milner and Maurice Hutton.

He was greatly disappointed in his first year. There were few opportunities for a shy student like himself to develop or display his intellectual abilities in large classes. His essays were being marked by women instructors, rather than by the professors, who he felt were unappreciative of his approach and ideas. He disliked the emphasis in the classics courses on grammatical structure through short weekly translation exercises of Latin and Greek prose. He preferred reflecting on the beauty and symmetry of the prose or on the ideas of the authors being translated.

Still, he stood first in both honour programs.[9] He claimed in later life that a good student would do well no matter how poor the opportunities, but would also have agreed that good teachers could help a student to develop his ideas and express himself.

Hard work became for Frank an escape from social obligations. He preferred burying himself in a book to meeting students in a club. He refused to join a fraternity because the 'snobbish' nature of the students who belonged. He believed he was one of the poorer students at the university, although there is no evidence to justify this status. He longed to be part of that inner circle of select students, such as Vincent Massey and Murray Wrong, son of George Wrong, both from prominent and well-to-do Toronto families, who had a decided advantage simply on the basis of wealth.[10] It was not their money that he envied but their social ease and cultured ways. He knew that he would have to achieve recognition the hard way: by the strength of his intellect rather than the power of his purse.

Second year was better. For one thing, he had more stimulating classes. He especially enjoyed Alexander's lectures on Shakespeare. He recalled coming out of those lectures 'walking on air.' 'He was the only professor of whom I was really afraid, because his judgement and his taste seemed so superior to my own. I was certainly a conceited young man.' He had Professor Wrong in British constitutional history. While disappointed in Wrong's lectures – disorganized, rambling, and factual – he was impressed with the personal interest that Wrong took in the promising students in the class. He enjoyed Medieval European history as well with Edward Kylie, associate professor and second-in-command to Wrong. He took a psychology course as an alternative to religious study. This enabled him to be absent from morning prayers and religious exercises, something he had not particularly enjoyed in first year.

He was going through a transitional period in his views on religion. He was still a practising Presbyterian, attending either Sunday morning or evening services at College Street Presbyterian Church with his parents. He joined the university YMCA for both religious and social reasons, and consented to be a member of the executive.[11] The club held monthly study groups on religious topics conducted by theology professors from Knox. These he found stimulating and informative, but he was becoming more discerning in his views of religion, more capable of separating religion as a faith from religion as an intellectual discipline. He had less interest in the former and more enthusiasm for the latter. Religion needed to be discussed rationally like any other subject, and he was better able to appreciate this need as he took a critical look at great thinkers in the past who were religiously influenced. Still, he was not yet prepared to move to an agnostic position. His ambivalent position was characteristic of students of his generation who were going through a period of healthy scepticism.[12]

He did well in his second-year courses but fell to second-place standing overall, losing out to Carleton Stanley of Victoria College in both honour programs. Accustomed to being first in his class, he was obviously disappointed. Fletcher Calvert, his former high school teacher, bolstered his morale by assuring him that a good summer of daily studying at the cottage would enable him 'to trim' his opponent next year.[13]

The turning-point in Underhill's undergraduate days came in third year. Classes were small enough to conduct tutorials, while some courses were strictly seminar courses based on readings, discussions, and student reports. His most enjoyable course was a seminar on 'Milton and his Age' offered by Malcolm Wallace of the English department. Wallace was a protégé of Alexander's, and Alexander considered the appointment of Wallace to the staff to be his 'greatest service to University College.'[14] Wallace was particularly good at drawing out diffident students. In his teaching he stressed ethical and political concerns when discussing the classical texts of the seventeenth century. Such an approach appealed to young Underhill.

In the seminar each student had to report on the ideas of one of Milton's contemporaries. Underhill decided, because of his interest in history, on Clarendon's *History of the Great Rebellion*. He began reading three or four volumes of the work, but found it heavy and dull. He knew that he could never show his true abilities if he stuck to Clarendon. Mustering up courage, he went to Wallace to see if he could switch topics. Fortunately, a woman in the class had made a similar complaint about Thomas Hobbes, and Wallace asked Underhill if he would like to switch to Hobbes. Underhill knew nothing about Hobbes, but felt any subject would be better than Clarendon. When he read the *Leviathan*, he experienced something akin to religious conversion; Underhill claimed he was never the same afterwards. Hobbes 'swept me off my feet,' he recalled. 'It was a landmark in my intellectual progress,' the beginning of a lifetime interest in the study of the history of political thought.[15] He wrote a first-rate paper for the seminar in which he received a grade of 90.[16] What he particularly liked about Hobbes's writing was its iconoclastic thrust, which he found a relief from the 'obscurity of those idealists' of his day. To this brilliant but shy university student, Hobbes's *Leviathan* revealed the power of the mind, the ability to persuade people to a point of view solely on the basis of the logic, precision, and persuasiveness of the argument. When Underhill finished reading his paper in the seminar, Wallace remarked: 'Well, Underhill, you must have got a lot of enjoyment from writing that essay.' Indeed he did, so much so that he followed up the subject with a second paper that year comparing 'Hobbes and Milton' and a third paper in fourth year on Thomas Hobbes and Edmund Burke.

Underhill's fourth year was even more rewarding. Now he knew where he stood on important issues, and he was able to judge critically the individuals he was studying. In his fourth-year English seminar on 'Nineteenth Century Thought' he disliked the moralistic preachings of Cardinal Newman, Thomas Carlyle, and

John Ruskin, while revelling in the emancipated secular writings of Matthew Arnold and John Stuart Mill. He discovered from reading W.E.H. Lecky's famous chapter 'The Rise of Evangelical Christianity' that he was not meant to be an evangelical Christian. In fact, he had become a confirmed agnostic, particularly after reading Leslie Stephen's delightful study *An Agnostic's Apology*. Agnosticism was, for Underhill, a logical position of a process of critical thinking about religion first initiated by those agonizing doubts as a young boy in Stouffville. The decision created no great trauma; it was a natural progression of his views. It was also characteristic of this age of religious emancipation.

He did two papers for this fourth-year seminar. One compared the ideas of two men whose writings he greatly enjoyed, Thomas Hobbes and Edmund Burke, in which he judged them as 'Guides to Modern Democracy.' It was a splendid essay: critical in approach, balanced in judgment, perceptive in its commentary, and cogent in style. It revealed four years of intellectual maturity. The other paper dealt with the ideas of John Stuart Mill, in which he showed them to be an outgrowth of Utilitarianism, placed them in the context of the time, judged their value for the present, and weighed their strengths and limitations. This second paper served another purpose. Each year the English department offered the Frederick Wyld Prize, valued at $75, to the student who wrote the best competition essay. In 1910 the selected topic was the poetry of Robert Browning. Underhill was determined to land the prize, but Browning's poetry left him uninspired and devoid of ideas. Observing in the calendar that a contestant might suggest an alternative subject, he went to Alexander to seek permission to do another topic. Alexander agreed, and suggested that Underhill expand his seminar paper on Mill as his submission. It won the prize. In later life he seemed to recall that he was the only one who had submitted an essay for the competition. Anyway, he immediately went out and used the prize money to purchase the complete works of Matthew Arnold and John Morley.

The history component in fourth year was supposed to cover British and European history, but in practice it concentrated on British imperial history because that was Wrong's particular interst. A group of keen students were interested in learning Canadian history, a neglected subject at Toronto, and persuaded Kenneth Bell, a visiting professor and Brakenbury scholar of Balliol, Oxford, to offer a seminar. He agreed. The course dealt with constitutional history in the context of imperial history, with the emphasis on the post-Conquest era, particularly the evolution from colony to nation. It was Underhill's first real exposure to Canadian history.

His other memorable fourth-year course was a seminar in classics with William S. Milner. A graduate of the Toronto classics program, Milner specialized in Aristotle's *Politics* and Cicero's *Letters*, both of which he used as a means to get at the broader issues of Athenian democracy and Roman imperialism, which in turn were political theories which could be related to contemporary political concerns.

Here was the opportunity Underhill had been wanting for three years: to discuss the political thought of the Greeks and Romans.

By the end of his fourth year Underhill had proved to be well in advance of most of his fellow students. He could think critically and discernibly about the ideas of the intellectuals he was studying; he had the ability to express his thought cogently and clearly; and already he had the rudiments of his own political philosophy. It was that of a liberal democrat, premised on a deep faith in the essential goodness and rationality of man and on the freedom of the individual. Underhill disliked Hobbes's negative view of human nature as inherently evil even while admiring this philosopher's iconoclastic writings and logical mind. If men showed evidence of being selfish creatures, Underhill conceded, their selfishness did not predominate over all other characteristics in the simple and absolute way Hobbes set forth. Equally, it was John Stuart Mill's inherent faith in the individual as the foundation of liberal democracy that made him Underhill's intellectual hero.

Underhill judged any proposed form of government on the extent to which it would maximize the freedom of the people under it. Thus he opposed Hobbes's faith in the sovereign's right to absolute rule, and drew a parallel (as he did in his thinking about each one of these earlier political philosophers, believing their message transcended time) to those individuals in his day who believed in the omnipotence of parliament or of a compact cabinet, or those socialists who believed in the supremacy of the state over that of the individuals who made up the state. Underhill was conscious of current British socialist thinking and sympathetic to the need for liberals to be more cognizant of the virtues of economic collectivism to strengthen democratic liberalism in the twentieth century, as expressed by L.T. Hobhouse in his classic text *Liberalism*. But equally he was fearful of the inherent danger of excessive power in the hands of any ruler or government bureaucracy in a socialist state. This dilemma would plague him for the remainder of his life.

Underhill had also opened up socially by fourth year. On the advice of his professors he had joined a number of clubs in an effort to overcome his shy and retiring nature. He joined the Letters Club, a literary society presided over by his student colleagues Vincent Massey and Murray Wrong, and presented a paper on 'The Philosophy of Thackeray' at one of the meetings. He also became president of the Classics Club. But his greatest pleasure came from membership in the Historical Club. Founded by George Wrong in 1904, it consisted of twenty-five selected students who met eight times a year at the home of an influential Toronto businessman or intellectual. The aim of the club was to cultivate an elite of promising students by encouraging them to develop their intellectual skills through presenting papers and debating such subjects as European diplomacy, service reform, imperialism, and municipal government, while at the same time fostering social skills through exposure to the intellectual, political, and business leaders of the country. Underhill remembered one meeting in 1910 when Sir John Willison, then editor of the Toronto *News* but previously editor of the *Globe*, remarked that there was no difference between Canadian Liberals and Conservatives, except that one happened to be in office and the other out of office; and another evening when Kenneth Bell challenged the host in a heated debate. 'The spectacle of a young history lecturer actually questioning the judgement of a leading business tycoon was another subversive experience in my young life,' he recalled some years later.

At two meetings Underhill presented papers: one on 'Lloyd George's Budget and the Land Tax,' the other on 'Commission Government in Cities.' He spent more time researching these papers than he did class essays. For the one on Lloyd George's budget he searched the files on *The Times* of London and various English journals to find evidence to support his thesis that Lloyd George's 1908 budget was a radical departure in English liberal thought towards a more socialist position. For the other on 'Commission Government in Cities' he read American progressive literature to learn about scientific government of modern cities, and also wrote to various municipal governments for information. This latter paper became Underhill's first published work when it appeared in the April 1911 edition of *The Arbor*, a high-quality student periodical founded by Vincent Massey the previous year. The paper greatly impressed Edward Kylie. He invited Frank to luncheon at the National Club with a group of civic reform leaders and academics who were attempting to get municipal housing started in Toronto. Underhill was flattered, but was so intimidated by these businessmen that he remained silent throughout the meeting, too nervous to express an opinion.

At the end of his four years at the University of Toronto Underhill had an overview of the history of Western civilization from ancient times to the present, along with an in-depth knowledge of the ideas of the major thinkers within that tradition. He had improved his writing style markedly thanks to his study of classics and knew he had 'a sensitivity to style' denied to many of his friends. Even socially he had matured; he had relaxed beyond his expectations and had come to know a number of fellow students and professors.

Little wonder he felt a letdown when the fourth year was over.[17] It would only be from the perspective of Oxford, and later from that of a professor at Toronto, that he would look back at his Alma Mater with a critical eye. Then he would complain about the restrictive approach of the classics program with its obsession for grammatical structure, the absence of American history and the neglect of Canadian history as an independent subject, and the failure to be exposed to the writings of contemporary European intellectuals such as Sorel, Pareto, and Freud who were critical of the European liberal tradition that he was studying as gospel truth.[18] In 1911, however, he felt well prepared to face the world as a sophisticated young scholar.

His final examination results justified the confidence that he felt. In a class of

twenty-two graduands of the highest academic program at the university he
stood first in the English and history option and third in the classics option, with
Carleton Stanley in first place and Charles Cochrane in second. His superior
performance won him the Flavelle Travelling Fellowship of $750 per year, tenable
for two years of study at Oxford.[19]

The year 1911 was the finest year that the university had witnessed in student
achievement. President Falconer publicly complimented the three top graduates at
spring convocation on 9 June 1911 and proudly noted that the university was
sending its top four graduates (Murray Wrong was the fourth) to Oxford. Some
fifty years later C.B. Sissons, who was a member of the faculty in 1911, still
recalled the superiority of that class of graduands: 'He was a member of our finest
year in Honour Classics, 1911, in which there were seven firsts. Here I am tempted to
quote scripture – 'And now abideth these three' – Stanley, Cochrane and Underhill,
"but the greatest of these is" Underhill.'[20] Underhill did not rest on his laurels. He
spent the summer holidays in a self-imposed, ambitious reading program. He read
Edward Gibbon's monumental study *The Decline and Fall of the Roman Empire*
and was 'being fortified in Liberalism by "Glorious John"' (J.R. Green),[21] the
renowned British liberal thinker. The summer passed quickly with one complica-
tion. In late July he was hospitalized for an appendectomy. It meant delaying his
passage to England until the fall. On 21 September he bid farewell to parents and
friends, took time to vote in his first federal election by casting his ballot for the
Liberal party and reciprocity, and then boarded the train for Montreal, where the ss
Teutonic waited in dock to take the three gifted Toronto graduates to Oxford.
Underhill and Charles Cochrane sat up much of the night on the train in debate on
the reciprocity issue, realizing that they had cancelled each other's vote.

3

A Scholarly Gentleman: Oxford

Oxford in the Edwardian Age was the intellectual capital of the English-speaking world. That reputation was built on a tradition dating back to medieval times when it first began as a religious institution to educate clerics. Until the eighteenth century, Oxford and its rival Cambridge were the only two English universities. They had the further distinction of being the only two non-territorial constituencies which returned members to parliament. The university was simultaneously a haven for scholars and a seed-bed of political controversy; throughout its history there was an ongoing battle of gown and town.[1] This tension, and the resulting political consciousness of its professors and students, appealed to Underhill.

At no time was the political awareness of Oxford greater than during those few years prior to the outbreak of World War I. Oxford mirrored the nation in this era of political ferment. The upheaval began in the general election of 1906, which swept the Liberal party into power under Sir Henry Campbell-Bannerman (and later Herbert Asquith) with a radical socialist contingent on its coat-tails. That contingent would grow to become the Labour party; it would also support the great Reform Budget – the 'People's Budget' of Lloyd George, chancellor of the exchequer, that would take England along the road to the welfare state. Socialism was in the air, and in the minds, too, of many Englishmen, particularly the influential and vocal Fabian Society. The House of Commons and the House of Lords waged battle over their rights and power. The struggle for Irish Home Rule was at its peak, guided by an able-bodied group of Irish nationalists at Westminster. The suffragettes were taking to the streets to battle for political recognition, and demands for self-government for India and South Africa added a global dimension to the struggles. These were life and death issues that were heatedly debated in parliament and in the common rooms of every Oxford college. Professors and students searched for meaning in the confusion that swirled about them. To be at Oxford in the twilight years of the Edwardian Age was to experience the university in its finest hour.

Balliol College, Oxford, was the intellectual centre of the university, the elite of the colleges. It admitted only honour students and had the pick of the best applicants from the top English public schools and the universities from around the world. Herbert Asquith described the mark of a Balliol man as 'the tranquil consciousness of effortless superiority.' To be in 'Greats' at Balliol College was to be *la crème de la crème*. It was a rigorous program which combined the study of philosophy and history on the basis of a knowledge of classical languages. In philosophy, students were expected to know about the ancient philosophers, in particular Plato and Aristotle, while studying modern European philosophy in order to appreciate 'the unity of philosophy as a whole and the essential identity of the questions discussed by ancient and modern philosophers alike.'[2] The history studied was ancient Greece and Rome, but in the context of general history through an emphasis on political philosophy and political economy. Thus, as a student of *Literae Humaniores* at Balliol College, Oxford, Frank Underhill had the best of higher education that the British academic world could offer.

In 1911, when he entered Balliol, Underhill was a healthy young man of average build but short stature, his blond hair receding at the forehead, his round face having a scholarly and serious appearance. He was a month away from his twenty-second birthday, older by three years than the majority of English students who came directly to Oxford from sixth form. He was embarking on a second Honour BA degree, the accustomed practice for Canadian students at Oxford, which he would complete in the usual two-year period. He arrived at Oxford in early October, having spent a few days holidaying in London, a city he grew to love. During his first year he boarded at 6 Parks Road, a three-storey grey building where the landlady, Miss Bellamy, rented out rooms for thirty shillings a week.[3] It was only a few minutes walk to Balliol College, so ideally located. He shared 'digs' with Carleton Stanley. The association provided familiarity in an otherwise alien environment.

He felt insecure as he first entered Balliol from Broad Street through the medieval portals and into the tranquil inner sanctuary. He was embarking on a way of life. Education at Oxford was more than academic pursuits; it was learning to perceive the world through the eyes of a gentleman scholar. First, however, he had to familiarize himself with the physical surroundings. He obviously had difficulty, because he wrote to Calvert, his Markham high school teacher, that he had been fined for a wrongdoing. What the misdemeanour was is unclear, but Calvert replied: 'I hope you have learned where all the walls are now.'[4] He spent considerable money on clothing, feeling the need to upgrade his wardrobe in keeping with the upper-class English students. He enjoyed roaming in the numerous first-rate bookstores, particularly Blackwells, where he went on a book-buying spree of texts and other books of interest. He remembered in later life that the first two books he purchased were two that were being remaindered: Volume I of Karl Marx's *Das Capital* and André Siegfried's *The Race Question in Canada*. Siegfried gave him a new insight into Canadian politics, but Marx bored him and he never finished reading it. He found life at Oxford incredibly expensive, and was unable to keep within his self-imposed limit of $1500 per year.

Underhill had a variety of good courses and enjoyable professors in 'Greats' that first year. He took courses from J.A. Smith of Balliol on 'Schools of Logic,' F.J. Haverfield of Christ Church College in ancient history, and Cyril Bailey, registrar of Balliol, in Latin literature.[5] He found Bailey to be one of the few Conservative fellows in what was otherwise a radical, socialist college. His tutor, A.D. Lindsay, was an active Fabian socialist and a member of the Independent Labour party. In 1911, although only thirty-two years old, Lindsay was, as Jowett Lecturer in Philosophy, a well-established fellow of Balliol. In 1924 he would succeed A.L. Smith as master of the college. He had a reputation of being an 'indefatigable teacher.'[6] His strength lay in his strong convictions and outspoken views on moral issues, a characteristic which created enemies among his colleagues but generated respect from his students. Underhill came to know Lindsay well through his weekly tutorial meetings and through frequent Sunday afternoon visits to his home. Here he met Mrs Lindsay, an active suffragette. Discovering that Underhill was on the left politically, she tried to persuade him to accompany her on the suffragist campaigns in the towns and villages around Oxford. He declined out of shyness.

He did become a member of the Oxford University Fabian Society through Lindsay, who was president in 1911–12. There were numerous Balliol dons and students who belonged, including the young G.D.H. Cole, already making a name for himself as a brilliant Fabian socialist; Harold Laski, soon to become a noted Marxian socialist; and Gilbert Murray, Regius Professor of Greek in the *Literae Humaniores* School. The society had formed in 1895 as a branch of the London Fabian Society. Consisting of university members only, it was committed to 'the accurate investigation of social questions and the formation of a body of definite opinion in the University as to Social and Economic Reform, on the principles of collective ownership and state or municipal control of industry.'[7] It was the open nature and high intellectual quality of debate rather than the socialist ideology of the society that appealed to Underhill. In fact, he decided to become only an associate member, rather than a full member, because he recalled later, 'I wasn't quite sure that I believed in the full socialization of the means of production, distribution and exchange.'[8] He remembered attending the first meeting at which Ramsay Macdonald, leader of the new Independent Labour party, discussed current political and social issues from a socialist perspective. The speech 'swept me off my feet,' he claimed.

Most of his first term he spent studying. He quickly acquired the reputation of a very good student. Lindsay saw him as a potential 'First' and encouraged him by suggesting additional readings to help him prepare for the final examinations. Kenneth Bell, who had returned to Oxford that same year, reported to Wrong: 'Underhill and Cochrane are both very highly spoken of. Lindsay, the Greats tutor at Balliol [,] wrote to me specially to say that U. was doing unmistakeably first-class work and was a very able man.' In another letter Bell described Underhill as a 'Balliol Star of the first magnitude.'[9] His early success was evident in his winning a Williams Exhibition during his first term. Exhibitions were one notch below scholarships as academic awards and were awarded yearly on the basis of a rigorous examination consisting of an essay, two papers in Latin, Greek, French, or German, two general papers, and two papers which were the option of the candidate in either ancient or medieval or modern history. The Williams Exhibition was ordinarily for £40 a year, but the examination committee decided to give Underhill £50 for two years – '£25 a year with tuition free, but that in other respects the tenure should be the same as in the case of ordinary Williams Exhibitions.'[10] The exhibition boosted his confidence, insured him a more respected place among his peers, and eased his financial strain, although he still had to cable his father to send additional money.

Underhill thoroughly enjoyed 'Greats.' He was conscious of studying political ideas at the time when they first burst into the Western World, and he was learning to perceive the world through the eyes of these intellectual 'giants' of Western civilization. The ancient proverb 'the unexamined life is not worth living' took on a new meaning and became a guide-post of his intellectual enquiry for the rest of his life. He was equally aware of the relevance of Greek thought to present society. 'Greek philosophy is truly educative when you have it impressed on you all the time that what they were discussing were the same problems as meet us today, whether in metaphysics or politics,' he wrote George Wrong in February 1912.[11] Professors were constantly drawing parallels between the Greek city state or the Roman empire and modern Britain and the British empire. He was conscious of being in the centre of the greatest empire the world had known, when great moral issues – imperial dominance and the right to national self-determination, democracy, and aristocracy – were heatedly debated in the context of the political controversies of that day. Both past and present came alive, as the wisdom of the ancients spoke to him over time about 'the meaning of the good life.'

There were other benefits of 'Greats.' He was coming to appreciate good style – the simple act of putting sentences together in a crisp, clear, and cogent manner; to maximize his thoughts in the minimum of words; to say something effectively by the art of arranging words in a particular pattern; to detect and appreciate the rhythmn of writing. The study of classical texts also reinforced the importance of a critical enquiry, no matter whether the subject was an ancient text, an archaeological site, a medieval document, or a current newspaper. Classics prepared him for the creative art of historical writing by providing the intellectual tools of the trade in a way, possibly, that a study of history could not have done. What classics did not, and could not, do was to familiarize him with the sources or the historiography. These he would have to acquire in his year in modern history. Another appealing quality of the program was the elite undergraduates it attracted. They formed 'a sufficiently stimulating society of themselves.' They kept the level of discussion in tutorials high, and the dons intellectually alive and alert. What a contrast to the University of Toronto, he informed Wrong, where many professors did not have 'an idea later than 1860 ... [because] they never get interested in people who have been assimilating ideas since that date.'

In praising the noble qualities of English society and Oxonian education Underhill frequently made comparisons with the inferior nature of Canadian society and education. Although he greatly resented the colonial stigma placed on him by upper-class English students at Oxford, he perpetuated the image himself. He lamented that Canada was indeed a colonial society that could never measure up to the finer aspects of British society. From this lofty seat of higher learning, Underhill took a condescending attitude in judging his native country.

Yet he was far from uncritical of Oxford and English society. While enjoying his academic studies and the general intellectual atmosphere, he thoroughly disliked the social situation. For one thing, he felt removed from his professors. He was accustomed to teachers who took a personal interest in him at Markham and Toronto, and he found it difficult to accept a relationship with a professor that was purely intellectual. 'I had imagined that your tutor would look after your goings out and comings in, in a paternal sort of way,' he confessed to his former mentor, Wrong. He felt that he did not meet with his tutors frequently enough to get to know them as persons or for them to know him, and admitted that he needed that personal contact and encouragement. It was the aspect of his Toronto education that he had found most rewarding, he recalled from Oxford. Much more upsetting was the cold, indifferent, almost hostile, nature of the upper-class English students. '[T]hose who declare that the Englishman is self-centered, and hard to get acquainted with and uninterested in strangers can count me among their supporters,' he informed Wrong. He found it difficult to get used to passing students in the quad who knew him from class but who would ignore him in public. He could not simply pass it off as a peculiar English habit. Instead, he took the snub personally, and allowed it to reinforce his already evident feelings of inferiority and loneliness.

Underhill had a love/hate attitude towards the English while at Oxford. He greatly admired their polished ways, their sophisticated culture, and their social graces. He was impressed, for example, with the ease and elegance with which English students spoke on subjects about which they had less information than he did. He longed to be part of the elitist society. 'The best thing about Oxford,' he wrote in 1912, 'is undoubtedly the common life of the undergraduates. To be sure, it is appallingly expensive, but in a way it is a fine conception that you should waste a large part of nearly every day in eating absurdly good meals and talking on all subjects with your fellows.' He admired Massey and Murray Wrong, the only two Canadian students who seemed to fit readily and comfortably into British society. He attributed their social success to their wealth. He regretted that he would never belong to this elite society simply because he grew up in a middle-class family in a small Ontario town in a colonial society. He was equal intellectually to these English students, but he could never be socially. At the same time, he felt that the polished manners and social graces were often substitutes for serious thought and moral ethics. The university was more concerned with producing a social class with polished manners than an educated elite with a social conscience, which he believed was the hallmark of an intellectual. This initial encounter with the elite would colour his perception of the British for the remainder of his life. He would fluctuate between periods when he idealized the British, as he reflected on their intellectual greatness and cultured ways as evidenced by the students he met at Oxford, to periods when he condemned the British ruling class because their haughty ways and self-righteous attitudes reminded him too much of the snobbish upper-class students who were his Oxford colleagues.

Underhill's immediate reaction was to become more nationalistic. Convinced that the English rejection of him was a result of his colonial status, he became a patriotic Canadian. 'I had made up my mind during my stay at Oxford,' he recalled years later, 'that I was a Canadian, I wasn't an Englishman. I had that strong national feeling, that was deeper than reason.' He already knew that he could never be happy living in England, that Canada would always be his spiritual and temporal home. He became more critical too. 'The shameful luxury in which we live should, one would think, make anybody with a heart at all a ferocious radical.' he pointed out to Wrong. 'But it only makes the majority good-natured, brilliant, superficial Tories.' In his first year, too, he became even more introverted. Bell described him as 'a little clammy and prefers the part of a satiric spectator.'[12] Underhill associated with the poorer English students or with a group of Scottish students at Balliol who resented the haughty ways of the upper-class English as much as he did. But most of the time he clung tenaciously to fellow Canadians – Stanley, Cochrane, Wrong, Massey, Walter Sage, and Henry Angus. He forced himself to join the Oxford Debating Club and even participated in a debate on the topic of whether Oxford should be open to students of any social class. He found the experience so nerve-racking that he dropped his membership, convincing himself that he was not cut out for debating.[13]

His introspection concerned his Toronto professors. Edward Kylie, in particular, urged Underhill to get 'to know Englishmen better – you will be with Canadians all your days.' He advised him to move into residence, where there would be more opportunity to socialize, and to give more speeches at clubs. Otherwise he would miss out on, perhaps, the most important aspect of an English education: to learn to become a refined gentleman scholar, capable of being at ease in upper-class society and of speaking out on important subjects. George Wrong encouraged him to forget his social conscience and to enjoy the luxuries for his few brief years at Oxford. 'A year or two of luxury will do a Canadian youth no harm. I doubt whether the soul is after all much injured by the luxury of good pictures, carved furniture, comfortable easy chairs and beautiful rooms.'[14]

Underhill took their advice. He moved into residence during Michaelmas term of his second year and forced himself to join more clubs. Vincent Massey nominated him for membership in the Russell and Palmerston Liberal Club, while he continued his membership in the Fabian Society, claiming it was natural to belong to Liberal and Socialist clubs at the same time. He was invited to join a Balliol Fabian research group of about ten members headed by G.D.H. Cole which met occasionally to give papers on the development of labour socialism in England. Underhill's paper was on 'The History of English Trade Unionism,' in which he argued that the British trade unions, both in make-up and in ideas, were a logical outgrowth of earlier British liberal-socialist co-operative movements rather than a product of Marxist revolutionary socialism.[15] His information had come from Sidney and Beatrice Webb's monumental work on British trade unionism, as did his main argument that British trade unions needed a highly organized and bureaucratic form of socialism to succeed.

These extracurricular activities contributed to rather than detracted from his academic excellence. He was doing even better work in his second year than in his first, especially in his course on 'Philosophical Theory of the State.' It was a topic that complemented his interests perfectly. His tutor Lindsay would listen attentively to Underhill's weekly papers, only interrupting occasionally to press him further on a point he was making. He enjoyed Underhill's witty prose and epigrammatic remarks, for Underhill had, by second year, come to accept more readily the flippant style of Oxonian students that he had denounced in first year.

Underhill was concentrating his energy on those all important final examinations at the end of his two-year program; they were constantly on his mind. In December, at the end of the first term, he took a holiday on the Isle of Wight to relax before the big push in the second term. Clearly he was under stress to the point where he had eye-strain by mid-March and had to wear glasses for reading. Still he complained to friends about being lazy and letting the standard of his work drop; this was a technique to prepare himself for the examinations. He decided to forgo a trip to Europe in the lengthy Easter break as a means of relaxing for the finals, as most Oxonian students did, preferring instead to take a canoe trip with Charles Cochrane down the Thames to Windsor.[16] He was mentally and physically prepared for the rigorous six days of final examinations. 'In fact,' he recalled in later life, 'I reached the apex of my intellectual efficiency in the six days I spent writing the final Great exams. I had never been so good before and I've never been so good since.'[17] He rose to the challenge when under pressure to produce, and his ideas crystallized. Everything that he had learned in the last two years – in fact, in the last six years of classical studies – came together. It was as though he were writing himself into existence by displaying his knowledge and his intellectual skills. What he proved – as he knew when he finished the examinations – was that he had a first-class mind, that he had become a gentleman scholar.

The good news came in late July – a 'First' in 'Greats'! Carleton Stanley was the only other Canadian student in that graduating year to receive a 'First'; Charles Cochrane got a 'Second.' Balliol College did not fare well overall, which made Underhill's 'First' even more spectacular.[18] Murray Wrong wrote that Underhill's 'Greek history paper was a marvel – Sandy [A.D. Lindsay] said probably the best he'd ever seen.' Lionel Curtis heard from Harold Prichard, a Balliol tutor, 'what I already knew, that you were in every word and deed a first-class man.'[19] Letters of congratulation and praise also came from Toronto professors and friends.

As a reward for his accomplishment, Underhill took a six-week vacation in Europe with Charles Cochrane and Daniel Harvey, another Canadian student who would later become a distinguished historian of the Maritimes. There is a picture of the three of them in a scholarly pose, in three-piece suits with books in hand, standing among the ruins of the Palace of the Emperor, Palatine Hill. The photograph captures their image of the trip: an academic study abroad to enrich their bookish knowledge of Western civilization. Much time was spent in the art galleries, churches, and museums of Italy, Germany, and France. In Italy, he found Renaissance painting and sculpture more moving than the architectural ruins of Ancient Rome. He remembered Florence as the greatest cultural centre that he visited on the continent, because of its wealth of Renaissance art, but in Rome he enjoyed an unusual opportunity to observe a dig beneath the Roman Forum, arranged through a chance meeting with a fellow Oxford student who was working on the excavation. Opportunity seemed to be a positive quality of an Oxford education, he came to realize. It opened up so many avenues and new acquaintances. There was no need to prove yourself; you had already done that simply by being there. Society might ridicule the erudite scholar, but it did so out of envy at the prestige which the scholarly life provided. Underhill reflected in that glory, although he never let it blind him to the need for the scholar to be an intricate component of society at large. He could be elitist in his attitude without being haughty or aloof in his ways.

At the end of his two-year program, Underhill was offered a job as assistant lecturer in ancient history at Manchester University for the academic year 1913–14.[20] He declined the offer, however, because he had decided, on the advice of Lindsay and his Toronto professors, to stay another year at Balliol to take modern history. He was also holding out for a Canadian academic position which his Toronto professors were encouraging him to expect.[21] The big question was money to fund this extra year. There could be no additional support from the University of Toronto, Kylie informed him. His Flavelle Scholarship expired at the end of his second year, as did his Williams Exhibition. He had tried in second year for a Jenkyns Exhibition worth £100 for history and philosophy and had received honourable mention but no remuneration. He wrote asking his father to help support him for a third year. Kylie also applied pressure on Underhill's father by forwarding Lindsay's letter on to him, with a personal note urging him to support his son's education for one final year. Underhill helped cut costs by moving out of residence and into 'digs' with Henry Angus[22] at 45 Winchester Road, Oxford. Underhill also tried the All Souls' examination in the fall of 1913 but lost out because of a low mark in history. In the end his parents covered the entire costs of his additional year in modern history at Balliol.

The School of Modern History was well established by the time Underhill entered in 1913. In theory, the program covered modern European history; in practice, the focus was narrower, with an emphasis on English constitutional and political history from Roman time to present.[23] Candidates had to know the entire period, but specialized in depth in one era. Underhill chose the medieval period, and did papers on the working of political institutions as revealed in the historical documents. He was also expected to be knowledgeable about the social and literary history of the period and about its geography. In addition, a candidate had an area of concentration in European history, which for Underhill was Renaissance and Reformation, and one special subject; he chose Canadian constitutional development.[24]

The usual time to complete the program was two years, except for candidates with a degree in *Literae Humaniores*.[25] Underhill was part of a pattern at Oxford, but it was an ambitious undertaking, especially when taken immediately after a rigorous two years of 'Greats.' He also had the disadvantage of not having the extensive background in English history that most of the British schoolboys had received in public school. He had stiff competition. His tutors and mentors realized the pressures on him and warned him not to overextend himself. 'Don't work yourself to death in the effort to pull off a first in history in one year,' Lionel Curtis advised. Lindsay suggested that he let his academic studies slide in favour of more socializing. Until Underhill felt more at ease with others, Lindsay predicted, he would not make a good teacher.[26]

One club in which Underhill took an active role in his third year was the Ralegh Club (deliberately spelt without the 'i' in recognition of Sir Walter Raleigh, the first British imperialist, who signed his name this way in his early correspondence). Underhill had joined the club back in January 1913 as a founding member.

He had not been present at the initial planning meeting on 6 December 1912 in the room of its first president, J.G. Lockhart of Trinity College. The two Canadians present were Murray Wrong and Vincent Massey, the latter being elected secretary. At that meeting it was decided to begin a club of not more than twenty-five members representing Britain and the dominions 'to debate questions concerning the British Empire.'[27] Massey nominated Underhill out of 'high regard' for his intellect.[28] The club also had honorary members, including Viscount Milner, Winston Churchill, A.J. Glazebrook, George Wrong, and Lionel Curtis. Of these honorary members, Curtis became most active in the club. He saw the new organization as a part of his Round Table movement where he could convert potential young men to his vision of imperial unity through a single imperial government.[29] Assisting him in this task was Reginald Coupland, lecturer of ancient history and a member of the club. Coupland organized a subgroup made up exclusively of the colonial component, who met to draw up a constitution for a future commonwealth. Coupland invited Underhill, along with a few other students, to Curtis's country estate near Ledbury, sixty miles northwest of Oxford, where they could continue their discussions. Here Underhill came to know personally these two British imperialists, and met as well other British intellectuals and politicians who visited from London, Oxford, and Cambridge.

In the Ralegh Club, Underhill played the role of 'devil's advocate.' In a paper on doctrinaire imperialism, he launched an attack on the club's 'most depressingly unanimous' views on the subject of imperialism. In an indirect reference to Curtis, he complained that 'those green covered books have grown into a sort of repository of revealed truth which it is the mission of our devoted brotherhood to preach to a somewhat apathetic world of party politicians and parochial colonists.'[30] He attacked both the military and political arguments for imperial federation. Under military, he argued that the empire was already moving towards a decentralized position with the request by Australia and New Zealand for navies of their own. Even in Canada there was no unanimity on the issue of a contribution to an imperial navy or the establishment of an independent naval force. Such a decentralized empire, he noted, would prevent 'dry rot at the centre,' a common affliction of centralized bureaucracies. Under the political question, he emphasized the need to reorganize and accept the growing spirit of nationalism in the colonies. The dominions were no longer immature adolescent colonies, but mature adult nations ready to assume positions of responsibility in the world. The main question, therefore, was whether they could best assume this position of responsibility in a tightly knit imperial federation or in a loose imperial association. Underhill argued that in an imperial federation, in which each nation sent representatives to some central federal parliament, the dominions would have an inadequate voice, thus weakening their sense of importance and responsibility. While Underhill was clearly opposed to the popular view of the time of imperial unity, he was not willing to go to the other extreme to propose independence for the dominion, as many nationalists were. He was essentially defending the status quo position of colonies which were half-in and half-out of the empire – wanting more freedom but unwilling to consider separation.[31]

Underhill presented a second paper on the subject of imperialism at the Acton Historical Club on 9 March 1914.[32] In this paper he went further in his criticism of imperial federation by implying that it was motivated by economic interests and materialistic concerns rather than by ideals and spiritual values. The tone of the paper indicates that he was attempting to evoke debate rather than state an unequivocal position. Strong statements are hedged with qualifying words or phrases to tone them down so as to make them appear less emphatic. He presented a general but persuasive argument that throughout the history of the British empire enthusiasm for imperial consolidation coincided with the particular economic or military needs of the mother country. It was a thesis popularized by J.A. Hobson in *Imperialism: A Study*, published in 1902. Whether Underhill had read Hobson's work when he gave the paper is unknown; he made no reference to the author. It is likely, however, that Hobson's views were well known since he would have provided fuel for debate in imperial circles. Still, this interpretation of imperialism was uncommon at Oxford in the prewar era and no doubt set Underhill apart from his contemporaries.

Despite his involvement in numerous clubs, or possibly because of it, he received only a 'Second' in modern history. He was obviously disappointed; it was the first time in his brief academic career that he had not stood at the top. He rationalized his lower standing by realizing that he had his 'First' in 'Greats'; that a year was too short a time for a colonial student, without a strong background in English history, to prepare adequately; that he was now qualified to teach modern history; that he already had an academic position for the following year at the University of Saskatchewan, the position having just been finalized; and that he had matured socially through his affiliation with a number of clubs, as he had been encouraged to do by his mentors. What he could not realize at this time was the importance of this year for his future career as a historian.

Underhill's social activities during his three years at Oxford do not appear to have extended beyond acquaintances with males in this bastion of male dominance. There is no evidence that he knew any girls while at Oxford. He wrote to a few female friends in Toronto, but his letters dealt with academic pursuits, involvement in clubs, his views on Oxford, or his opinions on current topics of interest, particularly politics. It is true that sex was not an open topic of discussion at Oxford in the prewar era, as it became in the 1920s, but there was somewhat of a sexual revolution in England in general, and particularly at the universities.[33] Underhill does not appear to have been a direct participant in this freedom. His puritanical and strict Calvinist upbringing kept 'a tight hold on him.' He claimed in later life that the Bohemian life-style did not appeal to him.[34]

He channelled his energy into the social revolt of the day: the rebellion against the Establishment and traditional social customs and beliefs. One of his greatest pleasures while at Oxford was discovering the plays of George Bernard Shaw and the novels of H.G. Wells. 'There have never been any two men since in the English-speaking world so effective in getting their whole society excited about political and social questions,' he claimed in his eightieth-birthday speech. He remembered seeing the first production of *Androcles and the Lion*, a play which purported to be about the early Christians in Rome but was really a satire on the early Fabian socialists in Britain. Underhill revelled in Shaw's satire and wit by which the dramatist attacked the Establishment.[35] It was satire at its best, because Shaw was not only attacking the status quo but offering something constructive in its place. He was forcing people to think about values and institutions that they took for granted so as to evoke discussion and debate on important issues. Underhill realized that he too would delight in pricking the conscience of those in authority; he had discovered his mission.

4

Academic Apprentice
and Soldier

W.S. Milner, classics professor at the University of Toronto, was responsible for Underhill securing the appointment at the University of Saskatchewan. Milner had hoped that his student would get an appointment at Toronto, but when he was passed over for an opening there[1] he recommended him to President Murray at Saskatoon. 'I cannot think of anything that would give you fuller personal development,' he advised Underhill. 'Saskatchewan is a pivotal province in Canada – *the* pivotal province – in the same way as the Middle West States in the American Republic. Everything in our immediate future will turn upon what happens there.' Milner also spoke highly of the president. 'I may say too that literally no man in Canada knows our country as well as President Murray. You will find this is the deliberate opinion of many public men, and he is a glorious man to work with.'[2]

Underhill was upset with his failure to get an appointment at Toronto, but the Saskatchewan offer was attractive: a full professorship (Underhill joked in later life that he never got a promotion), a generous salary of $2500, and the opportunity to shape the education at a new university in an expanding region of the country. In the initial offer he had the option of either the Greek or the history chair. He replied that 'he would unhesitatingly take the History. I should like the Aristotle and the Ancient History very much, but my knowledge of Greek is far too slight, and I enjoy the study of politics far more than that of literature.' In the end he was asked to do mainly Greek for one year, with one course in medieval English history and the directing of honour students in English history. In his second year he would be free of the Greek and able to offer courses to his liking in the history and political science departments.[3]

Underhill's two close friends from Toronto and Oxford days, Carleton Stanley and Charles Cochrane, who were both teaching at Toronto, were conscious of Underhill's disappointment at not getting a Toronto position and tried to convince him that he would be better off at Saskatchewan. Stanley wrote: 'the University's admirable system of weeding out the best men has prevented you coming here ... And if you had come here you would have found yourself in such a slavish position with a $1200 or $1500 salary that you could have done nothing but "to lie in cold obstruction and to rot." One cannot buy a book, or go to a concert, or entertain a student, or respect oneself when invited to the houses of the Toronto rich, who are the dullest, crudest oysters into which human beings were ever debased. I get more and more discouraged.'[4]

Underhill left for the West in early September in order to arrive in time for the beginning of term. The train ride through wilderness country gave him ample time to reflect upon his future in Saskatoon. He knew very little about the West, and less about the University of Saskatchewan. He did recall reading about the Prairies, while at Oxford, in a series on Canada by Rupert Brooke, the well-known English scholar, poet, and travel correspondent, who had made a trip across the country in 1913 and recorded his impressions in a serial in the *Westminster Gazette*, later published as *Letters from Canada*. Brooke was critical of the West, describing it as 'a lonely place to live in.' Underhill agreed as he looked out the windows of his sleeping-car at the flat expanse only occasionally broken by small frontier settlements. He searched for positive indications that he had made the right decision. He was struck by the fresh, crisp, cool prairie air in contrast to the hot, humid, and stuffy air of late summer in Toronto. He was even more impressed with the first editorial he read in the *Manitoba Free Press* during his stopover in Winnipeg. The editor, John Wesley Dafoe, was discussing on that particular day Canada's involvement in the war 'not as dutiful colonial children of Britain but as grown-up responsible citizens of Canada exercising the international responsibilities of an adult democratic people.' 'That's just what I believe,'[5] Underhill exclaimed to himself, or so he recalled in later life. This initial introduction started him on a lifetime's reading of the *Free Press*; it also buoyed up his optimism about the West. Maybe the Prairies would not be as backward as the architecture indicated and Easterners assumed.

Unfortunately, his enthusiasm did not last. Reading the *Free Press* would be one of his few pleasant diversions during the year. He found Saskatoon a raw frontier town, all the more evident coming from the sophisticated society of Oxford. By western Canadian standards, Saskatoon was a thriving prairie city in 1914 with a population just over 12,000; in fact it had the proud title of 'the fastest growing city in Canada, the hub city of the West.'[6] The university was the focal point of the city. It had first opened its doors to students in January 1909 with a student population of seventy and a faculty consisting of the president and four professors (later known as the 'Old Contemptibles'): Reginald Bateman in English, Edmund Oliver in history, Arthur Moxon in classics, and George Ling in mathematics. By the time Underhill arrived the faculty had expanded to twenty-one and the student body to 445. Four faculties were in operation – Arts and Science, Agriculture, Law, and Engineering – and two religious colleges, Emmanuel and the Presbyterian Theological College. This rapid expansion had resulted in openings in Greek and History, when Moxon joined the Law faculty and Oliver became principal of the Presbyterian College. Two men replaced Oliver:[7] Arthur S. Morton and Underhill. Morton, twenty years Underhill's senior, became head of the two-man history department.[8] They respected each other, but Underhill found Morton a garrulous colleague and grew tired of hearing his standard stories over and over again. Morton in turn found Underhill's debunking radical ways hard to take – 'the jeers of the Phillistine, like Frankie Underhill,' as he once put it.[9]

During his first year in the West, Underhill found difficulty in adjusting. The open spaces did not appeal to him; he felt cut off from the academic world beyond Saskatoon. He took long walks along the South Saskatchewan River, reminiscing about the glorious days at Oxford. As early as October he had decided to return to Toronto during the Christmas break as a reprieve from Saskatoon.[10] He tried to improve his immediate surroundings by re-creating a cozy English sitting-room in his bachelor suite. He lined the walls with numerous framed prints he had brought back from England, including his favourite of Oliver Cromwell and one by Michaelangelo. Yet it still did not look 'cozy as a sitting room should,' he informed his mother, because it lacked a fireplace and a tea-making outfit. He picked up the latter in Toronto at Christmas time, but he realized that it would take more than a kettle to overcome his negative feelings about the Prairies.

Adjusting socially was no easier. Being single, he was left to his own initiative to meet friends and plan social events. Once again his shy nature held him back. In his first letters home he seldom mentioned other faculty members or social events. Instead, he complained of being lonely and depressed. He could not concentrate on his work; he was continually tired. His life was so dull that he contemplated attending picture shows, even church services. 'As far as one can judge this place is even worse for church-going than Toronto or Edinburgh,' he wrote his mother. 'But I shall ward off the day when I start as long as possible.' Before long, he was attending not only picture shows and church services but also wrestling matches in an effort to get himself out of his feeling of self-pity. He frequently ate alone downtown at Cairn's department store to avoid the dining hall and social situations. Reginald Coupland of Oxford perceptively noted the strong impact that environmental conditions had on Underhill's mood: 'I am somewhat depressed by what you tell me of the 'deadness' of Saskatchewan life. It's a terrible thing if material interests have obtained so deep a hold that, when they chance to collapse, there are no springs of energy left.'[11]

By November the situation had improved. He became acquainted with three other bachelors on staff – Brehaut, Bateman, and Eaton. He wrote home: 'I don't feel nearly so lonesome as I did at first, and I'm working rather better in consequence.' From that time on, he had a more active social life – attending theatrical performances and musicals that came to the city as well as a variety of events at the university, such as guest lectures, debates, and clubs – and was in a better frame of mind. But he never fully adjusted to his new situation during that first year, and did not get over thinking of Saskatoon as a 'backwoods settlement.'[12] As late as 1925 he would complain to his friend Stanley that 'it is easier for a camel to go through the eye of a needle than for an Oxford man to fit in out here – at least if he is a very young Oxford man.'[13]

The most memorable social event of the year was his favourable meeting with J.S. Woodsworth, the popular prairie minister, social reformer, and author. In an address to a group of farmers on the topic of immigration as part of a short course on agriculture, Woodsworth stressed, to Underhill's delight, the need 'to find out what we could learn from the new European immigrants, and not to be too insistent on what they must learn from us.'[14] Underhill had occasion to talk further with Woodsworth at a reception at the president's home. He wrote to his mother: 'I have only heard him once and he was splendid.'

He found relations with students difficult in his first year. He disagreed strongly with the mixing of male and female students either in casual social situations or in the classroom. 'Among various horrors of the University hall,' he informed his mother, 'there is one unique one – men and women students sit together, two or three women and four or five men at each table. They also play tennis together a great deal, which probably accounts for the fact that the only persons who know how to use a racquet belong to the staff.' He separated men and women students in his tutorials, believing that shy females in the group inhibited the men from expressing themselves freely, thus lowering the quality of the tutorial. Although he admitted to having some very good female students, he doubted that their interest went very deep.[15]

Overall, he was disappointed with the quality of the students. Accustomed to associating with first-class scholars all his academic life, he found it difficult to accept the second- or third-class student. He did have a few undergraduate students who met his rigorous demands of weekly reading assignments and an essay in the Oxford style, a couple of them doing as much work as his MA students.[16] But such students were 'few and far between'; most seemed to be 'taking the class because they have to.' He tried to interest them in history by dividing the large classes of twenty-five into three small tutorials which met fortnightly to present papers on relevant topics in the course. He abandoned the experiment after the first term, however, because only the student presenting the essay did any reading.[17] He was also disappointed with the unenthusiastic response of students to his lectures. He admitted that his initial lectures were not the best, crammed with detail and presented in a nervous voice and jerky manner. He also relied heavily on his notes from Oxford in teaching his English history course, and much of the material was too advanced for undergraduates in an introductory course whose knowledge of English history was negligible. Still, he spent long hours preparing clear and well-organized lectures written out in full, because he did not have confidence in his ability to talk informally.[18]

He found that his lecture preparation left him little time to devote to his own research and writing. He did not begin any research project during the year. His Oxford friend Reginald Coupland encouraged him to submit articles to a new publication of the Ralegh Club, or to consider writing 'a really great history of Canada.'[19] He was conscious himself of the need to get something published, but could not find a topic that interested him. He felt like a nonentity on the edge of nowhere. His seven years of vigorous intellectual training and his top honours were unappreciated here in the West, or so he felt. 'I wish I were doing something worthwhile myself instead of spending my time away off from everything out here,'[20] he concluded in a letter home in reference to a note from Coupland which referred to the involvement of the Round Table movement in the war effort. He wanted to be part of a greater cause where he would be recognized. Could the war provide the opportunity?

From the time of his arrival at the university, Underhill felt compelled to enlist in the army. He received letters from former student colleagues at Toronto and particularly Oxford who had joined; Coupland forwarded a Ralegh Club card to show 'how nobly its members have responded to the call to arms.' Daily that fall he observed the tally sheet in the *Saskatoon Phoenix* of the local boys who had signed up, and editorials extolled the virtues of the war.[21] The university was particularly under pressure because of the large number of qualified young men. The student newspaper, *The Sheaf*, contained articles written to inspire students and faculty to join the cause. One such article, 'Saskatchewan Men at the Front,' concluded: 'All honor to those who have responded so nobly to our Empire's call in the hour of great need. For freedom and for right they go forth to fight.'[22] As further enticement, the university governors granted leaves of absence with half pay to a faculty or staff member who enlisted.

Underhill reacted to the events about him with a mixture of guilt and envy: guilty that he was not enlisting and envious of those who were. He wanted to join, chiefly for the recognition, glory, and excitement, but he did not feel qualified – at least to be a commissioned officer which was what he wanted. He regretted not having joined the Oxford Officer Training Corps so that he would already have training, and lamented that Saskatchewan did not have one. In October he decided to enlist in the 105th Regiment in Saskatoon so as to 'get some training and then volunteer sometime next spring.'[23] Then he changed his mind. He did not feel physically fit to join. He also feared that if he joined a local company he would never be considered for a commissioned position.

Guilt and envy were mixed with nobler thoughts of honour and duty. Like many

English Canadians, Underhill believed the war to be a moral struggle for democracy over autocracy. In such a battle, Canada had a part to play at Britain's side. In an article 'Imperial Architecture' written for *The Sheaf* in March 1915, Underhill claimed that 'sending soldiers to Europe is not an act of generosity but of duty, that we are in the war on the same basis as England, that being part of the Empire means that we have obligations to fulfil just as much as she has.' He hoped the war would also arouse the dominions, and particularly Canada, into a more responsible role in governing the empire – a contrast to J.W. Dafoe, whose views Underhill claimed in later life to have accepted.

He returned to Toronto in May, when the academic year was over, to find the city in a war fever. The Germans had made a strong push into Belgium and northern France that spring, putting the Allies on the defensive. The government was appealing for more recruits to fight a war which was seen as much Canada's as Britain's.[24] The University of Toronto was far in advance of Saskatchewan in its recruiting. It had its own Officer Training Corps and Speakers' Patriotic League, to drum up support for the war effort. Charles Cochrane was secretary to the University Speakers' Bureau and persuaded Underhill to take over his responsibilities while he was away at training camp. The task of recruiting others for the cause was the final act which confirmed his own decision to join: 'I was engaged for several weeks sending out people to deliver patriotic speeches and I thought what the devil am I doing sending people out to try to induce other people to sign up and I am not joining up myself.'[25]

Underhill notified President Murray that he would not be returning when classes resumed in mid-September. 'I ought to be doing something after having spent a whole year as if I were an American neutral,' he wrote, 'and I'm afraid I'll lose my own self-respect if I put off matters much longer.'[26] Yet he did not enlist until 29 September 1915. The delay was part of his plan to get a commissioned position. When he did enlist, he joined the 4th University Company, Montreal, a regiment in the 11th Reserve Batallion of the Canadian Expeditionary Force recruited to go overseas as reinforcements for the Princess Patricias. It was made up exclusively of university graduates who, it was believed, were destined to become officers after a short training program. Underhill wanted to do his part for the war effort, but as an officer, not as an ordinary soldier. He received the recognition and praise that he craved. *The Sheaf* noted Underhill's enlistment in glowing terms: 'It is hard for us to realize what a great sacrifice Professor Underhill has made. After spending the best years of his life in the best Universities preparing for his Professorship to be called away at the very outset of his career is indeed a notable case of self-surrender.'[27] In addition, President Murray wrote to say that he was 'being very much missed this year. I know it would be gratifying to you if you could hear the inquiries of your former students, more particularly the advanced students. You seem to have succeeded wonderfully well in making them think and in awakening their interest.' This praise was in marked contrast to his low opinion of himself as having done 'very poor work'; he even offered to decline the half-year's pay given to staff members who enlisted, feeling that he was not worthy of it.[28]

He threw himself into army life with vigour. He left Toronto for Montreal on 30 September and was examined and in uniform by 1 October.[29] His two-month training consisted of drill exercises, long marches, and fatigue duty which involved cleaning up the barracks and keeping the fires going. At first he found difficulty adjusting, and complained of making stupid mistakes, but he thoroughly enjoyed the vigorous physical activity of army life in the outdoors. 'My chest will be 2 or 3 inches bigger in a few weeks if we get work like this all the time,'[30] he informed his mother. At the age of twenty-six, he looked and felt at his peak physically. He had put on some weight and had grown a moustache which, along with his uniform, took away from his youthful appearance. He related well to his fellow soldiers, whom he described as 'a fine lot' of friendly guys. He also carried on an active social life, attending theatre, dining out, and visiting friends. If this was what army life was all about, then he would throughly enjoy it.

But things would change. On his birthday, 26 November, he boarded the troop train in Montreal enroute to Halifax, where the ss *Lapland*, converted into a troop ship, was anchored in harbour. Underhill, along with two thousand other soldiers, embarked at daybreak on Sunday, 28 November, 'amid cheering and bandplaying.' The five-day Atlantic crossing he described as terrible, even though he enjoyed comfortable quarters in a first-class stateroom. The food was 'simply rotten,' and his fellow soldiers equally hard to stomach. 'If ever I am ship-wrecked,' he informed his mother, 'I hope there are no Canadians or Americans among the company with me. Their absolute lack of intelligent interests would drive me crazy.' It was his first exposure to non-university soldiers; the experience reaffirmed his earlier decision not to join an ordinary regiment. Still he objected to the poor treatment given these regular soldiers. They were stuck in steerage with worse food than he had, that had to be eaten 'at long tables beside their bunks in the foulest smelling places I've been in. Such are the delights of being a common soldier.'[31]

He hoped for better in England, but it was not to be. He was stationed at Shorncliffe in Kent, and he hated every moment of his five-month stay. He could find nothing positive in sitting around a cold, damp camp, the monotony broken only by menial tasks on fatigue duty that were 'blunting his powers of appreciation and concentration.' He was so miserable that his friend Stanley could not recall a time when Underhill was so low. 'So it must be pretty bad with you. I've given myself a day or so to recover from the effects of the mere reading of this [letter].'[32] He was depressed at failing to get a commission. When he joined, he had expected to have his training completed by the end of the year and immediate promotion to a commissioned position. That time had passed and he was no closer to his goal. The realization spurred a round of requests, in particular to Lionel Curtis and George Parkin, for help. Equally upsetting was the indifferent or hostile attitude of Canadian officers towards their men. He personally resented having to take orders from men less educated than himself who were simply on 'power trips.' Still, his dislike for officers did not alter his low regard for his fellow soldiers. Characteristically, he went into a state of self-pity and depression. The reality of army life was a far cry from the ideal he had envisioned while teaching in Saskatoon. 'I suppose I might as well get reconciled to it and be content to go through the war as an experience,' he confided in his diary, 'but I had some high-flying ideas of service when I enlisted. However if I stick at this business much longer I'll soon lose all of them.'

Adding to his frustration were the reports in the Canadian newspapers of the desperate need for more men at the front. The year 1915 had been especially devastating for Canadian soldiers who had been sent 'over the top' and into no-man's-land to face the machine-guns, artillery, barbed wire, and poisonous gas of the Germans – simply to try to regain lost ground. Thousands had died or were critically wounded and more recruits were badly needed. Prime Minister Robert Borden had pledged, in a surprised New Year's Day address in 1916, to get a total of 500 000 recruits. Underhill was ready and willing to fight – to be one of those badly needed men at the front – yet he was wasting away in training camp. He concluded that army life was 'nothing but waste – waste of time, waste of material, waste of ability.' Its only virtue was his need to keep physically fit. He got depressed if he felt out of shape, evidence of that puritanical self-discipline in the physical world that he had shown to possess many times before in the mental realm.

He showed restraint in his private life too. Living within his means was important. He kept track of daily expenses and only allowed himself one item of luxury, chocolate, for which he had an insatiable appetite. He expected his parents to contribute to his material comfort. Letters home were full of demands for items of clothing and food packages. He was willing to spend on trips to London and Oxford to attend theatre and the occasional musical, but these excursions he considered necessities for his mental well-being. He did not enjoy going on drinking sprees with fellow soldiers, although he began to drink moderately while in the army. He preferred to keep to himself. Small talk and gossip he found to be low and unproductive activity and he seldom indulged in it. He did not venture to learn about other people's personal activities, and he did not want them to know about his. Letters to friends while in the army (and later) were predominantly accounts of his activities or his views on current events. There was one exception, his letters to Edith Alexander, the daughter of Professor Alexander and sister of Isabelle Stanley. Here he opened up more than to anyone else, but still held his feelings back. When their correspondence did verge on the intimate, Isabelle ended it.

Underhill regretted this because of the incisive insights that Edith provided into his personality. She described him as 'conceited and too much concentrated on [him]self,' which she attributed to an over-protected life; he had never experienced great worries or sufferings. She chided him for his reserved nature and his overly rational approach to life – a quality which prevented him from showing his emotions. He agreed. In a different context, he wrote in his diary on 28 January 1916, after hearing a concert at Albert Hall in London: 'To hear good music or see good pictures by myself has a peculiar emotional effect on me at times when I am not quite sure of it. It may be a spurious emulation or it may be the real thing. I often doubt if I am capable of any pure emotion because I've got so in the habit of imagining myself in various moods – an actor on the stage of my own mind.' Even emotions had to be rationally explained, and his shifting moods understood in relation to cause and effect. Enthusiasm and 'letting go' were out of character. Yet fantasizing about the future was a very real part of his existence.

He had little opportunity to keep up with world affairs while in the army, except when on leave. Then he would go to London or Oxford to talk with informed people. In mid-February, as a result of an injury to two fingers on his right hand, he was given a week's leave of absence and went, without notice, to Ledbury to visit Curtis and Coupland. His arrival coincided with a meeting of members of the Round Table movement; it was a chance to reflect on the war from an intellectual viewpoint – a rare opportunity since joining the army. Underhill took a 'realistic' view of the war and its outcome to counterbalance the overly optimistic view espoused by these zealots. He had come to question the war rhetoric that had initially aroused his enthusiasm to join. The liberal ideals of a moral war fought for freedom and democracy were incongruous with the reality of army life. All he knew for certain at this point was his personal need to fight at the front, to satisfy his ideal of service and prove his self-worth.

He seemed thwarted in his attempt. In March, for example, his battalion was scheduled to go across to France, when a measles epidemic quarantined the men for three weeks. Discouraged, he decided in April to enrol in an eight-week machine-gun course, believing that the experience would give him an area of military expertise to use at the front. The training part of the course was in West Sandling, near Ashford, where his battalion had been transferred in March. The change of scenery and the new challenge improved his disposition. He set out to be the best in the class, duly recording his progress in his diary. But by July the novelty of the course had worn off, and he was back to complaining about the boredom and waste of army life. What initiated this bout of depression was the drafting for active service of those men from his 4th University Company who were not taking the machine-gun course. That left himself and four others as the only men in his battalion who had still not reached the front. It was as though fate were against him. He feared that friends and relatives would associate him with the 'cold-footed ones' who were avoiding fighting, and that he would have to return home a failure. 'I think I can honestly say that none of the delays so far have been of my own conscious choice,' he assured his mother, 'but I wouldn't believe a story like that if anyone else told it to me, and I don't expect other people will believe me if I tell it to them after the war is over.'[33]

Finally, on 13 July 1916 his British commission came through, thanks to the influence of Lionel Curtis. Now he wished it had not materialized; he tried to delay accepting it to the point where he got into a row with his commanding officer. He heard that he was in line for a Canadian commission which he had been pressing for and which he much preferred. In the end, he decided to accept the British position for fear that the Canadian one would never materialize. If it did, he would transfer.

His four-month officer training course was in Denham, Berkshire, fifteen miles outside London. Once again his expectations were greater than the reality and he was unhappy. The life of an officer cadet in the British army was no better than that of a private in the Canadian army. He admitted that he ate better and had more comfortable accommodation, but he felt estranged and lonely. He did not relate well to his superior officers; they appeared indifferent and snobbish – a viewpoint that would change once he became an officer himself. His only thought was to get through his examinations and out of the place as quickly as possible. He was nervous he might fail, especially the practical part on company drill. 'My turn hasn't come yet and I hope it doesn't,' he confided to his diary, 'because I seem to have very little control over my nerves after all and anyway I shan't shine in Capt. Woodhouse's presence.' In the end, he did well enough to be one of the fifteen to pass the course. On 6 October 1916 he was gazetted second lieutenant in the Hertfordshire Regiment. Next day, he happily departed for Halton Park in northern Berkshire to join the First Reserve Battalion as a machine-gun officer.

Shortly after his arrival he was hospitalized with jaundice for a month at Aylesbury. The convalescent period gave him time for sustained reading, though throughout his army career he kept up an ambitious reading program of books, periodicals, and newspapers forwarded by his parents or Mrs. Angus, Henry Angus's mother, who looked after his possessions in London. He ordered some history books, and found that history 'bucked [him] up enormously.'

What he wanted to know was why the Great War broke out at a time when liberalism had reached its finest hour. He began reading in mid-nineteenth-century German, British, and American history, since these were the major world powers of the time. He discovered that liberals were totally unprepared for the cataclysmic event that occurred in August 1914; their idealism blinded them to the reality of power in the world. The war, therefore, threw them into a tail-spin from which they had still not emerged. The resulting identity crisis was healthy, Underhill believed, since so many liberals were sentimental Christians or spiritual idealists who needed to be wakened to the fact that brute force was a real part of human nature and world politics. The only danger in this soul-searching would be if liberals went to the other extreme of cynical realism and the worship of materialism. The true path lay between idealism and realism. Underhill predicted that the postwar period would be a creative period for liberals, and that it would therefore be wise to study current conditions and attitudes in England 'so as to find out what is in the air and what may be expected after the war.'

He left hospital on 24 November, in time to go to Oxford to celebrate his twenty-seventh birthday with the Gerrans, the uncle and aunt of Walter Sage, a fellow Canadian at Oxford. The occasion made him pensive, and he indulged in one of those rare moments of self-analysis in which he reflected on the changes in himself since joining the army:

A year ago to-day I was on a troop train travelling from Montreal to Halifax and getting my first taste of army food. Two years ago I must have been in Saskatoon tho' I can't remember a single circumstance connected with the day. I must have learned more about life, concrete life, and people this last year than I ever knew before. In some ways I feel so enormously more mature, as if I had acquired real individual judgment; and then again, in matters of practice I find myself as ineffective and as without confidence as ever – so totally unfit to be an officer and have charge of men and so entirely an egoist in the way I habitually view the world that I am always unhappy and miserable when facts make me contrast the actual me with the person about whom I am always weaving fantasies. Well, if I am to make a birthday resolution it must be to give up always thinking about myself and to try to view my surroundings objectively. And I must put more energy into my military work. If I fail in it I shall be no good for anything afterwards.

Three days later, on 29 November, he got his second posting, but first sustained job, as a British officer. It was in Darlington, a railway centre in northern Yorkshire, where his new battalion was defending the northeast coast of England against a possible German invasion. His task was to instruct in machine-gun tactics an unruly gang of youngsters who had been in France already and who resented having to return to England to do over again the drills they had done before. Underhill enjoyed the challenge and loved the life of an officer, claiming he felt 'much better' than at any other time since coming to England. He had the service of a batman, the responsibility of training soldiers for active duty at the front, and the companionship of a fine lot of fellow officers. The men teased him for his Canadian accent, but he was encouraged to feel that he was one of them.[34]

Underneath the enjoyment, however, there lingered a feeling of loneliness and a sense of uneasiness with his comrades that brought back memories of Oxford days. Something about the British officers irritated him, thus arousing his feeling of nationalism. 'It is very curious how much a Canadian I have come to feel since I joined the army, and I can't express what it is that makes me feel the difference between the two nationalities.' British officers did not take the war seriously; war was just an extension of British sports. He concluded that the British, although good regimental officers, were incompetent staff officers.[35]

In September, exactly two years after enlisting, Underhill was notified that he was being transferred to France. 'It will be a great weight off my conscience when once I'm in the firing line,' he wrote home. He looked back on his army career with a feeling of contentment unexperienced before: 'I don't suppose anything that could have happened to me would have done more good than those last two years, though I haven't exactly enjoyed it. I think I'm lazier than I used to be but otherwise improved in every respect and much more generally capable. When I look back now I'm astonished at how little I knew about the world and human nature – in spite of or because of 8 years university life.'[36]

   'Here I am at last within sound and almost within sight of the firing line,' he wrote enthusiastically to his mother on 9 October 1917. He had crossed the channel on the 3rd, taken the train to Calais on the 4th, and had gone on to the 17th Infantry Base Depot at Bailleul, near Ypres, where he joined No 4 Company of the First Hertfordshire Regiment as part of the 118th Infantry Brigade of the 39th Division.[37] He was part of the British campaign in Flanders, officially known as the Third Battle of Ypres, popularly known as 'Passchendaele.' The great British offensive had begun on 31 July; before it ended, on 12 November, it would come to embody all the worst and most repellent connotations of the war of trenches. It would cost the British 244 897 men.[38] Underhill described for his parents his surroundings with the shell holes, the shallow trenches, the endless mud, and the stinking mustard gas. 'The whole sky was lit up with flashes and there was just a constant roar.' His platoon was on the firing line. The strain on the nerves was excruciating, the casualties high. He marvelled at the stamina of his men under such pressure of death. It was as though they had found reserve energy in their struggle to survive the horror. After three days they retreated amidst the shell fire to rest-camp to recuperate for three days, before returning to the front line again – a pattern they followed throughout October. Underhill accepted his situation stoically. Even the threat of imminent death did not move him to express his deep inner feelings or to turn to religion. Yet for the first and only time in his life he became interested in poetry, particularly Rupert Brooke's war poems.[39] Brooke was able to express the emotions which he felt but was unable to show.

   For five weeks in November and early December, Underhill left his battalion at the front in order to instruct a platoon in arms drill some thirty miles behind the front line. It was not strenuous work, and he enjoyed the relaxation. In fact, having now proved to himself and to others that he was not a coward, he was not anxious to return to the front. When the course ended, he was granted leave, and he went off to London. He was away when his company headquarters, where he had been instructing, was struck by a German bomb. Two fellow officers were killed, one being his best friend, Second Lieutenant F.M. Brown. Underhill was cabled the news in London, and he went to Reading to visit Brown's wife and to offer his condolences.

At the end of January 1918 the First Battalion of the Hertfordshire Regiment was transferred to 37th Division in the region of the Somme. Underhill's platoon was in reserve until the middle of March, when it was brought up as part of the Allied supreme effort to withhold the all-out German attack. It was a critical time in the war. The French were all but defeated and the Germans were concentrating on beating the British. What was needed was a final push to break through the Allied line and put them on the defensive. The outcome of the war still hinged on the battle of the Somme. March 21st was a morning of dense fog, mingled with smoke and gas. At 4:40 AM a 'skilfully "orchestrated" barrage supplied by almost 6000 guns burst forth on the fronts of the British Fifth and Third armies from the Somme to Cambrai.'[40] The German offensive was on, headed by 'storm troopers,' followed by the infantry of sixty-two German divisions. The Germans succeeded in cutting the Allies' lines of communication with base camp, and the soldiers at the front fought alone in the dense fog.

Underhill's platoon was manning the sides of a chalk pit near Villes-Fauion during the German offensive. On the morning of 22 March he felt a sharp pain in his right leg. Shrapnel had entered at the back of the calf and come out at the side, narrowly missing the bone. He limped back to the nearest dressing station, dodging shells as he went, only to find it packed with wounded soldiers. He continued on foot, since there were no stretchers available, to the nearest town, some two miles away, where he got a ride to Perrone. His leg was treated at the local hospital, and he was immediately transported to Hyde Park Hospital in Plymouth, England.[41] As a result of his involvement in this sixteen-day offensive he was promoted to lieutenant, 1st Hertfordshire Regiment.

On 25 September he rejoined his regiment in France and took part in the final Allied offensive which had begun in August with a brilliant British and Canadian victory at the Somme. It required going over rough terrain strewn with barbed-wire fences. As the Germans retreated, they continued a barrage of firing. Again, Underhill was shot in the leg, but the wound was not serious enough to require his returning. He pushed on with the rest. His battalion was on the French-German border when welcome news of Armistice came on 11 November. The war was over.

Now came the problem of demobilization. Men were restless to get home;

mutinies broke out as rumours of favouritism and delays in demobilization spread through the camps. Educational classes were begun to keep the men occupied, and Underhill became the logical choice for educational officer for his battalion. With the help of a few fellow officers who were qualified school teachers, he began elementary classes, but it proved to be a farce. Too many men were illiterate, and supplies were inadequate. Also, by the end of January, British school teachers were released, because they were badly needed back home. This left Underhill and a couple of other colonials to carry on. He asked President Murray to request his immediate release since he too was needed for educational purposes back home.[42]

In the mean time, Lionel Curtis had passed on one of Underhill's letters to George Wrong with a note attached requesting that Underhill be considered for a teaching position at the Khaki University of Canada. Wrong, who was already teaching there and was in need of assistance, mentioned Underhill to Colonel Henry M. Tory, president of the University of Alberta and acting-president of Khaki University. Tory interviewed Underhill on 24 February and hired him on the spot. Underhill returned to the Canadian army without loss of service or pay.[43]

The Khaki University was the work of the Canadian YMCA. Since the sending of the first Canadian troops overseas, the 'Y' had provided limited educational facilities for Canadian soldiers in Britain and France. In the summer of 1918 it established the Khaki University. Its main campus was in Ripon, an ancient cathedral town in Yorkshire, with additional classes at University College, London, and the University of Bonn, Germany. A number of Canadian professors had been selected to teach, but with increased enrolment after the Armistice, more instructors were needed. It was a demanding job. Immediately upon arrival Underhill had to mark some 150 matriculation essays. In April he had sole responsibility for lecturing in European, British, and Canadian history. He enjoyed the challenge; it also had a practical benefit, since he could prepare lectures which he could use on his return to Saskatchewan. It was his first opportunity to teach Canadian history, and he learned more than the students. He emphasized military history, comparing, in particular, the military strategy of the War of 1812 with that in the recent war. He was happy being back among Canadians, although he admitted that he missed the leisurely life of a British officer with afternoon tea, servants, and drinks.[44]

Classes ended in June, and Underhill left on 18 July, after finishing his marking and packing his materials. A short final holiday in London and Oxford followed before he boarded the ss *Winnifredian*, a 'slow old tug' destined for Halifax and home.

It was the second time in five years that he had left England's shores for Canada (and, interestingly, his last visit to England). This time he felt much more mature and worldly wise. He had learned to handle men, to live with people with radically different values and interests, to survive the harshest of physical conditions, and to come to grips with his own feelings of insecurity and inadequacy. He knew that the war had changed him and wondered if it had had a similar beneficial effect on others. He heard about postwar unrest in Canada that spring, particularly the Winnipeg General Strike, and questioned whether the war had transformed his country into a new and mature nation.

5

The Saskatchewan Years

On his return to the University of Saskatchewan, Underhill hoped to convey to his students the new wisdom and insights he had acquired from army life. He wanted to teach them to become excited about the revolution that was occurring around them. He believed that the Great War was a watershed in the history of Western civilization, the beginning of a new millennium when the full flowering of liberal man would show in all its splendour. His chief concern that first year back was making sense of the war. It was constantly on his mind. He would have flashbacks to the horrors of the trenches and the sight and smells of dead bodies. At low periods, he would feel sorry for himself and go on drinking sprees with other veterans on faculty to release his pent-up feelings. He felt bitter towards those faculty members who had not enlisted. '[W]hen you looked around you at all these fat civilians who had made no sacrifice and who had done well out of the war you got that bitterness and that led you to too much self pity.'[1] An inordinate number of them, he noted, were American born or American educated; this brought out his pro-British feelings. He had mixed feelings about discussing his involvement in the war. He wanted to talk about the war in hopes of conveying the importance and meaning of the holocaust; but he feared that the experience was alien to civilians who would not understand it and might misinterpret his views. He found it easier to discuss the war objectively, by dealing with its significance for Canadians and Canadian nationalism.

This he did in what would be his only sustained piece of work: 'The Canadian Forces in the War,' a 208-page account of Canada's military contribution to the war as part of a larger two-volume work, *The Empire at War*, edited by Sir Charles Lucas and published in 1923 under the auspices of the Royal Commonwealth Society. It was probably Lionel Curtis who got Underhill involved in the project. Curtis was a friend of Lucas, and also had a high regard for Underhill's scholarly abilities. Lucas interviewed Underhill about writing the chapter sometime in the spring of 1919, while Underhill was teaching at Ripon, and the two men finalized details by July. Lucas was very precise as to what he wanted from Underhill: '200 pages of 400 words each on the purely military work of Canada during the war: that is to say of the fighting, the units concerned, and everything that is of a purely military nature, beginning with the composition and enlistment of the first expeditionary force.' (Lucas intended to do the section on the political side of the war himself.) He had one year to complete the project, for which he would receive a fee of £100.[2]

Underhill was an unlikely candidate for the project. He was not a military historian by training; his active service had been in the British, not the Canadian forces; and he had limited acquaintance with the sources. It was also an unlikely project for him to accept: there was no opportunity to express personal opinion; the style had necessarily to be dull and mechanical given the nature of the project; and he had no particular interest in the subject. If anything, his four years in the army had turned him off military interests. He agreed to do it, however, probably unaware of the magnitude of the task, and because he had no other research topic to interest him at the time.

He worked to his deadline. During the academic year, he familiarized himself with Canadian involvement at Vimy Ridge, Ypres, Passchendaele, and the Somme. In May he went to Ottawa to examine the unpublished material in the Department of Militia archives, and to interview Sir Arthur Currie, commander of the Canadian Expeditionary Force. It pleased Underhill that Currie concurred with his belief that the Canadians were superior to the British as staff officers owing to their more scientific approach to war. By early August the project was finished, but he was unhappy with the final product. '[I]t seems too purely military, and I'm not sure that I've made clear the main outlines of a battle in the mass of detail. I haven't felt qualified to pass judgment on tactics or strategy nor to praise living men, so that I'm afraid I've been dull.'[3] It was an accurate self-evaluation of the study; he simply failed to add that it did what he had been asked to do. Heavy, dull, detailed, and impersonal, it was untypical of Underhill both in subject and in style. He was so unhappy with it that he seldom listed it as one of his publications, despite its magnitude, and never mentioned it to his students in class.[4] The strong part of the study is in the concluding section where Underhill revealed his passionate admiration (probably against Lucas's wishes) for the tremendous contribution of the Canadian Corps to the war effort. His feelings of nationalism clearly emerge: 'Canada made notable contributions in food, munitions, and money to the Allied cause, but her unique contribution was the Canadian Corps ... [It] is the greatest national achievement of the Canadian people since the Dominion came into being ... The four years' career of her fighting troops in France forms the real testimony to Canada's entrance into nationhood, the visible demonstration that there has grown up on her soil a people not English, nor Scottish nor American but Canadian – a Canadian nation.'[5]

Underhill had also to adjust to being back in the classroom. While still in the army he had written his department head, A.S. Morton, to request teaching modern European and Canadian history to senior students 'so that they'll go out into the world knowing something about it.'[6] He believed he could excite students more about history if he could relate the subject to present conditions, something he found more difficult to do in medieval English history. There was, of course, the practical concern too that he could use his lecture notes from the Khaki University. He ended up, however, teaching 'Europe in the Nineteenth Century' to forty-two first-year students, 'English Medieval History' to twenty-three senior students, and topics in English history to special history students. Canadian history remained Morton's domain.[7]

In his European course he began with the French Revolution, seeing it as an epoch-making event comparable in impact to the introduction of Christianity or to the period of the Renaissance and Reformation. 'It was a revolution not only as a political upheaval but also as a social revolution and intellectual revolution. "Liberty, Equality, Fraternity" and the opening sentence of Rousseau's *Social Contract* "Man was born free and everywhere he is in chains" were words which fell like a thunderbolt into the society of the ancien regime.'[8] During the year he introduced students to the latest books on European history and to the most recent journal articles. They came to appreciate the impact that ideas had in the evolution of modern Europe leading to the Great War. By the end of the course, he was giving an almost on-the-scene commentary of contemporary changes in Europe to enable students to make sense of newspaper accounts, particularly those in the *Manitoba Free Press*. In these lectures he expressed a viewpoint he had held since Armistice day – that the victors were too harsh on the vanquished. The Versailles Peace Treaty left too many nationalities in the defeated countries of Europe without possibility of self-determination.[9] The thesis was not original, but he presented it with clarity and forcefulness. Clarity – the ability to make a complex subject comprehensible – would be his best quality as both a lecturer and public speaker.

It was during the second academic year after his return from the war (1920–1) that Underhill got his opportunity to teach Canadian history. He took a 'problems' approach, dealing with such topics as French rule, the Conquest, the two races, the struggle for responsible government, Confederation, development of the West, political relations with the empire, and present-day problems. Besides covering the standard political and constitutional developments, he discussed the 'climate of opinion' at various periods in the past, through use of primary sources such as documents and original writings of noted Canadian politicians and intellectuals. He lamented the lack of intellectuals in Canadian history. In a lecture on 'Canada: 1791–1837' he commented that 'Canada was too busy in its struggle to mature to have the leisure to produce thinkers … Only when a country has a certain start over nature is there leisure for it to devote its best energies to public affairs. Therefore Canadian history is not interesting in its early stage.' When he got to the rebellions of 1837 and Lord Durham's Report, he dealt with the ideas of William Lyon Mackenzie and Louis Joseph Papineau, and also discussed extensively the climate of opinion in England out of which Durham's Report emerged. For the 1850s, he dwelt on the ideas which formed the ideological base for the emerging two-party system in the Canadas.[10] He had embarked on his lifelong interest: Canadian political thought. It was a novel approach for the time, but indicative of a heightened awareness of Canadian history in the 1920s.

The students certainly enjoyed the course. They gave him a camera as a token of appreciation for his 'enjoyable lectures' which 'added to our information, gave us fair and unprejudiced views and altogether has given us a new interest in Canadian history. We realize that to prepare and give these lectures every week meant to you the giving up of otherwise free evenings, and we want you to know that we appreciate what you have done.'[11] Such response was indicative of Underhill's popularity as a teacher. He was a more confident and relaxed instructor than he had been in his first year before he left for the war. He now spoke with only brief notes, and his lectures were polished, rational, and well organized, though he continued to display some of his nervous habits while talking. He met with students after class, but the topic of conversation seldom deviated from the subject at hand. He was interested in students' intellectual development, not their personal lives, and made a point of not attending their parties. He could still be chilly with women students, chiefly out of shyness, but was encouraging to those who proved their capabilities. In tutorials, he could get flustered and blush if thrown off by an unresponsive group who refused to open up in discussion. But with a group of intelligent, well-read, and expressive students, the superb qualities of the British tutorial system was clearly evident. Students responded beyond even their own expectations.[12]

His popularity was not at the expense of high standards. Early on he acquired the reputation of being a demanding professor. Students were expected to read widely on their own, both in the subject and in recent periodicals and newspapers. He recommended a long list of British newspapers and British and American journals, whether the course was in British or Canadian history. He told one class to 'acquire the habit of reading good newspapers, reviews and general periodicals and you will become a well-informed person with an intelligent interest in the affairs of the world.' A good historian was one who was vitally interested in current events, he believed.

Students appreciated his efforts. While many were reluctant to praise him while taking his course, knowing that Underhill did not take kindly to flattery, they frequently wrote after the course to thank him. One student, for example, wrote:

I had intended writing you before to tell you just how much I enjoyed your lectures ... I wouldn't dare tell you that if I ever expected to take any more classes from you for I'm sure that you would be rather 'hard' on anyone whom you thought was trying to gain your good graces by flattery. But please don't think that the above is flattery for it isn't. I've taken lectures from quite a few professors but I think that you are the only one who always says what he thinks, and that was what appealed to me more than any-thing else. That and the fact that you were always fair. I remember that we always held divergent views about Lloyd George but you never held that against me; and it makes a big difference when one can hold one's own opinions without the fear of being plucked. I am afraid I have not said what I wanted to very well but I just wanted to tell you that not only myself, but all the others, who used to sweat and curse over those terrible essays that you set, appreciated your lectures more than you might imagine from the work we turned in.[13]

It was Underhill's extensive knowledge, and his precise, cogent, and logical mind that won him respect and even admiration among gifted students; these same qualities created anxiety and intimidation in poorer students. Hilda Neatby, one of the women students whom Underhill respected and strongly supported in her academic pursuits, recalled: 'Underhill could occasionally speak loftily of the mental outlook of the average undergraduate. But the mentally limited undergrad-uates trembling below were well aware that he took the trouble to give them his very best as a teacher – and we had an idea (a perfectly sound one) that his best would be very good anywhere.'[14]

Underhill was also busy establishing a political science department. Before 1918 Ira MacKay had taught the subject, but when he left that year there had been no one to replace him.[15] President Murray approached Underhill about reactivat-ing the program, and Underhill agreed. He offered his first political science course in 1921–2. Entitled 'An Introduction to Political Science,' the course, open only to upper-level students, covered a wide range of political topics: the nature of the state, sovereignty and political obligation, the structure of government, and a discussion of the political theories of Plato, Aristotle, Hobbes, Locke, and Rousseau. The prescribed text was *Elements of Political Science*, a popular and widely used text by the Canadian economist-cum-humorist, Stephen Leacock. Nine students enrolled in the course.

By 1924–5 Underhill had become professor and sole instructor of political science, 'with a department to myself which I can make or mar with my own efforts,' he informed one friend, and remained a lecturer in history. He saw no difficulty in switching subjects, because he found the two complemented each another – at least the way he taught them. He confessed that his history courses 'had become very much a study of government anyway.' He shortened the time period covered in the courses every year so as to concentrate more on the modern period. 'It is the problems of government which interest me more and more and therefore I think P.S. is where I belong.'[16]

There was a more important reason for the switch: he wanted to make political science a Canadian equivalent of the Oxford 'Modern Greats' program. What he had in mind he outlined in a letter to a prospective student: 'My idea in Political Science is that no one should be allowed to graduate as a specialist in it who hasn't made a fairly thorough study of the history and government of his own country, who isn't familiar with what outstanding men have thought about the problem of the state since men began the experiment of self-government, and who hasn't a working knowledge of how modern states conduct their internal affairs and their relations with one another. In Canada it seems to me that we should know Britain and the United States best of all foreign countries, and especially Britain since we are engaged in working out some kind of political co-operation with her.'[17] Students would have to take mandatory core courses each year and devote their last two years solely to political science. In the first year they would take the introductory course which would familiarize them with the major themes, issues, and terminology of political scientists. They would take core courses in their senior years in political theory, comparative government, international relations, comparative law, and social psychology. Only the last two courses would be taught by instructors outside the department. The courses were interdisciplinary in approach and concentrated, as in 'Greats,' or a few classic texts as the basis for an in-depth study of Canadian civilization. The approach was not novel, nor were the courses in relation to other political science programs across the country. What was new was Underhill's conviction that Canadian studies were worthy subjects of concentration. In this respect he was breaking new ground not only in the West, but also in Canada as a whole.

Academic concerns paled into the background, however, as Underhill became absorbed in courting the woman he would marry, Ruth Mary Carr. Ruth was the eldest of five children of George and Maybel Carr of Prince Albert, Saskatchewan, a town of some 12 000 people situated on the North Saskatchewan River, ninety miles north of Saskatoon. She had been born in England and received her early education at Ealing, near London. In 1912 the Carr family had emigrated to Prince Albert, where her father established the Northern Cartage Company, a moving, storage, and packing centre. They were a well-to-do family. Mr Carr was involved in various social clubs and became an alderman in the early 1920s; Mrs Carr was active in the Women's Auxiliary of St Alban's Anglican procathedral.[18] Ruth Carr (nicknamed 'Rufus') had entered the University of Saskatchewan in the class of 1914, the same year that Underhill arrived. She was a model student. She received high honours in French and English while carrying on an active student life, serving on the Student Council executive, the Athletic Directorate, the Literary Club, and the YWCA. She won the Ladies Senior Stick for 1917–18, an award given to the most outstanding woman student of her year. Her graduation picture of 1918 reveals an attractive young woman with delicate features and expressive eyes. In 1919–20 she went to the University of Toronto to do an MA in English. Here she heard glowing accounts of Underhill's brilliance from two of her English instructors, W.J. Alexander and Malcolm Wallace, both of whom had taught Underhill earlier. Alexander told her that Underhill was one of only two truly gifted and independently minded students that he had ever taught at Toronto.[19]

She returned to Saskatoon the following year to teach English at the university. She occupied an office next door to Underhill in Qu'Appelle Hall. Underhill, being shy, was slow to get to know her. He recalled the first time he escorted her to a public social gathering – a Progressive meeting during the election campaign of 1921: 'The meeting was in the Third Avenue Methodist Church, and when we got there the whole body of the church and the galleries were filled; so that we had to sit in the front row of the choir, behind the speakers, in full view of all my friends and colleagues in the audience. I still remember their amused comments on what was evidently happening to me.'[20] Their public outings were more frequent after that. The two could be seen taking long walks along the river, deep in discussion about Canadian literature, politics, or some book one of them had just read. He proposed to her during one of their walks in the winter of 1921–2 while she was staying with the Murrays, recovering from a bout of flu. The Carr and Murray families were acquaintances, and Ruth was a good friend of President Murray's eldest daughter. The couple were married on 22 June in St Alban's procathedral. Following the wedding and reception they left by train for their two-week honeymoon at Lake of Bays in Muskoka. They spent the remainder of the summer in Toronto with his parents.[21]

Underhill was able to provide financial security for his bride. Although he would be the sole provider, since Ruth resigned her position upon marriage, he was making a respectable salary of $4000. He had purchased the two-and-a-half storey, white-framed house at 815 14th Street where he had been living as a bachelor since his return to Saskatoon. During the summer he arranged to have it renovated into a family home. In addition, he had over $1500 as Victory Bonds and investments of $1000 in preferred stocks. He had also dabbled in real-estate property along with Professor Eaton (at the time, ironically, when Underhill was critical of the real-estate mentality of western Canadians), and was able to make sufficient profit to provide a down-payment on the purchase of his house. The couple would not be wealthy, but they would be able to live comfortably.[22] It took Underhill time to adjust to married life; he was thirty-three years old and used to being independent. Fortunately, his wife was herself an academic who appreciated his interests and supported him in his intellectual pursuits. She provided him with the free time he needed to read, write, and speak at public functions.

On 12 November 1924 the Underhills became the proud parents of a daughter and their only child, Elizabeth Joyce. Underhill adjusted well to fatherhood. He took an interest in Elizabeth's growth and development, and proudly informed his friends of her progress. He wondered what effect the new addition would have on his own work. He was pleasantly surprised to find himself even more productive in his studies that winter than he had been since the war. Marriage and a family gave him stability, security, and a personal commitment.[23]

Underhill's marriage to a westerner linked him to the West but his ambition was still in the East. He desperately wanted an academic position at Toronto. Every year he wrote to Wrong to find out what was happening and each time Wrong wrote back to say how interested the department was in acquiring him. But that was where it stopped. Part of his problem, he realized, was his lack of publications. A heavy teaching load, yearly revisions and updating of his lectures, and at least one new course every year had absorbed all his time. Still, he realized that his chances of getting back east were slim without a weightier curriculum vitae. He must keep an eye open for a research topic that excited him.

Instead of pursuing research, however, he got involved in a number of activities on campus and in the city. He helped establish a 'United Order of Canada' group in Saskatoon, a round-table organization committed to 'greater unity and a higher type of Canadian national spirit' through informed discussions of Canadian affairs. At the organizational meeting for a Canadian Officer Training Corps on campus he volunteered to become adjutant and then a year later the captain of the organization. He created his own history club (which barred women students) in competition with Morton's historical association, and began a League of Nations Club, of which he became honorary president.[24] He also wrote a series of six articles on the league for a school publication, *Modern Education*,[25] in an effort to interest young Canadians in this important international organization to which Canada belonged. Increasingly he found himself a consultant, providing information on a wide range of historical and contemporary issues for university colleagues, public organizations, and private citizens.

Underhill was also called upon to give public lectures. Though he found it difficult to make speeches, he enjoyed the challenge and knew he was an effective speaker. He saw his strength in his ability to see the fallacies and inconsistencies in conventional wisdom. He loathed and attacked sloppy thinking. He found giving speeches helped him to organize his thoughts, to present his ideas coherently and simply. He believed that academics should impart their knowledge to others, a lesson he learned from his Toronto and Oxford professors. And he felt that he had something important to say and the ability to say it cogently and clearly. His speeches in the early 1920s had a consistent theme: the need for an educated and informed public to encourage Canadians to take a more responsible role in international affairs. Within Canada, this theme was popular among intellectuals and politicians. Where Underhill differed from other speakers, especially John W. Dafoe, was in advocating Canadian involvement in the world through association with the empire rather than as an autonomous nation. In a guest lecture at the University of Alberta in March 1924 on 'Canada's National Status,' Underhill argued that the familiar constitutional achievements on the road to nationhood – the formation of the Imperial War Cabinet, the signing of the Versailles Peace Treaty, membership in the League of Nations, the Chanak crisis, and the signing of the Halibut Treaty – were 'not really so great as would-be prophets would have us believe.' Why? Because they lead Canada into two opposing directions which negate one another. Some resulted in closer co-operation with Britain and others moved Canada towards isolationism and autonomy. Canadians had to pursue one of these policies to its logical end. He left his audience little doubt which policy he favoured: 'Are we to raise ourselves to a part worthy of the position which is ours in the British Empire or are we going to be foolish enough to imagine that we alone of all peoples in the world can stand by ourselves in these hard times[?] Are we going to allow these vociferous busy bodies of all our past faiths and loyalties which the dominant school of nationalists is dinning into our ears today to commit us to this will-of-the-wisp of an independent isolated nationality which will lead us dancing into the bogs[?].'[26]

The argument was a familiar one among Canadian imperialists. While Underhill delighted in pointing out the inconsistencies in the logic of Canadian imperialist thought, he was not prepared to challenge their basic assumption that national status could best evolve through Canada's association with the empire. He still remained, in other words, a comfortable, middle-class easterner imbued with imperialist ideals from his student years at Toronto and Oxford and his army years in the Canadian and Imperial forces.

Responsibility was also the underlying theme of his speeches on the question of higher education. Donning the cloak of the critic and taking the popular American critics of higher education as his example – H.L. Mencken, Thorstein Veblen, and Walter Lippmann – Underhill proceeded to chastise his colleagues for failing to provide the best quality of education possible. Such criticism fitted naturally into the iconoclastic and debunking spirit of the 1920s. He argued that professors were too much concerned with product and too little concerned with process. The subject matter was secondary; instructors should encourage students to think critically and independently. This was the view of John Dewey and the 'progressive school of education' which Underhill accepted implicitly. The best way to encourage critical thinking was by having students concentrate on one discipline. The curse of North American education was the elective system which allowed students to wander in the intellectual wasteland, picking up a smattering of knowledge on sundry subjects, but never forced them to challenge their intellectual abilities on any one of them. He equated this system to the mechanized American factory after which it must have been modelled. In a whimsical style, he exaggerated the evils of the system: 'Every course, every detached segment of knowledge, every unit must be equated with every other. It makes no difference whether the subject is Kant's metaphysics or elementary French. They are all equal when the student appears on May 3 at the pearly gates of his B.A. paradise and demands admission from our St. Peter who sits on the Chancellor's Chair. And if perchance the Recording Angel in the Registrar's Officer on counting up his credits finds that he has only 19 or 19 1/2 instead of 20, he is sent back again to get another manufactured in the summer school or at Columbia or Chicago, or some other education factory. For the products of this American system are as standardized now as the parts of a Ford car, and the student can pick up spare parts in any up-to-date educational garage all the way across the continent.'[27]

While critical of the American system of education, Underhill looked increasingly to American intellectuals for ideas and direction for Canadian studies. Social scientists there were well in advance of Canada in both methodology and new areas of research. He realized too the importance of making contact with American professors for his own intellectual and academic advancement. His first opportunity to attend an American conference came in the summer of 1924 when he was accepted as one of 225 delegates to attend the Institute of Politics conference at Williamstown, Massachusetts.[28] Once accepted, he wrote to Dafoe to inquire whether he could cover the proceedings for the *Manitoba Free Press*.

The Institute of Politics was the brain-child of President H.A. Garfield of Williams College. In 1913 he proposed the establishment of a summer school in Williamstown where scholars of international repute could deliver university lectures to interested and informed scholars. Meanwhile the war intervened, and the first conference was not held until the summer of 1921. By that time the strictly academic nature of the original proposal had changed to make the institute a conference on international relations at which leading scholars and 'experts' could meet for 'the serious study of foreign affairs with a view to creating a more sympathetic understanding of the problems and policies of other nations.'[29] Underhill liked all aspects of the conference. The physical setting in the picturesque Berkshire Hills of northwest Massachusetts was ideal. The format, by which candidates attended lectures and round-table discussions in the mornings and evenings, with afternoons free for sports or other leisurely activities, suited him. It approximated the Oxford style more closely than anything else he had witnessed in the North American academic world. He was much impressed with the high level of discussion and the overall enthusiasm of the delegates. 'It was refreshing,' he reported in the *Free Press*, 'to find so many people gathered in one place on this continent who are trying to study world affairs seriously and dispassionately, with a keenness for knowledge and a distrust of catchwords and "isms."' Most valuable was the wealth of ideas that bombarded the participants: R.H. Tawney, the brilliant Balliol socialist, on 'The History and Policy of the Labour Party'; M.J. Bonn, the German scholar, on 'The Crisis of European Democracy'; Louis Aubert, representing France, on 'The Reconstruction of Europe'; and Sir James Arthur Salter, spokesman for the League of Nations, on 'The Economic Causes of War.' All these speakers agreed, he observed, that 'the main cause of war in the future will be that economic form of nationalism which drives nations to seek to monopolize raw materials and markets at the expense of their rivals. For this form of economic imperialism we must substitute some form of international co-operation or perish.'[30]

Here was 'food for thought' for the long winter in Saskatchewan, for his research in Canadian history, and for discussion with students in tutorials. How important were economic factors? They seemed to have played an important part in Canadian development according to J.S. Ewart, whose writings Underhill was reading with great interest. Charles Beard had used economic factors to explain the origins of the American nation in his *Economic Interpretations of the Constitution*, a book Underhill had read in the spring of 1923.[31] Could the Progressive political revolt in the West be understood in economic terms? Certainly spokesmen for the Progressives emphasized their dissatisfaction with the economic domination of the industrial and manufacturing interests by Bay Street and St James Street.[32] Had liberals been blinded to economic concerns in the past in their quest for political democracy? He himself had not thought of looking at economic and materialistic factors behind political events in his political science courses, preferring instead to explain political action in terms of political theory. For the moment there were only random thoughts, but they would begin a train of ideas that would lead him away from his idealistic perspective to a realistic outlook on current and past events and, ultimately, to his economic interpretation of Canadian history.

In the summer of 1924 Underhill embarked on a new research topic in Canadian history: a study of the ideas of George Brown through an analysis of his editorials in the Toronto *Globe* of the 1850s and 1860s. The topic was a logical outgrowth of his Canadian history and political science courses. In both disciplines he was interested in the 'climate of opinion' at various periods in the past, in particular the Confederation era. As a political scientist, he wanted to know more about the origins and nature of Canadian political parties. A study of Brown's life and ideas was an obvious means of getting at these broader subjects. Moreover, Brown's liberal views, political involvement, and rural Ontario appeal made him a natural subject of interest. Underhill felt that Brown had been unjustly treated in the standard textbooks and it was time for a new study of the man.

He presented his preliminary thoughts on the Confederation era in a speech to the Saskatchewan Women's Canadian Club in the fall of 1924.[33] He chose to speak on the origins and early development of Canadian political parties. Although the ladies in the audience would not be aware, Underhill introduced them to some novel ideas about the study of Canadian political history in his speech. He maintained that before 1867 Canadian parties had different philosophies and ideologies, each one closely reflecting the ideas of its English namesake. Only at this point in their historical evolution did Canadian parties resemble British parties. After 1867 the parties became more North American in nature, because Canada, like the United States, was confronted with the gargantuan task of creating a transcontinental nation. This task of nation-building became of uppermost concern, and the two parties differed in their response to this practical but vital undertaking. The Conservatives captured the imagination and political support of the Canadian people with their bold and challenging platform of territorial expansion. It was John A. Macdonald who alone 'had been seized with the conception of a great Canadian nation, and he inspired his nation-building enthusiasm into those who followed him.' He was a great Canadian nationalist. Only George Brown among the Liberals approximated Macdonald in these formative decades. Unfortunately, he left politics before the Liberals came to power. His successors, Alexander Mackenzie and Edward Blake, were unimaginative and parochial in outlook. Blake was a great intellectual, Underhill conceded, in fact 'probably the greatest intellectual in our history,' but a man without a national vision. Macdonald's ideal became tarnished in the late nineteenth and early twentieth century when the Conservative party fell prey to the ambitions of the Canadian Pacific Railway and the Canadian Manufacturers' Association. By this time, the Liberals had taken up the challenge of national expansion under Wilfrid Laurier. It was not as bold an undertaking for Laurier as it had been for Macdonald because this was a boom period, and the Liberal leader had only to ride the crest of prosperity. '[W]e have been a materialistic people,' he observed. 'And this has been the key to our party history from 1867 to 1914. First one party, and then the other, embodied in the person of a great leader, [sic] this idea of material expansion had captured the imagination and support of the country with it. Apart from this the words "Liberal" and "Conservative" and the struggles between the two parties were as meaningless as those party divisions which perplexed Mr. Pickwick and his friends in the Eatanswill elections.'

Here was a new look at Canadian history from the viewpoint of its continental development rather than its imperial relations. The decisive factor in our national history up to 1914 was not the decisions of the British Foreign Office but the response of Canadian leaders to the practical concerns of forging a nation. While

his interpretation emphasized economic factors, it was not yet the economic interpretation of Canadian history. He still maintained that the motivating force behind Canada's development was a spiritual vision of a great transcontinental nation that had inspired two great prime ministers. There was no thought that the territorial expansion and material growth in these formative years was a sinister plot perpetrated by big business interests to line their own pockets. He was still too much of a Canadian nationalist to believe that interpretation.

Underhill's concern with past political developments aroused his interest in the current political situation, and he decided to get involved in the 1925 election campaign. He came out in support of the Progressive party, an independent farmers party that had first come into political existence in the federal election of 1921. He gave a speech at one of their rallies, wrote two anonymous articles in the Saskatoon *Daily Star*, and explained in a non-partisan forum at the university why he was voting Progressive.[34] In each case he spent as much time attacking the Liberals as he did defending the Progressives. Clearly he favoured many of the Liberal policies – low tariff, Senate reform, and a more equitable national transportation system – but he was annoyed at Mackenzie King's failure to implement these programs during the Liberals' four years in office. He attributed their inertia to the stranglehold that the anti-liberal forces of Quebec – the Roman Catholic church and St James Street – had on the party. 'No party that is saddled with the support of 50 or 60 reactionary Quebeckers will ever make any sincere attempt to carry liberal ideas into practice. Quebec is governed despotically and has been for the last 2 generations by an alliance between the Catholic hierarchy and St James Street,'[35] Underhill claimed. In the end, there was no difference between the two major parties; the electorate could choose 'Tweedledee Meighen or Tweedledum King.' Or they could vote for a genuine alternative in the Progressive party. He admitted to the Progressives' ineffective action in parliament against the guileful Mackenzie King and their failure to become a national party able to win seats in all regions of the country. But he still persisted in voting for them on an 'act of faith.' He believed that the party was on the verge of becoming a meaningful third party that represented those people unrepresented in the two traditional parties. He looked at the Progressives in terms of their program and 'class representation,' seeing them as nationalistic as the two traditional parties which represented only the business interests of Ontario and Quebec.

Such a positive public political stance concealed an uncertain voter. In a letter to his father he admitted: 'I think I shall vote Progressive as I did last time unless it seems very certain that the Progressive has no chance in Saskatoon in which case I shall vote Liberal'[36] – hardly the reasoning of a political convert. Also, in his more academic speech to the Saskatchewan Women's Canadian Club only a year earlier, he had described the Progressives as a strictly western Canadian protest movement that was splitting the nation by irrationally attributing all their economic ills to the evil bankers and industrialists who happened to reside in eastern Canada. At that time he had concluded that the real blame for the narow sectional nature of Canadian parties lay with the Progressives. They had forced the 'two old-time parties to the position of being little better than sectional Eastern groups.' The one exception was the Ginger Group, that little band of rebels under J.S. Woodsworth who split from the Progressive party in 1924. They alone, he claimed, were confronting the real problem in Canada, 'which is how our political democracy is to control those in whose hands rest the concentrated economic and financial powers of modern America.' Clearly, therefore, Underhill's outspoken and definite public views were intended more to arouse debate than to express strong convictions, a stance that remained true throughout his life. Equally, his thinking in the mid-twenties revealed his search for the ideal Canadian political party, a search that would occupy a lifetime.

6

The Making of a
Canadian Historian

The term ended on 15 December 1925. There were only examinations to mark, then Underhill could put teaching and administrative duties behind him for eight glorious months of sabbatical leave. He had wanted to spend his sabbatical term in England renewing acquaintances at Oxford and revisiting the cultural centres of Europe, but it was simply too expensive. 'The cost of travelling and of having children in this damned protectionist country is so high that we are continuously poverty-stricken,'[1] he informed Kenneth Bell at Oxford. So he decided instead to spend the term in Toronto. He wanted to devote his time to his research. He planned in early January to begin reading the Toronto *Globe* of the 1860s in an effort to complete the research on George Brown that he had begun two years earlier. He was more convinced than ever that 'there is a good deal to George Brown which might be brought out yet besides the "trouble making politician," '[2] as the Canadian textbooks described him. Brown needed to be vindicated, and he was anxious to do it.

First he had to adjust to living in Toronto. Finding accommodation was no problem since they stayed with his parents. This proved to be a great saving, and he realized that the trip would have been impossible otherwise, since Toronto was such an expensive city. The weather was cold and miserable for the first month; he nearly 'froze to death in the badly constructed Toronto houses.' Both he and Ruth came down with colds.

The rotten weather was tolerable, however, compared to the attitude of the people. 'These Torontonians are the most self-centered complacent lot of conventionalists on the face of the earth,' he wrote to Bell. 'Our Canadian millionaires are beginning the practice of founding scholarships to send western students east to Toronto and Montreal. What is most needed is a series of free passes to enable some of these Eastern profs to visit Canada. The stuff you read in the Round Table and such organs is mostly by pundits who have never penetrated beyond Toronto farther than the surrounding golf links.'[3] Such snide remarks about the stuffiness of easterners was characteristic of Underhill ever since he moved to the West. But they had always been said half in jest; now he meant it. He attributed their self-centred attitude to their lack of national ideals. Torontonians were more under the grip of the 'cursed North American individualist civilization' than were westerners. They seemed to have few ambitions beyond acquiring more material goods. He concluded cynically that the main contribution of Toronto to Canadian civilization was not the Mendelssohn Choir, the University of Toronto, or any other cultural interest, but the T. Eaton and Robert Simpson companies.[4] He had come to Toronto under the illusion that eastern Canadians were more nationalistic and idealistic than his western compatriots. Now he wondered if any Canadian had national ambitions any more. Within one year, Canada would be celebrating its Diamond Jubilee. Yet Canadians were too busy making money to take stock of what spiritual goals they had achieved in the last sixty years or hoped to achieve in the next forty.

Most appalling of all were eastern academics. They should have been critical of such attitudes and loftier in their aspirations, yet they were accepting and mediocre – a far cry from the ideal he had envisioned in the West. He informed George Simpson that his 'opinion of the Saskatchewan faculty has gone up enormously. I have been labouring under the delusion that we were rather commonplace compared with the supermen of the East. But if I couldn't give better stuff than some of what I have heard down here, I should desert academic life for selling bonds.'[5] Was this sour grapes? He certainly had aspirations of being among these 'supermen of the East.' There was a defensiveness in his reaction, but that was only part of it. These outbursts were characteristic of his approach whenever a situation failed to match the ideal that he envisioned. Disillusionment was inevitable when he set his sights too high.

The same was true of his reaction to Toronto. What he disliked about the city was its failure to match his ideal. He had come naïvely hoping to find the perfect Canadian society, a city imbued with national interests and spiritual concerns that had inspired earlier Canadians and that seemed to be missing in the West. He had arrived disillusioned, hoping to find the spark to rekindle his flame of nationalism. Instead he found a society on the make, dominated by the businessman with his one aspiration of becoming wealthier. He became even more cynical and critical of the East. He had been primed for that reaction. His reading in American progressive historiography and his exposure to the Progressive movement in the Canadian West prepared him well for his negative reaction. He was also, at the time, reading works critical of current British and American society, such as F.C.H. Schiller's *Cassandra on the Future of the British Empire* (London 1926), Walter Lippmann's *The Phantom Republic* (New York 1925), Herbert Croly's *The Promise of American Life* (New York 1909), and Bertrand Russell's

Prospects of Industrial Civilization (New York 1923). Without this intellectual context, he might not have been so critical of the city. Still, it took a change of environment to trigger the reaction, an indication once again of the strong effect throughout his life that his physical environment had on his mental outlook. The return to Toronto was a turning-point in his life.

From this perspective, Underhill came to appreciate the nobler qualities and ideals of westerners. He now projected the ideals on westerners that previously he had projected onto easterners. He believed that the western Progressives were 'the only hope for a civilization in this country in which we won't all be abject slaves to a few vulgar ignorant money barons in Toronto and Montreal.' The West became in his imagination the golden region of the country, with the Progressives as the leaders in building up a new and meaningful Canadian civilization. His faith in the Progressive movement rose immeasurably.

His research reinforced his disillusionment. In reading the *Globe* he discovered that Confederation was not the great era of nationalism he had assumed. Even then, big business was operating behind the political scene. 'I always thought I was fairly sophisticated about the influence of big business on our present-day Canadian politics,' he confessed, 'but I never dreamt the conditions were so similar sixty years ago, although it is obvious that they must have been when you think about the matter.' Underhill had not wanted to think about such an idea. It was pleasant to believe that there was at least one era in Canadian history that had not been tarnished by the corrupting influence of big business. He could not ignore the evidence, however. He found 'the trail of the G[rand] T[runk] R[ailway] and the Hudson's Bay Company and similar institutions running across everything that happened, almost, in the two decades before Confederation.' He concluded that 'this country, like the United States, was chiefly made by successive generations of grasping unscrupulous businessmen and its political history is only a by-product of big business.'[6]

Now he understood clearly the unpopularity of George Brown in the standard textbooks. These authors accepted at face value the arguments of Brown's opponents, the Montreal businessmen, who accused him of religious bigotry and anti-French Canadianism in an effort to deflect attention from Brown's attack on themselves. 'Brown wanted a government which could stand above the lobbying of business interests. Montreal wanted one which should be their tool. And they made use of Brown's religious views to stir up the habitants against him just as they do today of Meighen's conscription activities for the same purpose.'[7] At a time of sordid politics, Brown was the one politician who stood for the interest of the Canadian people rather than of a few unscrupulous businessmen. Even John A. Macdonald, the great hero of Confederation, could not boast of such an ideal. 'His conception of politics never rose above that of the business man on the make,' he concluded. How blinded he had been to Macdonald's weaknesses and to Brown's strengths from his reading of distorted versions of Canadian history. His admiration for Brown now knew no limits. He admitted that he had been predisposed to Brown and his Clear Grit party, having lived in the heartland of Grit support and raised on its Bible, the *Globe*. He had sound reasons for praising Brown; he was a truly great politician.

Brown was more than that, however. He was also a great Canadian intellectual. His *Globe* was a medium to introduce intellectual currents from England and Europe to the raw frontier society of Upper Canada. 'What has struck me most in reading the *Globe* is that its editor was very closely in touch with the main intellectual currents of his time, as one gathers them from reading English history of the middle of the century, and that he was much more than a mere Canadian publishing a provincial paper in Toronto and leading a provincial party. The *Globe* constantly discussed broad general questions, such as the relations of Canada with the mother country and with the United States, which did not come within the range of party politics ... It acted, in fact, as an interpreter of English and European liberalism to the rough and pioneer society of Canada.'[8] Underhill admired Brown's faith in the intellectual capabilities of Canadians, a faith sadly lacking among Brown's political colleagues.

Underhill was equally excited to show Brown's importance in the political and intellectual evolution of Canada. His Clear Grit movement could rightfully be considered the antecedent of the modern western Progressive movement. The parallels were striking: the enemy was the same – the alliance of the Roman Catholic hierarchy and St James Street in Montreal; the ideas and ideals were almost identical; and both could be considered western frontier movements of revolt against the domination of eastern metropolitan and business interests. Canadian history had a radical tradition preceding Confederation. He must ensure that Brown's efforts lived on into the present. 'The more I read, the redder I become,' Underhill proclaimed. He was ready to take up the attack on big business where Brown left off half a century earlier.[9]

These revelations spurred his enthusiasm to do a first-rate biography, but he still had research to complete on Brown in the Public Archives in Ottawa. In May he went to the capital to work through the minutes of the Executive Council and the correspondence between the governor general and the Colonial Office for the period from 1857 to 1867.[10] He went down alone and stayed at the University Club for the first month until his family could join him in a rented house at 245 Powell Street.

It was a blistering hot summer in the capital, and the archives were stuffy. This alone was an excuse to leave his work to observe the parliamentary session, not that he needed an excuse. He knew that he had the opportunity to observe one of the most memorable and historic events in Canadian history: the Constitutional Crisis of 1926. Mackenzie King had decided after his marginal victory in the election of 1925 to hang on to office, despite the misgivings of the governor general, Lord Byng, and to let parliament decide his political fate. The session opened in early January with King wooing the Progressives for their support. At first the situation looked promising for the Liberals with Charles Dunning, premier of Saskatchewan, agreeing to join the party and with Mackenzie King winning a seat in Prince Albert. But the Conservatives had a trump card left – the maladministration of the Customs Department. They forced the appointment of a special investigation committee of the Commons which was ready to report its findings in June. By the time that Underhill arrived in Ottawa, the customs scandal dominated the political scene.

Research went to the wind for the month of June. He became a daily spectator in the Visitors' Gallery of the House, both during the regular parliamentary sessions and during the deliberations of the Customs Committee, coming away only 'when compelled to do so by exhaustion.' It was, he recalled, 'thrilling politics all that summer and I had a great time.' He listened to both sides of the story, weighing the evidence and judging the validity of their arguments. He was impressed with Mackenzie King's shrewd handling of the crisis, and his admiration for the man rose daily. King was obviously better in the political arena than he was on the political hustings at election time.[11]

Underhill's real admiration was for the political critics: Ted Garland, Henri Bourassa, and especially his friend J.S. Woodsworth. He admitted in later life that he saw 'the customs scandal through the eyes of Mr. Woodsworth.' Through watching him closely in the House of Commons and talking extensively with him in his office in the East Block, Underhill concluded that Woodsworth was a saint in politics. Here was a politician with principles and moral standards, a man who had ideals amid the practical and sordid politics about him – very much like George Brown in his day. To come to know Woodsworth better in itself made his sabbatical a great success.

There were other rewards too. He was in Ottawa for the annual meeting of the Canadian Historical Association on 17 and 18 May. The session attracted to the city historians and political scientists from across the country. He was unimpressed with the proceedings themselves. What he did enjoy was the opportunity to meet colleagues outside of the conference, especially at the Public Archives. He became better acquainted with his western colleagues: A.L. Burt of Alberta, and D.C. Harvey and Chester Martin of Manitoba. He talked with W.P.M. Kennedy, Vincent Bladen, George Brown, and Lester Pearson, all of Toronto; and he met for the first time W.A. Mackintosh, an economist at Queen's University, and G.E. Wilson, a historian at Dalhousie. He was part of the 'renaissance of Canadian history'[12] that got under way in the 1920s. It was a wonderful way to spend a sabbatical: combining original research with intelligent discussion of current events. It was the closest he had come to the 'academic's paradise' since student days.

Reluctantly, in mid-September he packed his belongings and research mater, bid farewell to family and friends in Toronto, and started the trip west. They arrived a few days too late to cast their vote in the 14 September election but he had confidence in the sensibility of western voters. He was returning with new insights into Canadian history to present in university and public lectures. He was already thinking of a paper for the 1927 Canadian Historical Association meeting in Toronto on the Upper Canadian reform tradition. It had been his idea to have a session on Confederation in commemoration of the sixtieth anniversary. Here would be an opportunity to present his economic interpretation of Canadian history, which he knew would arouse considerable debate among his colleagues. [13]

He was anxious to test his new ideas in his public speeches, yet he found himself in a quandary. How could he reconcile his belief in the need for a spirit of Canadian nationalism with his awareness that such nationalism had never existed? As a Canadian he believed in national unity, yet everywhere he turned, past or present, he saw only sectional interests. Were there national ideals which transcended regional, ethnic, or economic differences? He believed that there were, yet they were usually presented in sentimental terms which lessened their impact. It was important to reveal the truth in hopes that Canadians, if they could see the realities and ideals behind its evolution, would come to appreciate the history of their country. That was what American progressive historians believed. To present only one side of the story, the ideals, as traditional historians had done, distorted history and led to fatuous boasting.

As Underhill worked through these questions in public speeches, he contradicted himself. In a speech on 'Canadian Confederation after 60 Years' he began by lamenting that Canadians, unlike Americans, were unexcited by their history. 'From the beginning our federal union has been a prosaic commonplace business. It has never really stirred our blood or quickened our imagination. No generation has consecrated it for us in blood by a war of liberation to achieve it or a Civil War to preserve it. The Fathers of Confederation are still too near to us in time for us to be able to delude ourselves into the belief that they had many of those lofty or heroic qualities with which the fathers of their country are usually invested by patriotic myth. The political situation from which Confederation resulted is remembered only as a sordid struggle for office and the spoils of office.' [14] Yet there were aspects of Canada's past, he noted, which were interesting and different from the history of the United States: welding a nation out of two races with different languages, religions, and cultures; developing an autonomous nation while still remaining a member of the British empire; and creating a distinct nation alongside a bigger and more advanced nation that is similar in so many respects. Then he went on to downplay the greatness of these uniquely Canadian developments by revealing their limitations. The union of the two races was tenuous, held together only by political expediency. The imperial connection had served only to heighten English-Canadian and French-Canadian hostilities, while on this continent Canadians had failed thus far to find any feature in their country's make-up to distinguish them from Americans. He concluded on a pessimistic note: that Canadians lacked a national spirit. The speech appeared to be more of an appeal to westerners to prove him wrong than a definitive statement of Canada's development.

He developed his new ideas in a more sustained form in his paper for the Canadian Historical Association meeting on 27 and 28 May. His friend, Charles Cochrane, who was secretary-treasurer of the organization, had asked him the previous November to give a paper, but he had left the writing, as usual, to the last minute, and the due date was fast approaching. He had to have a copy of the paper in Cochrane's hands by mid-May for him to read at the session. He had decided against going east to deliver the paper himself, since he was too busy preparing for his permanent move to Toronto.

That urgent need taught Underhill an important lesson: he could produce good-quality written work only under pressure. An impending deadline or a moral obligation was the best assurance that he would do something. If it *had* to be done, he did it, and did it well. Otherwise, he would procrastinate. He could find too many distractions or excuses to take him away from his immediate task. That was to be a pattern of his life.

The paper was provocative as he had intended. He appealed to historians to take a new perspective on Confederation. It was time to study 'the atmosphere, social, economic and intellectual, in which the political movement took place.'[15] He saw his paper as an introductory study in Canadian intellectual history through an examination of the ideas of the Upper Canadian Reformers on such issues as the Grand Trunk Railway, the acquisition of the Northwest, and Confederation itself as revealed in George Brown's editorials in the Toronto *Globe*. Rather than present a thorough study of the assumptions and beliefs of the Reformers on these issues, he used the writings as a medium by which to offer some new insights into the writing of Canadian history. The points were all there in the paper: the need for Canadian intellectual history; the validity of the economic interpretation of Canadian history; the parallels of Canadian and American reform traditions, including the applicability of the Turner thesis to Canada; and the rivalry between the frontier and the metropolitan centres. None of these concepts was developed at great length and too often the central ideas were concealed in a wealth of quotations from the *Globe*. The real strength of the paper came through only after further reflection. The seeds were planted to be germinated in the minds of a younger generation of Canadian historians.

The major weakness of the paper was the uncritical view of George Brown. In his enthusiasm to debunk the traditional heroes of Confederation – the politicians who fought for its success – Underhill resurrected his own hero. Brown could do no wrong. Underhill accepted his ideas and his professed motives at face value. Even while outlining Brown's imperial ambitions for the West in the boldest economic and political terms, Underhill could only see noble national aspirations. Brown alone stood above the sordid politics to speak for the common man of Canada.

Underhill's CHA paper was his first presentation of the economic interpretation of Canadian history. The ideas had been latent in his mind, but it took the actual writing of the paper to clarify his views. He had read Beard and Turner much earlier, but without enthusiasm. Now their message seemed to ring out clearly. He presented his new interpretation boldly and convincingly, as though it were a self-evident truth to which he had adhered for all time. The 'conversion' was too much for one perceptive student from Saskatchewan who was truly amazed at Underhill's changed perspective: 'I am interested in the glimpses afforded me ... of the thorough-going intellectual revolution which has occurred in your mind in the course of the past four years. Four years and a half ago, in your seminar, we dwelt in the rarified mountain-top Idealist atmosphere of pure politics, save for the occasional economic effluvium which might exude from my essays, or some similar contaminated source ... You angrily dismissed Prof. Simpson's suggestion that a foundation of economic studies was needed before the study of Canadian history would become profitable; and you dismissed, as a crude, if original, adaptation from Beard the frontier theory which was worked out, in detail, with diagrams, and with a few of the necessary qualifications, in a study of mine ... You have the courage, I must say, of your announced conviction then that "consistency is the meanest of the intellectual virtues." '[16] Charles Lightbody attributed Underhill's change to 'delayed recovery from Oxforditis.' He might more accurately have seen it as a delayed reaction to Toronto – a distaste for the city and all it stood for – a dislike which would sustain his radical impulse throughout the 1930s.

From his research on George Brown's *Globe*, Underhill published in June 1929 a second important article in which he examined the views expressed in the *Globe* on the imperial question during the decade before Confederation. He analysed Brown's views on the role of the governor-general, the influence of the English commercial and financial class, the Canadian tariff, and Canadian defence.

These two articles are of interest for the insight they provide into Underhill's approach to the writing of history at this point in time. Both articles were more concerned with the ideas behind events than the political events themselves, thus showing Underhill's interest in the study of political thought. Both also present a novel thesis which illustrates the tremendous insights that Underhill provided for new studies and new directions in Canadian history. In the CHA paper he argued that economic influences more than political developments were the key to understanding the pre-Confederation era, and implicitly all of Canadian history – a thesis that would concern Canadian historians for the next decade. In his *Canadian Historical Review* paper on the imperial question his thesis was that imperialism was one form of Canadian nationalism. He stated in his concluding paragraph: 'It will be obvious from the many extracts quoted in this paper that there are two main tendencies running through the *Globe*'s discussion of imperial affairs. In the first place, it is sturdily Canadian. It is determined that the Canadian people in all matters which concern them directly shall be free to act as they see fit ... But, on the other hand, while it asserts Canada's rights with the utmost vigour, it glories in the traditions and power of the Empire. It has no use for the "Little England" ideas which were prevalent in the mother country. It is proud of the connection with "the grand old British Empire," and determined to maintain it "intact and unimpaired" ... Its fundamental faith that the two seeming opposites, Canadian autonomy and imperial unity, were the most reconcilable things in the world, has been justified by later experience.'[17] In both papers, the thesis is stated but unfortunately not developed. It remained for later historians to study in depth.[18]

Already Underhill's fertile mind was working out the dynamics of the new approach to Canadian history that would emerge from his recent revelations about the economic interpretation of Canada's past. He indicated the nature of that history in his Dominion Day address to the Men's and Women's Canadian Clubs of Saskatoon. He began by warning his audience that this would not be the conventional patriotic speech they had come to expect from public speakers on this occasion; they would get enough bombast in the newspapers and from other speakers. Instead he proposed to offer the essence of the new history of Confederation soon to be written: '[It] will be more interested in investigating how business was carried on than how politics was carried on; it will tend to see in the men who ran the Grand Trunk or the Bank of Montreal, or the men who ran the Catholic Church or the Methodist Church or the Toronto Globe, much more important figures than in the men who ran the Conservative or Reform parties.'[19] Much of the speech was an elaboration of the ideas in his CHA paper, but there was one new section. He noted the strong anti-American feeling among the Upper Canadian Reformers of the 1860s which he attributed to their determination to create a second and distinct transcontinental nation in North America. 'Confederation has been our Bannockburn.' Yet today, he lamented, the battle has been lost. Americans have invaded Canada in the form of economic and cultural domination. He gave two specific illustrations to prove his point. He recounted a visit to Thorold, Ontario, during his sabbatical term to visit the monument to Laura Secord, the brave woman who saved Canada during the War of 1812. 'At length we reached the spot and there stood the pathetic little monument overshadowed and almost surrounded by the immense plant of the pulp mill which makes newsprint for the Chicago Tribune.' His second story concerned his visit to Ottawa, where he found the dominating influence of the International Paper Company in the Gatineau Valley – another American influence. The implication was that American influence in Canada had been wholly negative in the form of big business and materialism. Was there an alternative? Underhill claimed there was in the Canadian National Railway, Ontario Hydro and the Wheat Pools – Canadian organizations designed to use 'the natural resources of ours for the common good rather than for the production of vulgar Americanized plutocrats.' This linking of big business in Canada with that of the United States and seeing the uniqueness of Canada in its co-operative adventures were a natural extension of his economic interpretation and would be a standard theme in his writings throughout the thirties.

This would be his last speaking engagement in the West. He was moving back to Toronto. He had known for the last half of the academic year that he was likely to be leaving Saskatchewan. The first indication had come in February when George Wrong wrote to say that he was about to retire and that he was putting Underhill's name forward as his replacement. Underhill knew that Wrong had some doubts about his effectiveness, although he had consistently indicated an interest in hiring him. He did not have any idea how the other members of the department felt about him. [20] In fact, he realized how little he knew about the Toronto history department despite his sabbatical term in the city. He dashed off a letter to Cochrane in classics requesting the names and rank of members of the history department, and information on salary scales and departmental 'politics.'

The official offer from President Falconer arrived on 3 May. Underhill took only three days to deliberate before replying, but he had spent the intervening three months since Wrong's letter thinking about it. He weighed both pros and cons. On the positive side he realized that he would become a member of the most prestigious Canadian university in a city which could be considered the intellectual and cultural capital of the country, certainly of English-speaking Canada. He emphasized his proximity to good libraries and to sources for his work on George Brown. This was important if he were going to make a name for himself as a Canadian historian. He had achieved little recognition in the West, and he was already thirty-eight years old. He wanted to get a book published, and certainly was being pressured to do so by colleagues, but he was not even close to his objective. The reason, he felt, was an unduly heavy teaching load of undergraduates, which made his teaching 'dull and mechanical.' He imagined that Toronto would be better with superior undergraduates as well as graduate students to stimulate a teacher. On the negative side were lower salaries, the probability of teaching history courses he did not particularly enjoy and abandoning his political science courses, living in Toronto which he did not particularly like, and leaving friends and a relatively comfortable environment. In the end, he accepted the position.[21]

By late August the Underhills were ready for their permanent move to Toronto. Their house was sold, their belongings packed, their goodbyes said. In Toronto Underhill felt as though he were home, yet so unlike the feeling that home should convey. There was a feeling of familiarity, yet a distance. He realized that the estrangement was not the result of new buildings, the faster pace of life, or the boom-and-bust mentality. It was the atmosphere of the city that made everything so foreign to him, the same stuffy and staid atmosphere that had repelled him during his student days and his sabbatical year. That had not changed. In fact, the staidness was all the more apparent since his sojourn in the West. Still he could not help thinking that this stale air symbolized the intellectual mood and spiritual stuffiness of the city's inhabitants, particularly its social elite. His friend, A.L. Burt, upon hearing of Underhill's move to Toronto, quite perceptively described him as 'a fresh wind from the West.'[22] Underhill thought of himself in similar terms. What Toronto needed, so he imagined, was a good dose of fresh thought to clear it of its dour, imperialist, Victorian mentality. He was the apostle from the West ready to preach the new gospel. He arrived in the city already prepared to shake it out of its lethargy.

Underhill's view of his role at Toronto stood in stark contrast to that of his mentor, Wrong. Before Wrong had nominated Underhill for a position in the department he had solicited the opinion of University of Saskatchewan's president, Walter Murray, and in doing so expressed his own misgivings of the candidate: 'My doubt in respect to him is whether he is not too quiet and retiring to be an effective leader in such a community as this. By leadership I mean a person who would make his influence felt as a factor in the life of the University. I have no doubt whatever that he has the needed ability. Has he been an influential person in your own University?'[23] Wrong's knowledge of Underhill was based on Underhill's undergraduate years. As Underhill's career at the University of Toronto unfolded he would rarely be regarded as 'too quiet and retiring' and for some he would 'make his influence felt' far too much for the good of the university.

7

Climbing Down from the Ivory Tower

Underhill had developed a westerner's dislike of Toronto during the sabbatical year he had spent in what was his home city. Now that he had returned on a full-time basis, he instinctively took on the role of critic of the city – its citizens, its institutions, and its university. None the less, he was to live in Toronto for the next thirty years, and his personal life there was happy, comfortable, and secure.

The academic situation at the University of Toronto he was to find ultimately frustrating and unsatisfying, even though his effectiveness and popularity as a teacher was to be one of his greatest achievements. At the same time he was soon to become increasingly enmeshed in extra-academic activities that kept him busy and increasingly well known.

The year of Underhill's arrival, 1927, was a transitional one at the University of Toronto. Two men who had dominated the university's academic life for the past two generations retired: George Wrong and Maurice Hutton.[1] With Wrong's departure, all the professors in the history department who had taught Underhill as an undergraduate had left. Wrong represented a certain type of historian: a gentleman scholar, educated in England but not necessarily in history, who believed that the role of a historian was to draw moral lessons from the past which could then be applied with benefit to present society.[2] Underhill was a product of Wrong's image of the historian, and was indeed, in many respects, one of his protégés, even though he did not always agree with him as to the exact role the historian should play in society. He did at least agree that the historian, as an intellectual, had a responsibility to society that should take him outside of the ivory tower. That image was being challenged by a new view of the academic as a detached, scientific scholar who researched and wrote from a position beyond and above the controversy that swirled about him. This view was upheld by the administration at the university and by politicians who paid the bill. As a result, Underhill was, from the beginning, on the defensive to justify his own position.

With Wrong's retirement the department was undergoing substantial change. There was a more even distribution of the work-load among senior and junior members. Attempts were made to diversify the program and to make more efficient use of manpower by enabling professors to teach their own specialty. Increased enrolment meant better salaries and new positions. Besides Underhill, one other member was appointed as a full professor: W.S. Wallace, the university historian who had published that year his *History of the University of Toronto*. He had been a full-time librarian, but was now dividing his time between teaching graduate students in history and performing the duties of a librarian. George Smith became chairman and, like Ralph Flenley, was promoted to full professor. George Brown and Lester Pearson were granted assistant professorships, while Donald Creighton, fresh out of Balliol College, joined George Glazebrook and J.C. Proby as lecturers. Hume Wrong took a leave of absence to join the Canadian legation at Washington as its first secretary.

In the division of teaching in the department up to 1927 George Smith and Ralph Flenley taught the bulk of British and European history, Hume Wrong specialized in imperial history, and George Brown carried most of the Canadian and American history courses. George Wrong had been easing up in his teaching of British or Canadian history. The junior members filled in wherever needed, having to be experts, if the occasion called, in European, British, American, or Canadian history. Underhill replaced Hume Wrong in British, imperial, and Canadian history.

Underhill had a heavier teaching load than at Saskatchewan (even though Smith assured him that his was the lightest in the department). He had to lecture to forty senior honour students in Canadian constitutional history and to over 130 fourth-year pass students in British history, 1815–1914; conduct two seminars on representative governments for third-year and fourth-year students; and take three tutorials in modern British history, two for men and one for women students. In addition he had to guide and counsel a number of pass students in Canadian and American history, and read three essays for each student during the year.[3]

Maurice Hutton's retirement also had a direct bearing on Underhill. Professors W.S. Milner of University College and J.C. Robertson of Victoria College, both of the classics department, decided to honour Hutton by producing a book on the virtues of honour classics at Toronto during his tenure.[4] Robertson asked Underhill, along with Cochrane and Hubert Kemp, to represent a younger generation of graduates on the nine-man committee. The committee's task was to elicit the views of classics graduates on the program, and then to weave their ideas together into a coherent critique. Underhill became the *enfant terrible* of the committee. Already feeling uncomfortable and uncertain about his new position, he could not stand the endless and uncritical praise which Toronto men had for their own university. In his mind, there were genuine weaknesses in the program which needed to be noted along with the good qualities.[5] Personally, he thought there was undue stress on classical literature at the expense of history and philosophy. Even the literary studies were second rate, because of an overemphasis on grammatical structure. The greatest fault, however, was the lack of vitality among the professors compared to his tutors at Oxford. Their aloofness from current events and their 'cloistered existence' were reflected in their unimaginative approach to the subject.

The report undoubtedly upset the committee members; some of them were after all the very instructors Underhill was attacking. It also seemed an inappropriate time for such an outburst given the nature of the task. Still, Underhill was not vindictive. He sincerely believed what he said. A good teacher was one who could relate his subject-matter to the world about his students. That was the current theory of education as put forward by John Dewey in the United States. To Underhill, however, it was more than an abstract theory. He knew that he was a good teacher, and he attributed part of his success to his ability to excite his students to the realities of history as a living subject. Past thoughts really did impinge on and help to elucidate current events. Unfortunately, his Toronto classics professors had not agreed in his estimation.

Underhill's report set the tone for his reaction to Toronto: he complained about everything. Within the history department he was unhappy with the emphasis on British and European history at the expense of Canadian and American. What Canadian history was taught was in the context of British or imperial history, a reflection of the colonial mentality of his colleagues. The Toronto program was further from his ideal of a Canadian 'Greats' program than that of Saskatchewan, in spite of, or rather because of, ironically, the strong British influence. He began a one-man campaign to get more Canadian and American history into the program.[6] He complained about the students as well. Too many were there simply because they were sons or daughters of the wealthy. The university was turning out Babbitts rather than cultured and critical students. The city lacked a healthy tradition of scepticism and ferment because the university failed to provide it.

Such criticism was a standard reaction for Underhill whenever a situation did not match his expectations. It was his nature to be critical, whether from his Presbyterian upbringing, his academic training, his background in classics, or his perceptive mind. By the time he moved back to Toronto he had acquired the confidence to write and say whatever he felt. He was ready to apply his critical mind; he had only to find the right platform.

Soon after he arrived in Toronto in the late summer of 1927 Herbert Davis, book review editor of the *Canadian Forum*, invited Underhill to submit reviews to the journal. Here was the chance that had eluded him in the West despite his enquiries to the *Manitoba Free Press*. That event would dramatically affect his life.

Underhill had been a subscriber to the *Canadian Forum* from the time that it began publication in 1920. He knew personally some of the members of the editorial board, such as C.B. Sissons, a professor of ancient history at Victoria College, and Barker Fairley, a distinguished artist and a professor of German whom he had met in the summer of 1921 while viewing an exhibition of Group of Seven art at the Art Gallery of Toronto.[7] That fall he met the other editorial board members, most of whom were British born and educated academics teaching at the University of Toronto: Gilbert Norwood in classics, Gilbert Jackson in economics, Peter Sandiford in education, and S.H. Hooke in religious studies. He was immediately attracted to them because they combined the finest of the English university tradition with a spirit of Canadian nationalism.

The *Forum* supported the two great nationalist traditions in the 1920s: the Group of Seven and the western Progressive movement. In fact, the board supported any progressive movement in art, literature, or politics, particularly if it had a Canadian bias. In this respect, it reflected the growing spirit of nationalism in the cultural realm, equally evident in the political and constitutional developments of the decade. The editorial board was also becoming increasingly more socialistic in outlook.[8] The journal had struggled along for the first seven years in a hand-to-mouth existence – a tradition that would long continue. But in 1927 it got a new lease on life when Hugh Dent of the English publishing firm of J.M. Dent and Sons agreed that its Canadian branch should underwite the deficit. The journal was ready for a new creative and expansive period in its precarious existence.

Now came Underhill's chance to make his contribution to the *Forum*. He chose for his first review Stewart Wallace's *The Growth of Canadian National Feeling*, a topic that he had reflected upon a great deal. He credited the author for doing well what he had set out to do, 'to illustrate the growth in Canada of a distinctive Canadian feeling.' But Wallace had failed to go far enough in his analysis. He assumed, like most Canadian historians, that only politics embodied a spirit of nationalism, whereas 'the real makers of Canadian national feeling have been the pioneer farmers, the lumbermen and millers and manufacturers, the merchants and railwaymen and bankers, whose united efforts have developed an independent and distinctive Canadian economic life.'[9] To anyone familiar with Underhill's speeches in the West the message was not new. The review, however, delighted the editorial board members, and Underhill was soon writing more.

Shortly afterwards, Barker Fairley asked Underhill to join the seventeen-member editorial committee.[10] Underhill could not think of a greater pleasure, and readily consented. Here was a chance to vent his pent-up feelings, to express his views on current Canadian events, and to reach a wider educated audience with the ideas he had formulated from his extensive reading in Canadian, American, and British literature. It would also be fun. There were other considerations too, of course. He could make a contribution to establishing a first-class journal in Canada comparable to the *New Statesman* and *The Nation* in England or *The New Republic* in the United States. What the *Canadian Forum* presently lacked and these other journals had, he felt, was 'political criticism and information,' and that was precisely his strength. Furthermore, the journal offered an alternative viewpoint to the conventional beliefs of the day – something that the country, and particularly Toronto – needed. He was a rebel with a mission.

Underhill recalled that his affiliation with the *Canadian Forum* 'got me started on current Canadian politics and ruined forever all chances that, as a university professor, I would achieve that austere impersonal objectivity which was exemplified by most of my academic colleagues who lived blameless lives, cultivated the golden mean, and never stuck their necks out.'[11] The truth was he had lost those chances long before joining the *Forum*; his very nature as a passionate and critical observer ensured that. If it had not been the *Forum*, it would have been some other journal or an organization that attracted him. His association with the *Forum* undoubtedly took away from time he might have spent on his scholarly writing, but he wanted that distraction. As he aptly described in his eightieth-birthday speech: 'I was seduced from the ivory tower of academic research and teaching out into the brawling market-place of day-to-day or at least month-to-month politics. Like that woman in Byron's "Childe Harold" who was heard to cry out, when the barbarian Turks were beginning to sack some Christian town, "When does the ravishing begin," I enjoyed this seduction thoroughly.'

On the positive side, his association with the *Forum* opened up a new, creative, and exciting era in his life, one which would win him popular recognition that otherwise he might not have received. For one thing, he had a medium in which to express his socialistic views, thus enabling him to become the chief intellectual socialist of the 1930s. He was also able to do what he did best: write book reviews, and short, provocative essays in which he could display his critical judgment and his extensive knowledge on current and historical subjects. The famous, or infamous, initials 'F.H.U.' became a familiar sight to *Forum* readers in the late 1920s and throughout the 1930s.

Underhill's regular contribution to the *Canadian Forum* was an 'O Canada' column which first appeared in March 1929 and ran monthly until October 1932, when he felt it had outlived its usefulness. It was not so much a column of political commentary as an editorial critique in which he made controversial and sarcastic comments in a witty, sprightly, and colloquial style on current topics of interest: Canadian-American or Canadian-British relations, constitutional reform, the nature of political parties, attitudes of Canadian businessmen, and the failure of arts education in Canadian universities. The common thread running through the variety of topics was a demand for a stronger spirit of Canadian nationalism, a desire to discover those qualities of our nation which were unique and positive. The column gave a decidedly political emphasis to the *Forum*, strengthened its nationalist stance, and spiced up its critical spirit as well.

Underhill's aim in his *Forum* writings was to arouse his opponents to action in hopes of enlivening and elevating debate of political and social issues in Canada. Ironically, however, his journalism often had the opposite effect. His views were presented so emphatically and with so little sympathy for his opponents that they gave the impression of gospel truths, unrevised and unrepented. They created confrontation rather than debate, and made him appear more dogmatic than he really was. This had two effects: if he altered his views, he was immediately attacked as inconsistent and a traitor to a cause; if he refused to recant, he came under barrage, from the people he attacked.

In fact, attacks on Underhill had begun soon after his arrival in Toronto from Saskatoon. In the fall of 1928, for example, the Ontario premier, Howard Ferguson, wrote to Canon H.J. Cody, at that time chairman of the Board of Governors of the university, about allegations that Underhill taught that the British were as much if not more to blame for the outbreak of the war as were the Germans. The premier claimed that if these anti-British statements had indeed been made, he might be compelled 'to take steps that might be thought drastic. I have always endeavoured to avoid interfering in University affairs, but I do not think it is quite called for that any member of the staff should be exploiting his own views to the students as to the cause of the war.'[12] When confronted by the president, Underhill denied the allegations. 'The only case in which I recall having mentioned the Great War was in dealing briefly with the growth of the British Empire during the last century. I then pointed out how British and German expansion brought the two powers into competition at various points in Africa and Asia and I said that rivalry in these matters had much more to do with the causes of the War than the neutrality of Belgium. This I thought to be a commonplace among informed persons ...'[13] The president reported Underhill's statement back to Cody and added, to placate the premier, that 'in the War Professor Underhill had a most enviable record.' In April 1929 Ferguson again complained about Underhill. This time he was more explicit as to what 'drastic steps' he might be forced to take: 'Some day when the estimates are brought over here I will be tempted to tick off a number of salaries of some men who seem to take more interest in interfering in matters of public policy and public controversy than they do in the work for which they are paid.'[14] The outburst was in response to Underhill's 'O Canada' column in the *Forum* in which he had associated the success of rum trafficking to the United States with the anti-American sentiment of Canadian politicians. Underhill was irate over such threats, especially when they were made by the very people who claimed to be upholders of British liberal ideals in Canadian society. The hypocrisy only fired his determination to make more-concerted attacks on the Toronto Establishment.

An opportunity arose in January 1931 in reaction to the latest of a series of raids by the Toronto police, under the leadership of its rabidly anti-communistic chief constable, D.C. Draper, against alleged 'communistic' demonstrations.[15] Underhill contacted a small group of 'radically minded professors'[16] to circulate a petition around the university declaring that citizens should have the right 'to free public expression of opinions, however unpopular or erroneous.' Sixty-eight professors, a number of whom were senior faculty members, signed the petition.[17] The publication of the letter led to a barrage of press editorials. The issue soon became a question of the right of professors in a public institution to get involved in allegedly partisan issues. Undoubtedly the majority of Torontonians, including professors in the university, were against such involvement and sympathized with the editor of the *Globe* when he demanded the dismissal of the protesting faculty should they fail to recant.[18]

Underhill again expressed his views on the role of the academic in another dispute that erupted only a few months later. His targets, both prominent Tories, were Prime Minister R.B. Bennett and Howard Ferguson, now Canada's high commissioner to Britain, having resigned as Ontario premier in 1930. Almost any one of Underhill's articles could have got him into trouble, but the article that the *Mail and Empire*, 'the Toronto Tory morning organ,' selected was one of his more moderate and mild-tempered efforts, a piece written for the British *New Statesman and Nation*.[19] Underhill had noted the discrepancy between the promised results of Mr Bennett's tariff revision of blasting Canada into world markets and the actual results. He recommended that the proposed Commonwealth Conference, to be held in Ottawa that spring (which was later postponed), be cancelled. Since the Bennett government was not prepared to make concessions to British manufacturers wishing a share of the Canadian market, the conference could only strain relations within the empire. The *Mail and Empire* demanded that Underhill 'be called upon the carpet by someone in authority at the university' for such partisan views. The *Globe* came to Underhill's defence. The editor admitted that he did not always agree with the views of university professors, but that there was no excuse for demanding professors to 'keep academic thought within the bounds of party exigency.' The next step, the editor feared, would be a demand: 'Burn the books and cast the professors into outer darkness.'[20]

President Falconer wrote to Underhill to express his opinion, which he had outlined more fully in a 1922 address on academic freedom, as to the inexpediency of professors taking part in political journalism: '[F]or a professor, whose salary and position are maintained by the goodwill of the people as a whole, to enter into party-politics, is in my judgment not only inexpedient but dangerous to the well-being of the University ... [I]n view of the best fulfilment of the duties of his teaching position, – which is surely primary, – he should I believe restrain himself from taking part publicly in party matters.'[21] Falconer, who had been appointed president in 1907, remembered the University Act of 1906, which had granted the university a new autonomy from political interference in academic appointments. He was not prepared to forgo the freedom enjoyed by all professors to teach and do research within the university for the right of a minority to speak on controversial issues outside the university. He agreed that it was only natural for academics to have opinions on current issues, but at the same time an academic could not be divorced from the institution to which he belonged. Thus, to take sides in a public controversy was tantamount to committing the institution to a partisan position. Only an impartial university could be free from public or private pressure.

Underhill agreed that the university needed to be autonomous; he also respected the president's efforts to protect the institution and its professors from outside interference. Nevertheless, he believed that there was no better way to prove the institution's autonomy than for a professor to be free to express his opinions on public issues no matter how controversial they might be. If a professor had to be silenced for the university to be autonomous, Underhill concluded, then 'that autonomy is already lost. A freedom that cannot be exercised without danger of disastrous consequences is not a real freedom at all.'[22] Furthermore, he noted, numerous Canadian academics, including some of his colleagues in the history department such as Chester Martin, George Brown, and George Glazebrook had contributed their views on politics in newspaper editorials and political journals without reprimand. He was inclined to think that he was chastised not because he was outspoken but because he spoke out against the wrong people, party, or cause.

While he was developing an increasing degree of notoriety as a speaker and writer both inside and outside the academic world, Underhill also became involved in one of the most sensational court cases in Canadian history: 'Deeks versus Wells.' It had begun in 1918 when Florence Deeks of Toronto submitted a manuscript entitled 'The Web" to the Macmillan Company of Canada. She received it back eight months later in battered condition with a letter of rejection. Subsequently, she read *The Outline of History* by H.G. Wells, the renowned British writer and Fabian socialist, and discovered marked similarities to her own work, both in style and in content. Her suspicions aroused, she started court proceedings in 1925, but the critical trial was in June 1930 when literary experts – including George Brett, William Irwin, and Lawrence Burpee of the University of Toronto – were brought in to compare the two texts. The three testified that 'the documentary evidence of Mr. Wells' copying was overwhelming.'[23]

Frank Underhill appeared as the sole expert for the defence. In a brilliant testimonial he showed that the two works resembled each other in their basic factual material and general format, both of which could be found in any elementary history text. Furthermore, Miss Deeks's historical facts were simply incorrect in a number of places, while her style was too poor to be worthy of Wells's attention. Underhill received a cheque of $750 (for his lengthy court-room appearances), the satisfaction of being on the winning side, and an accolade from the pen of Hector Charlesworth, the veteran journalist, in *I'm Telling You: Being the Further Candid Chronicles*: 'I have never heard a more convincing witness. He spoke as though he had himself lived in every historical epoch discussed in the course of his examination ... His manner was so crisp and decisive, he was so obviously the master of the subjects he was talking about that after he had been five hours in the witness box the contentions of Miss Deeks' experts were entirely washed out.'[24]

At the centre of Underhill's whirl of activity was the security and stablility of his home life. When they had moved to Toronto in 1927, the Underhills had bought a pleasant home on Walmer Road, in a well-to-do middle-class neighbourhood where they were to live for the next thirty years. His parents lived nearby and he remained close to them – later, when they were too old to look after themselves, they moved in with Frank and Ruth.

The house was often the setting for meetings of the *Forum* and for political discussions. Ruth as an agreeable if self-effacing hostess. She had abandoned her academic career when she married, but in Toronto during the thirties she taught at a little private school which the Underhill's daughter Betty and some neighbours' children attended.

The summers were invariably spent in Muskoka, first at a rented cottage on Acton Island (near Bala) on Lake Muskoka (and beginning in 1936 at Juddhaven on Lake Rosseau). Frank found Acton Island a place to relax and escape the oppressive heat of Toronto and irate politicans and academics. He enjoyed golfing at a nearby course, swimming, and reading for his classes or for general interest. The location was ideal: close enough to Toronto to keep in touch, but far enough away to be left alone. There was good rail service to the area, which was important since until the late thirities the Underhills did not own a car.[25] Underhill would look back upon these early years in Toronto as ones of excitement and accomplishment.

8

Socialist Colleague

On the evening of 29 October 1929 – Black Tuesday – Underhill travelled to Oshawa to give a lecture in an extension course. As the train left Union Station he overheard two women talking excitedly about the stock market crash in which they stood to lose their entire life savings.[1] Underhill, with a secure job and few investments in the stock market, listened with detached interest, perhaps with even a certain smugness. Had he not, just six months earlier, warned his *Canadian Forum* readers to beware of their naïve faith in the infallibility of the businessman?

Underhill had been consistent in his attack on the business community. It was not the individual businessman that he disliked, not even businessmen as a whole. Indeed, he sprang from a hard-working business family. He also knew a number of Toronto entrepreneurs such as J.S. McLean, president of Canada Packers Limited and a patron of the arts, whom he respected. Rather, he abhorred the image that the businessman projected of himself as a confident, conceited, arrogant individual, and the myth that had grown up about him among the public as a person naturally chosen to lead. He suspected any group that was elevated by the public to messianic heights. 'On this continent and in this generation,' he noted, 'there has been a concerted effort to make the worship of the big businessman our real religion.'[2] The businessman needed to be brought down from his pedestal as the God-ordained leader of Canadian society and presented as the selfish, economic animal that he was. This was an exaggeration, he realized, but a necessary corrective to the romantic view held by the majority of Canadians.

Six months after his train journey to Oshawa, the Crash of late 1929 had become the Depression of 1930. Still he held to his views and had a public forum in which to express them at the Conference of Canadian Universities on 'The Meaning of a General Education.'[3] Too many good students, he argued, were taking commerce instead of classics, economics instead of history or political science. The men and women who could lead Canada in a new direction away from this slavish admiration of the commercial elite were being educated to become 'those polished, efficient, well-behaved young Babbitts who are already so drearily familiar a sight on any big University campus.' The speech led to a lively discussion as late as two years afterwards at the next Canadian University Conference.[4] At the first conference Dean C.J. Mackenzie of Alberta expressed relief that the East 'had not cramped Underhill's style': 'Exaggeration sometimes makes the point clearer.'[5]

Underhill suspected a conspiracy of businessmen behind many national events during the thirties. Just as they were undermining the quality of education at universities, the reform-minded history professor claimed they also worked to weaken effective government action in dealing with the crisis of the Depression. He argued at a symposium at the 1931 American Political Science Association that big business supported provincial rights in Quebec and Ontario so as to keep the federal government weak and unable to thwart their efforts.[6] He had no empirical evidence to substantiate this claim, but argued on the basis of an analogy to the states' rights movement in the United States as outlined by American progressive historians.

Nevertheless, Underhill could see promising signs of reform in Canada in the early 1930s. Dissident groups of farmers, labourers, disenchanted liberals, socialists, and intellectuals had arisen across the country. They only needed to be organized to use their consolidated energy and intelligence to bring about substantial change in the system. The problem was the dissipation of reform groups in Canada because of physical, ethnic, and social divisions. Could these difficulties be overcome? At times he was doubtful; at other times he was buoyed up by the awareness that such groups already existed in Britain and the United States. 'Radicalism in Canada will have to import its philosophical equipment from the United States; it will have to go to school to men like Dewey and Beard and Lippmann.'[7] This was neither unhealthy nor unnatural. Canadians modelled themselves after the Americans and the British in every other facet of life, so why not in the intellectual realm as well?

What his writings did was to convince him of the need for a more organized and sustained radical movement in Canada. The chief weakness of political and social reform in Canada compared to that of Britain and the United States, he felt, was the failure of intellectuals to get involved. He and the other active members of the *Forum* board seemed to be working alone or at least in isolation. J.S. Woodsworth agreed with Underhill on the need for an organization of dissident intellectuals, and he was less pessimistic about changing the situation. 'My files contain hundreds of letters from "intellectuals" who are spiritually homeless,' he informed Underhill. '[T]he time is about ripe for the formation of something more or less corresponding to the English Fabian Society.'[8] Why not begin such a movement? Underhill was intellectually and emotionally ready to commit himself to a new cause.

In the fall of 1931 Underhill, refreshed by a summer holiday in the Muskokas, attended the third Williamstown conference. Again he persuaded Dafoe to let him cover the proceedings for the *Free Press*.[9] 'World Economic Planning' was that year's topic, a most appropriate subject in the confused and chaotic conditions of the Great Depression. The hope of the delegates present was to seek remedies for the world ills rather than to seek causes. Underhill found the sessions stimulating, if not entirely satisfying, since world experts seemed no more in agreement on how to solve the Depression than were Canadian leaders. There was much talk of fascism and communism as possible alternatives to capitalism, neither one having any appeal to Underhill.[10]

All the issues paled into the background, however, next to Underhill's meeting with Frank Scott, a tall, self-assured young law professor from McGill. They met on a hike to climb Mt Greylock, the highest peak in the Berkshire Hills just south of Williamstown. By the time they descended, they had agreed to return to their respective universities to seek out recruits to begin a Canadian-style Fabian Society.[11] That fall, Underhill and Scott gathered together their supporters. By November Scott had the nucleus of the Montreal group: Eugene Forsey, a young economist recently appointed to the McGill economics department; J.K. Mergler, an ex-Labour candidate in the last provincial election; and David Lewis, a young undergraduate law student fresh out of Oxford. King Gordon, an instructor at United Theological College, joined before the end of the year. Underhill could count among his supporters Irene Biss, a lecturer in the political economy department; Harry Cassidy from the Department of Social Sciences; and Eric Havelock of the classics department. He had no luck persuading any of his colleagues in the history department to join initially, although later Edgar McInnis, a young lecturer also educated at Balliol, became active.[12] The group invited J.S. Woodsworth to serve as honorary president.[13] Underhill was ecstatic about Woodsworth's affiliation with the organization. In the past Underhill had profited intellectually from Woodsworth's political position, and Woodsworth in turn had sought Underhill's advice on academics who might be of value to him as leader of the labour-socialist movement. Now Woodsworth could provide the essential link to radical groups throughout the country and act as a source of attraction to those outside the university.

The new organization prepared for its first joint meeting in mid-January. They met in Wymilwood Hall, Victoria College, once the mansion of the Toronto entrepreneur E.R. Wood. By the time the seventy-five met, the core groups at the University of Toronto and McGill had already agreed on a manifesto which simply needed ratification. The Montreal group had drafted it, with revisions made by the Toronto branch. Ironically, the Montreal contingent thought the revisions too moderate in style. 'We shall have to hit upon something a little sterner,' Scott suggested.[14] At the joint meeting, Underhill was chosen president. The group also agreed on the name League for Social Reconstruction, or LSR for short.

The Toronto branch held its next monthly meeting in a downtown restaurant, the Kit-Kat, where Underhill delivered a sterling oration on 'the need for radicalism in Canada.' The proprietor was not impressed and refused to let them return once she learned of their socialist leanings. They decided to meet the next time at Hunt's restaurant. 'Hunt is an alderman,' Underhill reported to Scott with pleasure, 'and what he'll do when he discovers that he is feeding socialists I don't know.'[15]

January 1932 marked the birthday of this new socialist organization. There seemed to be no answers to the riddles the economy posed. In particular, the two traditional parties seemed bankrupt of ideals to deal with the crisis. Underhill, aware that it was a propitious time for a new movement of radical reform, announced its formation to his *Forum* readers in December 1931: 'The time is ripe for a Canadian Fabian Society to organize itself, define its aims, and start campaigning ... The trouble with most of us professional radicals in Canada is our feeling that we're sure to get somewhere if we only keep on talking long enough. It is time for us to consider where we want to go.'

The LSR's manifesto offered the answer. Its preamble stated that Canada needed 'a new social order which will substitute a planned and socialized economy for the existing chaotic individualism and which, by achieving an approximate economic equality among all men in place of the present glaring inequalities, will eliminate the domination of one class by another.' The new social order would replace the present capitalist system which had shown itself 'unjust and inhuman, economically wasteful, and a standing threat to peace and democratic government.' Bold words, and great promises; but that was, the members of the LSR believed, what was needed to end the Depression. There followed a nine-point program of 'essential first steps towards the realization of this new order.'[16] The founding members of the league believed the organization could work for Canada as the Fabian Society had in England: providing research and political education in preparation for the new social order they would help to usher in. It was a utopian dream of a better world emerging out of the ruins of depression and world tensions, where all would live in freedom, equality, and harmony. It was a humanitarian organization dedicated to improving the lot of the common man – the farmer and the worker – by improving the social and economic conditions in which he lived and functioned.

In the context of the time, and within the Canadian reform tradition, the LSR was radical. LSR members believed in a root-and-branch reform of the capitalist system and in the establishment of a new order, where brotherhood, democracy, and co-operation would replace individualism, competition, and plutocracy. But it was radical in more than principles and program. The very concept of a group of intellectuals, especially university professors, actively working together to bring about direct social and political change within Canadian society marked a radical departure from past experience. There had been groups of intellectuals in the past, and there had been individual social reformers and critics, but never before had the two come together in one group to bring about radical social change.[17]

To Underhill, the LSR was also a forum of informed, intelligent, and like-minded individuals who met to debate ideas and to provide guidance for the new society. That society, he believed, should be a conscious, moral, and rational one, a society freed from the bonds of ignorance, prejudice, and privilege and dedicated to accomplishing great things.[18] His role in the LSR reflected this perception. He would, for example attack the organization, or individual members, whenever he felt they put practical or political concerns above educational functions. Over the years, Underhill provided many of the themes for the league's public lecture series. He saw the league as another means to reach an audience (besides the classroom and the *Forum*) with the abundance of ideas that flowed from his fecund mind. It was also a fraternity for him, a meeting-place for men (and a few women) who accepted and respected one another and enjoyed each other's company. It had many of the qualities of an Oxford club. Underhill established friendships in the league which filled a void left from his estrangement from members of the history department. These LSR friendships, established in the 1930s, lasted a lifetime. It was not surprising that at his eightieth birthday celebration he chose the members of the LSR to sit at the head table and ended his speech on 'The Education of Frank Underhill' for the formation of the LSR. The LSR served a moral purpose as well. 'Having lost my Christian-Calvinist faith,' he recalled in later life, 'I guess I needed something to excite me and these political movements took the place of a religion.'[19] In his commitment to the league and its socialist and reform cause he had the passion and zeal of the religious convert. Socialism became his secular road to both personal and social salvation. It gave him a purpose in a world that seemed to lack meaning and purpose. This was true for many LSR members; an inordinate number were 'sons of the manse.' As a result of his involvement in the league, he could look back positively on the thirties as a time when he felt fulfilled, while others around him felt alienated.

Underhill took an active role in the LSR. As president, he oversaw the organization's development and kept local branches across the country informed on the decisions of the National Executive. He gave the speech at the inaugural meeting of the Toronto branch in February and offered a lecture series under the auspices of the league on socialist thought. Then, of course, there were the regular meetings, not to mention his correspondence with leading members such as Scott, Forsey, and Gordon, and with local branches.[20]

While Underhill fully endorsed the educational role that the LSR should perform, he had doubts about its political role. On this divisive issue the organizers had left the manifesto deliberately vague. It stated simply that the league would 'support any political party insofar as its programme furthers the above principles,' but it did not indicate the nature and extent of that 'support,' or the type of political party that it was prepared to endorse. The 'principles' were clearly socialistic, yet the organizers avoided using the term 'socialism' in the document for fear of alienating potential moderate Liberal supporters.

Underhill was uncertain what direction the LSR should take. He believed, for example, that the two dominant Canadian parties were replicas of their American cousins, loose conglomerates of sectional interest groups without definite philosophies. In an attempt to please a variety of interest groups, the parties ended up pleasing only one group: 'those interest-groups which are themselves best organized and most strategically located for applying effective pressure upon the party leaders ... The net effect of all this ... is that for all practical purposes our two parties are normally and regularly the servants of big business.'[21] It was his first attempt to apply Beard's economic interpretation of American political parties to the Canadian situation. Where, he asked, would the LSR, a British-type political phenomenon, fit in this North American political pattern? Was it not un-American and therefore destined to go the way of other unsuccessful radical movements in North America? This was true as long as Canadian parties remained in their present form. The Depression, he believed, would create new parties in which the LSR could play an important role. He pointed out that other classes (by which he meant economic interest groups and not Marxist classes) such as farmers and labourers were organizing and would be demanding a stronger voice in the decision-making process. Could the LSR not become the spokesman for such groups, just as the Fabian Society spoke for the working class in Britain? If so, then would this political realignment come about in a new party or in a transformed Liberal party? Initially, he seemed to anticipate a revitalized Liberal party which would be truly liberal, and therefore socialistic, in its philosophy. He outlined, for example, a liberal program for the party to adopt that contained policies that were supported by the LSR. Although he expressed a little confidence in Mackenzie King as leader, he realized that the man was malleable enough, and sufficiently educated in liberal-socialist writings, to be pressured in a time of crisis like the present to move the party to the left. Certainly, liberally minded intellectuals belonged to the party, such as Vincent Massey, Norman Rogers, and Francis Hankin.[22] That spring Hankin had requested a meeting with Underhill to learn more about the LSR and its possible assistance in reforming the Liberal party. Underhill appeared initially quite happy for the league simply to provide the Liberals with ideas.[23] During the debate over the terminology of the league's charter, Underhill appeared more conscious than most members of not appearing too extreme, for fear of alienating moderate left-wing liberal supporters. In this respect, an inconsistency, or at least a wide gap, often existed between what he was writing publicly in the *Forum* and what he was thinking in private. His bark was worse than his bite. Evidently, as a publicist, he got carried away with the rhetoric, and with the delight in stating the case in the extreme.

He soon changed. On 1 August 1932 the Co-operative Commonwealth Federation was launched in Calgary. While he had not been involved in the initial planning behind the organization, Underhill became extremely enthusiastic. Here seemed to be the answer to his appeal for a radical socialist tradition in Canada. Now there appeared unlimited opportunity and activity for the LSR; it had a medium by which to get its message to a wider public.

In his enthusiasm Underhill forgot his customary academic caution. He overlooked the non-partisan and strictly educational nature of the LSR and proposed that it affiliate directly with the CCF. He feared that without intellectual leadership the CCF would go the way of the Progressives in the 1920s and be absorbed by an opportunistic Liberal party. Frank Scott was more reserved and reminded Underhill of the pitfalls of too close an association. He suggested that 'the LSR should keep itself to itself until it knows itself better.' Even Woodsworth cautioned Underhill about the implications of formal affiliation for those members of LSR branches who were civil servants or who joined for strictly educational purposes.[24] In the end Underhill's proposal for affiliation was defeated at the LSR's national convention in January 1933.[25]

This did not deter Underhill from becoming active in the CCF on his own. He helped Woodsworth to call together the leaders of several radical groups in Ontario in the hope that they might form the Ontario wing of the national party. They met in Underhill's living-room one Sunday morning in mid-September, and it was here that the Ontario CCF was born.[26] He found the meeting a real eye-opener into the inner workings of a political party. To his surprise the most arrogant, aloof, and almost aristocratic of the political bosses were the leaders of the trade unions who appeared on his doorstep dressed in bowler hats and vested suits. In some respects, his was one of the 'plaintive vegetarian bleatings in the midst of the carnivorous jungle'[27] that he accused other party innocents of being.

Underhill urged league members to do all they could to keep the new party intellectually respectable. In particular, he urged them to write pamphlets, especially on economics and trade. He intended to write a couple himself, particularly on socialist theory, but he never completed them. Instead, he chaired a twelve-man committee responsible for establishing CCF clubs in Ontario and eventually in other provinces as well. This required him to be out two or three nights a week at organizational meetings or giving speeches in support of the party. He held the position until forced to resign by the university authorities some months later. It was his contribution to a cause to which he was totally committed. But at least one of his friends perceptively noted that 'practical political activities and the reading of books and writing of them' made for 'strange bedfellows.'[28]

The contribution to the CCF that brought Underhill more fame and recognition than possibly any other event in his life was drafting the Regina Manifesto. In later years he jokingly exaggerated its importance: 'I used to say in those days of youthful pride, that just as Thomas Jefferson had directed that there should be inscribed on his tombstone, not the fact that he had been twice president of the United States, but the fact that he had drafted the Declaration of Independence, so I intend to instruct my executors to put on my tomb the fact that I had drafted the Regina Manifesto. As time went on, however, I realized that the Regina Manifesto wasn't going to be quite as earth-shaking as the American Declaration of Independence, and so I have rescinded those instructions to my executor.'[29] Woodsworth had asked him in the autumn of 1932 to head an LSR group which would draft a manifesto for the party in time for the CCF's January meeting of council. Underhill consented to do the initial draft himself, which would then be reviewed by other league members. January came and went without a completed draft. Again, in April, Woodsworth reminded him of his promise[30] – the date for the CCF national convention in Regina was 14 July. Characteristically, Underhill waited to the very last minute – one weekend in mid-June, at his cottage in Muskoka – when, under pressure, he put together a typed draft. His version was then reviewed by a three-man committee of LSR members, Joe Parkinson, Harry Cassidy, and Escott Reid, before it was sent off to Scott and Woodsworth who would guide it through the Regina Convention. Underhill had decided against going to Regina, confident that the document was in good hands.[31]

In its final form, the Regina Manifesto was a 'popularized' LSR Manifesto. The preamble of the two is strikingly similar on the deficiencies of the capitalist system and the nature of the new social order that the CCF and LSR would usher in. An added section in the Regina Manifesto elaborated on the nature of a CCF government which, of course, was absent in the LSR Manifesto. All ten planks in the LSR Manifesto appeared in the Regina Manifesto in a more detailed form, but premised on the same assumptions. The Regina Manifesto had four additional planks not present in the LSR Manifesto: agriculture, freedom, social justice, and an emergency program. Finally, that last sentence in the Regina Manifesto, 'No C.C.F. Government will rest content until it has eradicated capitalism and put into operation the full programme of socialized planning which will lead to the establishment in Canada of the Co-operative Commonwealth,' was not a part of either the LSR Manifesto or Underhill's original draft; it was added at the convention. Underhill denied in later life ever wanting such a sentence added, and implied that it was out of tone with the rest of the document. Yet he did not appear to voice objection to it at the time, and it certainly said nothing that was not already implied in the preamble and planks of the Regina Manifesto. In 1933 Underhill would have concurred whole-heartedly with the emphatic assertion of that last sentence, one certainly in keeping with the strong negative opinions about capitalism in his *Forum* writings.

Another important task remained for the LSR: to publish a book on Canadian socialism, outlining in detail its views on the failure of the present economic and political situation and on the nature of the new social order. It was Woodsworth who suggested the study, and Underhill was in full accord. A research committee was struck in the fall of 1932 under Harry Cassidy, editor-in-chief, with Graham Spry, who in 1930 had founded the Canadian Radio League, as associate editor. Individual chapters were assigned to various LSR members according to their areas of expertise: Irene Biss, Eugene Forsey, and Joseph Parkinson were responsible for the chapters on the economy; Scott looked after constitutional questions; Reid was assigned the chapter on external affairs; and Underhill assumed responsibility for politics.[32] Little was accomplished, however, until a four-day organizational meeting was held at the Burlington home of Mrs W.B. Somerset, a socialist sympathizer and member of the Toronto branch of the LSR, in late April 1933.[33] It was a 'think-tank' session in the true sense of the word. Discussion continued all day and well into the night, with the delegates breaking only for short walks to clear their heads. Underhill returned home with his head 'still buzzing with four solid days of argument.' He realized how rude he and his colleagues had been in neglecting the hostess during the meeting, and wrote to apologize: 'I write to you at once to say how much indebted we all are to your kindness in entertaining us. We could not have met in more pleasant surroundings and, if the book comes off, it will have been mainly due to the days spent together in your house.'[34] It was just one example of Underhill's sensitivity to people and his kindness to friends.

As a result of their active participation in drafting the manifesto, and writing a tract on Canadian socialism, the members of the LSR soon earned the reputation of being the party's 'brain trust,' a term popularized in the United States to describe the academics and other intellectuals who were active in F.D. Roosevelt's government. It was George Ferguson of the *Winnipeg Free Press*, a long-time friend of many LSR members, who first used the term jokingly in an article on the Regina Manifesto in July 1933. Underhill had no objection to the term, since it reflected his perception of the role that the LSR ought to play in the CCF. In fact, he regretted that the CCF did not have 'an effective brain-trust' which could do more of the educational work so badly needed if the party were to bring in a socialist government in a democratic state. But he regretted the undue publicity that the LSR was getting from the use of the term, implying that 'Mr. Woodsworth and his fellow leaders were submitting themselves to the crafty influence of a group of intellectual malcontents and revolutionaries who were diabolically guiding the movement towards the upsetting of all our cherished institutions.' Such sinister ideas, he concluded, should 'be abandoned by our journalists to the editorial page of the *Mail and Empire*, where all good Canadian bogies go when they die.'[35]

Underhill was content being a member of the 'CCF brain trust' and its chief critic. He had no desire to run for political office, feeling that he was ill-suited to be a politician. He did not, however, object to other academics getting directly involved in politics and was instrumental in supporting M.J. Coldwell's right as a school principal to run as a CCF candidate despite the opposition of the Regina School Board. Underhill wrote letters to Vincent Massey and Joseph Atkinson, editor of the *Toronto Star*, to appeal for their public support of Coldwell and then expressed his own views in a letter to the *Winnipeg Free Press*. He admitted to the potential danger of partisanship entering the classroom by teachers getting involved in party politics. But 'if you deny to teachers, or to any other group of citizens, the right of taking part in political party activity you are, in the long run, effectively denying them the right of free discussion.'[36] At the heart of the issue was Underhill's unyielding faith in the freedom of the individual as the foundation-stone of a liberal society.

9

Socialist Intellectual
and Critic

Frank Underhill's socialism in the 1930s rested on three fundamental principles: liberal democracy, anti-capitalism, and anti-imperialism.[1] Underhill argued consistently that socialism was a logical outgrowth and a natural extension of British liberal-democratic ideals. In an important article on 'Bentham and Benthamism' for the *Queen's Quarterly* of 1933, he showed how Bentham and his followers, the Utilitarians, in their development of a liberal-democratic, collectivist, and egalitarian political and economic system, were the precursors of the modern British Fabian socialists. '[T]he Benthamites did as much as anyone else to forge the instruments through which the collectivist state might be achieved ... English socialism has always emphasized that it is only another method of seeking the same ends which the individualistic generation that preceded it had in view. Its end is the emancipation of individuality, the free development of personality.'[2]

These liberal-democratic ideals – the freedom and equality of the individual and the brotherhood of mankind – were premised on the assumption that man was an essentially good and rational creature who was capable of creating the perfect society through the exercise of reason. In the nineteenth-century era of individualism, Underhill argued, liberal reformers attempted to give practical expression to these ideals in two ways: in the political realm, through a democratic government based on universal suffrage; in the economic realm, through a capitalistic system based on the philosophy of laissez-faire – the right of each individual to achieve his economic goals without outside interference or governmental regulation. Liberal reformers had achieved their ideal in the political realm, but not in the economic sphere. What was needed in the twentieth century was to extend democracy into economics by creating an economic system in which each individual was equal and therefore inherently free. As Underhill expressed it: 'It has been slowly dawning on great masses of people that liberty without a substantial measure of equality becomes meaningless and that our political democracy in the face of economic plutocracy is largely a sham.'[3]

Thus followed the second premise of Underhill's socialism: anti-capitalism. The capitalistic system, he argued, led to excessive competition among individuals and eventually to monopolistic control, the antithesis of the liberal beliefs in liberty, equality, and fraternity. Capitalism was wasteful, inhumane, and undemocratic. It benefited a few businessmen at the expense of the well-being of society as a whole. As Underhill put it in an LSR radio address: 'A philosophy which spelt liberty of opportunity for thousands while we were in the pioneer stages of our growth is now being propagated by these corporate interests to protect their own selfish exploitation of resources and labour at the general expense of the community ... The system of rugged individualism has worked out in our generation so as to distribute the individualism to a small privileged minority and to leave the ruggedness for the masses of the population.'[4] Thus capitalism had to be replaced by a new economic order: socialism. He assumed, like most socialists of the decade, that the two ideologies were antithetical; the choice was one or the other, not a mixture of the two.

Another assumption he made was that imperialism was the extension of capitalism into the international realm. Imperialism, a severe form of the disease of nationalism, was a means for businessmen to do on an international scale, through wider markets and new areas of exploitation in underdeveloped countries, what they had already done on a national scale – exploit the people. Underhill expressed the idea in an exaggerated form in the *Forum*: 'The enthusiasts who preach a wider Imperial loyalty as a substitute for our nationalism are only innoculating us with a worse form of our present disease. Their Empire is a fighting organization in a world at war. Their imperialism is only a more ambitious nationalism.' This was particularly true of the British empire. He became as critical of the British empire by the 1930s as he had been supportive in the 1920s. He claimed in one *Forum* article that 'Pax Britannia' really meant 'Rule Britannia,' and that 'peace in our time' meant 'peace on our terms.'[5]

Underhill was attacked as being anti-British. Some simply denounced him as a heretic; others tried reason. W.L. Grant, the son of the prominent Canadian imperialist George Munro Grant, argued in a letter to the *Forum* that Underhill saw only the negative features of the British connection at the expense of its good qualities. Underhill retorted that he was quite capable of distinguishing between the negative aspects of the imperial connection and the positive aspects of the British connection. 'I am not anti-British; I am anti-Chamberlain and anti-Amery.'[6] He agreed that the unique aspect of British history was 'a spirit of political liberalism, the belief in fair play, the conviction that things turn out best when differences are adjusted by free discussion.' But such liberal values could not be sustained through British imperialism; indeed, imperialism was the very antithesis of this liberal-democratic tradition.

Along the same lines, he argued that war was the means by which imperialists expanded their economic interests over other areas of the world. 'The real cause of modern wars,' he informed his *Forum* readers, 'is the competitive struggle for overseas markets and raw materials which goes on between groups of capitalist magnates who have acquired control, each group of its own national government.'[7] He was critical of Canada's involvement in the last war, since it had only furthered British interests in world markets, and he fought diligently and consistently in his *Forum* articles to keep Canada out of the next world war, which he saw, as early as 1933, looming on the horizon, and which he assumed would be fought for the same selfish materialistic reasons as the last war. This anti-imperialist component of his socialist thought most frequently got him into trouble in loyal Tory Ontario. The Establishment could accept criticism of the abstract concept of capitalism and the nebulous term 'big business' so long as there were no names attached to these labels. But to attack its sacred faith in the British connection or to undermine its devotion to the imperial cause was heresy. Increasingly as the 1930s evolved and war became more apparent, Underhill was devoting his writings and speeches to the subject of Canada, the British empire, and war.

The attacks on him in the newspaper had a certain continuity and consistency. They were by now an annual event, usually around the end of summer or in early fall when he had delivered a paper at a public conference. In August 1933 he attended his first meeting of the annual Canadian Institute on Economics and Politics, better known as the Couchiching Conference, at the YMCA camp at Orillia on the shores of Lake Simcoe. Modelled after the Williamstown Institute of Politics, the conference, which had first met the previous summer, was an opportunity for academics to discuss Canadian political and economic problems. Underhill was invited to open that year's session, at which he made yet another appeal for Canadians to find some way to amend the BNA Act so as to be able to deal effectively with the current economic problems. In his address he poked fun at Canadian judges, whose antiquated views on the constitution reflected their physical age more than their intellectual maturity. The local newspaper, the Orillia *Packet and Times*, picked up on the comment, and chastised the professor for his outspoken, unacceptable, and unamusing views.[8]

The waves from this incident had not settled when the same newspaper reported Underhill's heretical views on Canada's external relations as presented in a series of four extension lectures in Orillia. The full-page editorial claimed that Underhill's lectures made 'no pretense of maintaining academic calm, moderation of language, a sense of balance and proportion, or a sympathetic attitude towards those called upon to steer the ship through stormy seas.' Indeed,

Our political leaders were held up to derision, the Prime Minister in particular; and the opinion expressed that there was no hope for better things from the two old parties. The tariff policies of the past had been all wrong. The effort to build up trade within the Empire was silly and hypocritical, as also was the opposition to trading with Russia. The Englishmen who came over to Canada to make speeches habitually advocated policies to the advantage of England, at the expense of Canada. Lord Beaverbrook was a 'pest.' Canada's economic interests lay with the United States, not with the British Empire, the States being our best customer. Canada was destined always to remain 'a hinterland of New York' in financial matters ... Our ideas, business methods, institutions were American, even our banking system – which will be news to the bankers. Englishmen had always made a failure of business in Canada – witness to Hudson's Bay Company and the Grand Trunk Pacific Railway – whereas Americans had always been successful ... Sympathy was expressed for China, admiration for the policies of Spain and Denmark, excuses made for Germany and Japan, but from beginning to end there was not one kindly or appreciative word for the mother country.

Could Canadians afford 'to pay university professors to undermine the foundation of her political and economic system, vilify her public men and loosen the bonds that bind her to the Empire,' the editor, C.H. Hale, asked rhetorically.'9 Underhill was flattered to think that his academic lectures could draw such public interest and rousing response, but Canon H.J. Cody, the new president of the University of Toronto, was not impressed as letters of protest came across his desk.

From the beginning, the two men did not get along. Henry John Cody was an Anglican clergyman who had higher aspirations than remaining a mere cleric. Early in his career, he decided to distinguish himself in the fields of politics and education. He was secretary of the Royal Commission that brought in the University Act of 1906. From there he moved into politics, where, in 1918, he became the Ontario minister of education for one year. He was appointed a member of the Board of Governors for the university in 1917 and was its chairman from 1923 to 1932, when he became Falconer's successor as president. From the beginning, his appointment smacked of political patronage. To Underhill, Cody had the worst qualifications for the position of university president: cleric, politician, administrator. When it was rumoured in the spring of 1931 that Cody was to be the next president, Underhill wrote to Brooke Claxton: 'He has refused so many archbishoprics now that he must be reserving himself the University – damn him. If he does get the job I expect that those of us who are connected with the Forum will have to watch our step.' There is an amusing story, probably apocryphal, that when Cody was seeking the chancellorship at the university, he met Underhill on campus and asked him if he wished to sign the petition for his support. Underhill replied that 'he never mixed in university politics.'10

Cody was upset with the adverse effect that Underhill's critical views were having on the university image. It was wise for 'universities and churches' to 'divorce themselves from actions of political interest,' he claimed at a public gathering in which Underhill's name came up. Such a blatant inconsistency of word and deed was too much for the editor of the *Toronto Star*, who reminded Cody that he was the worst offender, having mixed politics, religion, and academic interests during his career.[11] Underhill was not concerned about Cody's rebuke. In fact, he would have been more upset had he heard that Cody agreed with what he was saying. Earlier, when a *Forum* reader had written to remind Underhill that 'reputable people' like Sir Arthur Currie and Canon Cody disapproved of the journal, Underhill had replied: 'If they approved of it I should begin to worry.' Even the *Varsity*, the student newspaper, referred jokingly to 'Sexton Toady's' attempts to encourage 'Thunderhill' to speak out.[12]

But for Underhill the reprimand was harder to accept when it came from friends and respected colleagues. R.G. Dingman, a lawyer friend, spoke for many when he pointed out to Underhill that his problem was not much what he said but the way he said it. Approaching the subject in a more subtle way than Underhill would have done, Dingman remarked: 'It strikes me that sometimes you put a little more sting into your remarks than a judicially-minded Professor should find necessary ... Couldn't you in the University and in your extension work deal with the principles involved and leave personalities, (Bennett etc.) and parties, to the imagination of your hearers? ... I respectfully suggest that you would thus be more persuasive and would further more the causes you have at heart.' Underhill disagreed. The reason why his criticism was so effective was precisely because he could go beyond abstract ideas to name names. Not to do so would be to lessen the punch and therefore weaken the attack. George Wrong, who had been responsible for bringing Underhill to the University of Toronto in 1927, was of the same opinion as Dingman, and much more direct in expressing it: 'I do not regard your opinions as "deplorable" though I should have such a word in mind, I fear, if I were discussing your mode of expressing them.' He added a warning that if Underhill did not stop these personal vendettas, then his job might be in jeopardy. Wrong's letter hurt, for it was Wrong as a teacher who had encouraged his students to express their opinions in public. Underhill reminded his former mentor that circumstances had changed since the time Wrong was active in political journalism.[13] The conscientious academic of today found himself having to fight the tide of popular opinion and therefore had to expect to be unpopular. To be otherwise was to be ineffective.

Undaunted by friend or foe, Underhill continued to be outspoken in public. At the Couchiching Conference of 1934 he surpassed his performance of the previous year to give 'the most provocative' address of the series, 'probably to his delight,' as the Orillia *Packet and Time* rightly concluded. He proposed 'the disruption of the British Empire' and the consignment 'to the scrap heap not only the British Empire, but the League of Nations too.' Those who fought in the last war were 'suckers' and 'boobs.' Why do it again? The speech was intended to generate debate, and it did. *Saturday Night* reported that Underhill's speech was followed by the 'longest question period of the week.' It was Underhill at his best, the *enfant terrible*, or as *Saturday Night* described him, 'the Big Bad Wolf with sharp teeth,'[14] getting his licks in at his opponents through witticisms, half-truths, and logic. He believed the message when stripped of its extremities and exaggerations, but it was more of a challenge thrown out for debate than an authoritative stance based on a wealth of documentation and facts. The trouble was that his opponents lacked his ability at light-hearted attack and responded with a heavy hand of censorship designed to cut off debate.

The annual 'witch-hunt' was on again – ironically, while Underhill was off to the Institute of Politics in Williamstown, where 'this bane of the Ontario Imperialists' was stoutly defending British imperial policy towards India in a round table conference on the British empire.[15] J.L. Ross, a prominent Toronto lawyer, wrote President Cody requesting that his name be disassociated with the university so long as its professors were undermining the empire. 'I would prefer to have my Canadian grandchildren brought up in France under the shadow of the next war,' he went on to say, 'rather than to see them stall fed and listening in the class-rooms of the University of Toronto to Prof. Underhill.'[16] The president placated the discontented by assuring them that Underhill's 'silly utterances' in no way reflected the views of the university or even the majority of its professors. In fact, they were not even indicative of the ideas that Underhill was presenting in class. 'It seems that he breaks out only in public utterances away from the University,' Cody informed one irate correspondent.

Cody pinned Underhill down to a promise not to make further public speeches for one year.[17] It was the beginning of a short reign of intermittent peace between the two men, brought on less by Underhill's willingness to toe the line than by his ability to express his controversial anti-imperialist views without arousing public indignation. He had to be careful, however, since he was undergoing surveillance by J.M. MacBrien, commissioner of the RCMP, who reported at least once to Cody about Underhill's 'subversive' activities.[18]

Underhill's stinging attacks were not reserved only for his enemies. Even colleagues and close associates in the LSR and the CCF felt the point of his pen and the lash of his tongue. By the winter of 1933–4 the CCF had had a year and a half to prove itself. It was time to take stock. Did the CCF warrant the initial enthusiasm and support that he and his LSR colleagues had given it? It did not, according to Underhill's presidential address at the third annual meeting of the LSR in Toronto on 10 February 1934. Underhill regretted that ' "left-wing thought" had made so superficial an impression on Canadian thinking in the last four years, and expressed the opinion not only that the CCF had lost some of its original impetus, but that in the main, a great opportunity had been largely missed for the creation of a strong nation-wide socialist movement.'

It was the beginning of a persistent public and private criticism of the CCF which Underhill kept up over the next few years. He complained that the CCF would never become a truly national party until it had all the trappings of a national party: a well-organized bureaucracy with a full-time paid secretariat at a national headquarters in Ottawa, a widely publicized program with specific proposals that appealed to the populace, and a dynamic and aggressive leader. While Underhill admired Woodsworth as a friend and principled individual, he was frustrated with his humble and tolerant attitude towards the 'cranks and simpletons' in the party, by which he meant the farmers with their half-baked ideas of referendum, recall, and group government. As long as this group dominated the party, it could never get beyond being a 'collection of individual missionairies' to become 'a highly organized machine capable of carrying on a fight against the powerful organized interests who control Canada at present.'[19] Underhill pleaded with Woodsworth to be more assertive: 'You have no idea how great masses of people are looking to you for a lead and how willingly they will accept from you a definition of exactly where the CCF is going and how it proposes to get there.'[20] In a moment of self-confession that revealed a great deal about himself, Underhill admitted: 'The only way I know how to make myself useful is to be constantly critical.' Even the urbane and tolerant Woodsworth found his criticism overpowering. He reminded Underhill that leadership could not be imposed on a democratic movement unless a grass-roots organization already existed and an educated and informed party membership was established; the CCF had neither.[21]

Underhill wanted the CCF to put off its long-term prime objective of social reform for the immediate concern of achieving political power. CCFers had to be practical and hard-headed to succeed in the world of politics or else they would go the way of the Progressives and end up being a mere pressure group or an ineffective wing of the Liberal party. He was critical because he genuinely believed that the party had a good chance of forming the government or at least the official opposition in the next federal election. His buoyant optimism in the CCF's potential was the result of his perception of what was happening or more accurately what could happen in Canadian politics. Influenced by the ideas of Paul Douglas, the American socialist leader, in *The Coming of a New Party* (New York 1932), Underhill argued that the Liberals and the Conservatives were about to be forced to unite into a single right-wing party, since both represented the same interest groups and had the same philosophy.[22] This would then leave room for a new left-wing party – the CCF – to emerge to represent those interest groups that were left without party affiliation and wanted a party that genuinely represented their needs. For the first time in Canadian history there existed the possibility of a genuine two-party system based on parties with distinct ideologies and interest groups. This is what

Underhill believed to be happening in the United States with the Republicans emerging as the party of big business and the Democrats under F.D. Roosevelt as the party of the common man. Underhill was impressed with Roosevelt's 'New Deal' which he saw as being liberal-socialist in nature. 'American liberalism has shown us the way,' he wrote in the spring of 1934, 'and we are now witnessing an heroic effort in the United States to adapt the American liberal tradition to the needs of the crisis and to reform American economic institutions without transforming them.'[23] If true of the United States, then why not Canada, only with the CCF rather than the Liberals being the genuine party of the left.

The 1935 election results greatly disappointed him. With the Liberals winning 173 of the 245 seats, the country was in for five years of indecisive Liberal rule. That was depressing enough, but more upsetting were the few CCF seats. The party had contested 119 out of 245 seats, but had elected only seven members. 'The old two-party system turned out to be much stronger in the affections of the voters than I had expected,' he admitted to Hugh Keenleyside, serving in the Canadian legation in Japan. He rationalized the party's poor showing by pointing out that 25 per cent of the electorate had voted against the two traditional parties but that unfortunately this protest vote was dissipated among three new parties: the CCF, Social Credit, and the Reconstruction party. The CCF had critical newspaper publicity and insufficient funds for radio broadcasting. Most of all, the single-member constituency voting pattern denied that party a number of seats that, according to its proportional vote, rightly should have gone to it. Since this voting pattern favoured the Liberals, Underhill expected that there would be no attempt to change it. 'I take it for granted,' he informed George Ferguson of the *Free Press*, 'that any radical ideas which Mr. King may have about changing the system will remain deep down in his heart where apparently he has stored away quite a collection of radical opinions.' The only positive aspect of the results was a lesson to party members on the need for more educational work and better national organization – familiar recommendations.[24]

Finally, in September 1935, *Social Planning for Canada* arrived off the printing press. It had been a long time in the making (having been begun in the fall of 1932), much longer than anyone involved in the book expected. Underhill disliked the title and felt the book was too long and too expensive for the general public. Nevertheless he considered it 'in a class by itself' in attempting to present 'a thorough and comprehensive treatment of our economic and political problems.' He proudly sent a copy to J.S. McLean of Canada Packers with a note that read in part: 'You will no doubt find our case full of flaws, but I know you like to be aware of what your enemies have to say.' McLean replied jorkingly: 'I try to keep in touch with what you reds are doing, as I would like to know at least 6 months in advance when I have to hand over my job.'[25]

Publication of the book got Underhill involved in more public controversy as he felt the need to defend it against adverse criticism. One critic was Harold Innis, professor of economics at Toronto, who ironically would come to Underhill's defence later. The issue at stake was their opposed views of the role of a professor in public controversy. Underhill believed that the academic had a moral responsibility to attempt to find solutions to present-day problems, especially during critical times like the Great Depression. This viewpoint he presented in a paper on 'The Conception of a National Interest' at the 1932 Canadian Political Science Association meeting. He argued that in the present era, with society deeply divided on values and ends, the social scientist could no longer maintain the illusion of objectivity. Either he accepted the prevailing ends and values, in which case he played the role of propagandist for the Establishment, or else he risked 'his academic integrity by making up his mind to the best of his ability as to what our social objectives ought to be and to publish his conclusions to the world for criticism of his fellows.' The role of the academic to date had usually been to give intellectual credence to the prevailing conception of the national interest. In a jocular passage, he poked fun at the roles of the economist and the historian:

> Our economists have played the humble self-imposed role of minor techni-
> cians, never questioning the major purposes of the capitalist system in which
> they found themselves, never venturing any opinions about the general plan-
> ning of the machine or the powering of its engines, pottering about with their
> little statistical measuring instruments, doing occasional odd repair jobs on
> Royal Commissions, such as putting new brake linings into the financial
> mechanism, happy in their unambitious way as the intellectual garage-
> mechanics of Canadian capitalism. Our historians have played a rather flashier
> role. Not for them the greasy grimy jobs of testing and repairing in the work-
> shop. They have been among the white-collar boys in the sales-office in front,
> helping to sell the system to the public with a slick line of talk about responsi-
> ble government and national autonomy.[26]

The paper could have ended there. Instead, Underhill went on to make *ad hominem* attacks on three Canadian economists, Stephen Leacock, Harold Innis, and Gilbert Jackson, for their failure to offer solutions to the present economic crisis. Such attack was not customary in the academic community, where issues were usually debated in public on an objective and impersonal level, but it was characteristic of Underhill's personal attacks on the political and social elite in the *Forum*. He believed strongly in what he was saying, and was willing to expose himself to attack and abuse. After all, he reminded the audience, 'in a dangerous age there is no escape, even for social scientists, from living dangerously.'

Innis replied in his review of *Social Planning for Canada*. He compared the contributors to a tailor and his cloth, importing ideas from external sources, then putting them together in a patchwork fashion to produce a garment ill-fitted for the home market. Then he took swipes at these politician-professors, with Underhill in mind, who turn 'to political activity and popular acclaim during depressions ... The confusion of volubility with intellectual interest, and of symptoms with cures, are reflections of the fundamental effects of the depression.'[27]

Having attacked his colleagues, Underhill was now ready to take on the Montreal Establishment, especially its major company, the CPR – always a favourite target for his pen. What initiated his attack was a convocation address by Sir Edward Beatty, president of the CPR, in which he deplored the extent to which socialism was being preached in Canadian universities. Underhill rebutted in an unsigned *Forum* article, 'Beatty and the University Reds.' He assured Beatty that he had no cause 'to come roaring up' at economics professors in Canadian universities 'like a traffic cop and to bawl them out for reckless driving,' since most of them were supporters of the Establishment with respectable, bourgeois, and capitalistic sympathies. The remark infuriated Beatty,[28] and there were rumblings around McGill against the LSR members there, but Underhill emerged unscathed and ready for his next battle with the Establishment.

That occurred fifteen months later in May 1937 when, during a CBC radio debate with George Ferguson on the subject of 'The Freedom of the Press,' Underhill decried the monopoly of the Toronto press by capitalists. The statement that got him into trouble read: 'At present in Toronto I have no alternative to reading at my breakfast table every morning whatever a couple of gold-mining millionaires may think is good for the people of Ontario.'[29] It was an indirect reference to the recent amalgamation of the Toronto *Globe* and *Mail* newspapers under the ownership of William Wright and the editorship of George McCullagh, both millionaires.

McCullagh replied in one of his editorials in which he demanded to know, first, why the CBC 'chose a Socialist college professor to go on the air to criticize the newspaper business' and, second, when such professors would be 'turned out en masse and the public purse ... relieved of the burden of supporting the kind of "education" they support.' During his spirited attack McCullagh accused Victoria College of 'seething' with socialism and atheism. 'Many a parent hesitates to send his son to these institutions because of the subversive doctrines in which he is likely to be "educated."'[30]

The unfortunate reference to Victoria College, which was not Underhill's college, prompted the chairman of the Board of Regents and the chancellor of the college to deny such allegations. Such statements 'indicated lack of knowledge of the facts ... and created an erroneous and harmful impression.' McCullagh owed the college an apology. In his rejoinder, McCullagh tried to whitewash his accusations by denying that they referred specifically to Victoria; the whole University of Toronto was guilty. He agreed to withdraw the accusation if he were

assured by the administrators that all was well in the ivory tower. Underhill
escaped yet another attempt at his dismissal with only a tongue-lashing from the
president.[31]

Underhill's socialist views were subjecting him to verbal attacks outside the
university, but within, they were a cause of delight among his students. For
example, at the Christmas celebration of the University College Literary Society,
of which Underhill was the honorary president, the group composed an appropriate whimsical song to Underhill, based on his socialist leanings, and entitled
'Honorary President':

I am the very pattern of an honorary president,
In dealing with the students I am never shy or hesitant;
I speak at groups and meetings in a manner very affable
And all my jokes and stories are without exception laughable.

About the party system I can give you facts historical,
From Conservative to C.C.F. in order categorical.
My speeches get publicity and make the headlines in the papers,
For to be a notability one must be always cutting capers.
Chorus: He is a notability and must be always cutting capers.

But it really doesn't matter if I'm criticized or glorified
So long as my employers show no signs of being horrified.
And since with undergraduates I'm neither shy nor hesitant
I am the very model of an honorary president.
Chorus: He is the very model of an honorary president.

I'm definitely leftish in political economy.
I make an awful fuss about Canadian autonomy.
I associate with socialists, I've communistic tendencies.
And think that Britain ought to give up half of her dependencies.

I have a fixed aversion to the stupid fat capitalist
From Herby Holt up in his tower right down unto the little-est.
And how we should administer our wealth of natural resources
I will expound at length if you enrol in any of my courses.
Chorus: He does expound at length to all enrolled in any of his courses.

For I am very proud to be a lecturer in history
(Though why the Board appointed me is something of a mystery).
But since with undergraduates I'm never shy or hesitant.

I am the very model of an honorary president.
Chorus: He is the very model of an honorary president.[32]

A great deal of Underhill's time outside Academe was spent supporting the socialist cause. He continued to serve on a CCF committee that advised Woodsworth and his fellow party MPs on subjects to be discussed in parliament. He was giving speeches to LSR groups in the province, and was 'on call' as the most popular speaker for the meetings of the more active Toronto branch.

Then there was the *Canadian Forum*. Underhill continued to give generously of his time to keep the journal going. It had undergone substantial changes since Underhill joined the editorial board in 1927. From 1927 to 1934 the *Forum* was operated by J.M. Dent and Sons. The relationship was a friendly one in which the publishers allowed the editorial board full licence for the opinions expressed. From the beginning that viewpoint was left-wing, but by the early thirties it was decidedly socialist. After the CCF was formed in the summer of 1932 the journal showed a clear bias towards this new party.

Such partisan affiliation concerned Hugh R. Dent, owner of the *Forum*. He complained to the editorial committee in October 1932 that the journal had gotten away from his original conception of it as an 'open Forum' where different viewpoints were presented and had become instead a propaganda piece for left-wing sympathizers. He pointed out, in particular, the 'incessant attacks on Bennett and Ferguson.' These vituperative comments, he implied, were hurting his educational book sales in Tory Ontario. Underhill admitted to being the chief culprit, but was not about to repent. A good journal of political commentary had to have a definite viewpoint on current controversies in order to 'build up a subscription list of steady readers' and attract writers who wrote out of sympathy for the viewpoint expressed. He reminded Dent that only left-wing professors were 'interested enough or foolish enough' to write for mere pleasure. Such criticism was particularly needed in Canada just because there had been so little of it. Nevertheless, he promised Dent, 'I will hold myself in a bit.'[33]

Evidently satisfied, the Dent Company continued to support the journal until April 1934, when the association ended. The parting was cordial, and the existing editorial committee disbanded. Underhill's name disappeared from the masthead and his familiar and sprightly style vanished from the editorial page. He decided to leave because the new owner and editor, Steven Cartwright, a young Liberal, intended to carry the journal 'further to the right in politics than it has been under the present editorial committee.'[34] His 'retirement' was brief, however. In the spring of 1935 Graham Spry purchased the journal from the bankrupt Canadian Forum Limited for one dollar and Underhill was back writing editorials; it was a labour of love. But within one year, Spry was forced to sell out to the League for

Social Reconstruction. It undertook the financial venture with $200 of its own money, subscription funds, and a generous $1000 grant from Carlton McNaught, a wealthy member of the LSR's Toronto branch. One of McNaught's conditions for putting up the money was that Underhill 'continue to write for the magazine and participate in its editorial direction as in the past.' That he did with a vengeance. Consistently each month throughout the remainder of 1936 and in 1937 he contributed his fair share of editorials along with at least one article on a subject of national concern, not to mention his frequent book reviews. In addition, he was soliciting articles from British socialists and American liberals in an effort to broaden the *Forum* scope and to inform its readers on left-wing developments and ideas in these countries.[35]

Prior to the LSR's take-over of the *Forum* there had been a disagreement between Frank Scott and Underhill over the general tone of the journal. Scott complained to Underhill that the *Forum* was too negative and prone to meaningless criticism, which might be clever but hardly substantial. It was time for the journal to win new converts by offering constructive proposals. '[W]e should be much more honest-to-goodness enthusiasts, believers, idealists, go-getters, uplifters, and general Babbitts in a socialist way,' Scott claimed; he was tired of the name-calling and the glib criticisms. 'I shall scream if the present Forum board regurgitates the stock grievances of 1929–33. It's too damned reiterative. I know that good editorial notes are hard to get, but bad ones are not hard to throw out.' Underhill was not accustomed to that kind of outburst from his closest associate, and he resented it. He was working hard on the *Forum*, doing what he had always done and done well – criticize. He conceded that more positive and constructive suggestions were needed, but not at the expense of criticism or for the sake of trying to win over a few of uncertain faith at the possible expense of losing their committed supporters. 'I am not going to become any damned combination of Christian apostle and American Babbitt,' Underhill infomed Scott, 'merely for the sake of converting a few distressed members of the Montreal bourgeoisie.'[36]

Despite this disagreement, Scott, as president of the LSR, asked Underhill to become the new editor-in-chief of the *Forum* while under the LSR's aegis, responsible for seeing the journal through its various stages to publication, checking consistency in policy, and taking charge of the editorial notes. Underhill was the obvious man for the job, Scott claimed, 'though I still reserve the right to criticize when you have twisted your knife too viciously in some unfortunate victim.' Underhill consented to do the job at a time when the *Forum* was going through another of its regular financial crises.[37] It was a demanding task but had its enjoyable times too, such as the monthly get-together to paste the final edition together on Underhill's dining-room table. One member of the editorial board recalled: 'The committee would meet on Sunday evenings at Frank Underhill's home. Ruth Underhill kept us going with tea and cake and glasses of beer, while Frank's devastating and witty commentary on the current political scene would provide the background for the upcoming issue of the *Forum*.'[38] Once again Underhill played a major role in keeping the journal during difficult financial times. But by October he asked to be relieved of the responsibilities as editor-in-chief. 'I find that I am writing with more and more difficulty on the Forum ... [because] I feel less and less that I have anything that I want to say.'[39]

The need to clarify Canada's foreign policy in a world moving inevitably towards another major war dominated Underhill's writings in the *Forum* in the late 1930s. On one point he was absolutely clear and consistent: Canada needed to control its own foreign policy independently of Britain so that the country would not be dragged into another European holocaust against its will.

Underhill's opposition to Canadian involvement in another war stemmed from two factors: his anti-imperialism and his pro-nationalism. From the beginning he believed that the next war, like the last one, would be fought in the interest of imperialism. Wars were simply a means by which imperialists could extend their territorial ambitions. For Canadians to fight on Britain's side was to commit the country to British imperial interests. The alternative to siding with Britain was for Canada to pursue an independent foreign policy. It was time Canadians showed maturity by taking responsibility for their own decisions.

Underhill presented his argument most cogently in a memorandum on 'Canadian Foreign Policy in the 1930s' for the Canadian Institute of International Affair's eighth international studies conference on collective security in February 1935. The international situation in the 1930s, he stated, had reverted to the pre-1914 position: two armed camps ready to attack over any small incident. At that time, Canadians had two choices: pursuing a common imperial policy or working towards an independent nationalist position. Laurier had favoured the latter, and diligently worked for Canadian autonomy. Yet when war broke out, Canada became automatically involved owing to her imperial connection. The situation was no different in 1935. Despite Mackenzie King's diligent efforts in the 1920s to free Canada from her dependence on Britain, the country was still legally and emotionally tied.

Underhill wanted to believe that the League of Nations offered an alternative, yet he felt little confidence in the existing league. Like the empire-commonwealth, the league was an international organization manipulated by the imperialist nations for their own selfish ambitions. The real division in Europe was not the democratic against the fascist nations, but the satisfied against the dissatisfied. Once again, it was a balance-of-power position. He made his point most emphatically in his strongly worded conclusion, intended to arouse the ire of his opponents:

We must therefore make it clear to the world, and especially to Great Britain, that the poppies blooming in Flanders fields have no further interest for us. We must fortify ourselves against the allurements of a British war for democracy and freedom and parliamentary institutions, and against the allurements of a League war for peace and international order. And when overseas propagandists combine the two appeals to us by urging us to join in organizing 'the Peace World' to which all the British nations already belong, the simplest answer is to thumb our noses at them. Whatever the pretext on which Canadian armed forces may be lured to Europe again, the actual result would be that Canadian workers and farmers would shoot down German workers and farmers, or be shot down by them, in meaningless slaughter. As the late John S. Ewart remarked, we should close our ears to these European blandishments and, like Ulysses and his men, sail past the European siren, our ears stuffed with tax-bills. All these European troubles are not worth the bones of a Toronto grenadier.[40]

The passage was written to shock all 'right-thinking' Canadians. He warned Escott Reid, national secretary of the CIIA, not to amend or edit any part of the paper without his consent. 'I am not going to have a bowdlerized – or Masseyized or Rowellized – version appear under my name, and if your bosses don't like this as written it is to be returned to me, not watered down so that it will be safe for public consumption.'[41]

This paper was an almost verbatim account of his chapter on 'Foreign Policy' which he had done with Reid for the LSR book, *Social Planning for Canada*, except that this controversial last paragraph was excluded and replaced by more constructive and specific proposals for Canadian contribution to world peace. In particular, he made an appeal to turn the League of Nations into a genuine collective organization of security by freeing it from the dominance of profit-seeking interests and by putting it under the control of socialist nations dedicated to co-operation and peace. Canada's contribution could be 'to establish a socialist commonwealth within [its] own borders.'[42] Reform had to begin at home.

The League of Nation's inability to reprimand Italy for its attack on Ethiopia in the late summer and autumn of 1935 reinforced Underhill's worst fears about the weaknesses of this international organization in its present form. Underhill wanted the league to impose economic sanctions on Italy, although he opposed Canada taking the initiative in proposing such a move, because then the country would not have an excuse for staying out of war when it came. He was definitely opposed to going beyond economic to military sanctions, seeing this as a sure step to getting involved in another war on behalf of the imperialist interests. Marvin Gelber, a young business executive, turned Underhill's argument on himself by pointing out that in denouncing the imperialists, he was lending support to Hitler and the fascists. Underhill replied: 'Mr. Gelber wants to take sides in Europe because he can see nothing there but Hitler ... Having myself taken part in a fairly recent war for the elimination of Kaiserism from Europe, a war which eliminated Kaiserism only to replace it by Hitlerism, I have lost my faith in the effectiveness of the policy of burying more Canadians in the continent – whether we profess to bury them for the sake of liberalism or democracy or socialism or communism.'[43] To those Canadians who were already inclined to want to stay out of European entanglements, it was, in 1936, a persuasive argument.

By October 1936 Underhill had abandoned all hope for the league. The collective security system was dead, 'a subject for learned investigation by professors of history in their PH.D. seminars.' 'It is obvious,' he informed his *Forum* readers, 'that there is now no more hope that the League may be used as an instrument of genuine collective system for enforcing peace, and that if we let ourselves become entangled in its coercive machinery we are in danger of throwing our support blindly to one side or the other in the European balance-of-power which is now in the course of construction.'[44] Such a view was in line with the thinking of British left-wing critics of the international organization. In fact, Underhill borrowed heavily from their writings. For example, in July 1936 he was reading *Towards a New League* (London 1935) by H.N. Brailsford and *Why The League Has Failed* (London 1938) by the Vigilantes, a pseudonym for a group of British Labour intellectuals. The former argued that international developments in the years from 1920 to 1936 would not have been essentially different if the league had never existed; the latter claimed that the league had failed because it was dominated by imperialist powers who were using it for their own selfish ends. Only a league of socialist states, genuinely dedicated to peace, could revive the organization and ensure world peace.[45]

There were two – and only two – choices for Canadians: go to war at Britain's side or pursue an isolationist policy. His own position was clear: 'Keep Canada out of War,' the title of his article in the 15 May 1937 issue of *Maclean's*, summed it up precisely. Isolationism, he argued, was not a negative, fatalistic, or irresponsible position. On the contrary, it was irresponsible to trick Canadians into going to war on the pretense that it would be a war for freedom, democracy, or any other noble cause, when in reality it was just 'another of the good old balance-of-power imperialist struggles like all of the great world wars of the past.' That was the main point made by Underhill during a debate on the topic '1938! Canada Looks Abroad: Which Way Should We Go?' sponsored by the League of Nations Society of Toronto in January.[46]

Underhill marshalled an array of arguments to justify isolationism. Canada was in a good geographical position, protected as she was by 'Generals Atlantic and Pacific'; there was no immediate threat of attack on her borders. Close to half of the nation's trade was with its friendly neighbour to the south, which could still continue in spite of war; Britain would be forced to continue her trade with Canada simply because it was to her advantage to do so. Isolationism would help to keep the country together. In the past, war, more than anything else, had been the chief threat to national unity. 'War will put such a strain upon our national structure as it may not be able to withstand,' he warned Canadians. Underhill argued strongly and consistently for an independent and neutralist Canadian position until the bitter news came on 1 September 1939 of war in Europe. On that fateful weekend he was in Montreal to meet with a concerned group of academics of different political persuasions to try to find ways to head off the drift towards war. As they discussed the alternatives, they heard over the radio early Sunday morning that the King was going to address his people at 3 PM. That afternoon Britain declared war. Canada was still neutral, but those present knew that Canadian involvement would inevitably follow. The group disbanded, and the members went out to 'drown their sorrows.' Their struggles had been in vain. That weekend, the Angry Thirties came to an end for Underhill.[47]

10

The University Crisis

'These men are rats who are trying to scuttle our ship of state.' That was how Colonel Fred Fraser Hunter, member of the Ontario legislature for the St Patrick riding in which the University of Toronto was located, described Frank Underhill and George Grube during debate on a motion to dismiss the two professors from the University for 'hurling insults at the British Empire.'[1]

Hunter's speech climaxed a debate in the House on 13 April 1939, six months before the outbreak of war. It began when Dr L.J. Simpson, the Ontario minister of education, denounced George Grube, a Belgian-born, Cambridge-educated classicist who was active in the LSR, for stating that 'the expenditure of Canadian rearmament was a waste of public funds in the interest of British imperialism.' 'It is most unfortunate,' Simpson went on to say, 'that a professor in one of our universities should have had the audacity to make such a statement,' particularly at such a critical time when war seemed imminent and the democracies threatened. He lamented that only the government could discipline the professor, since he was a member of Trinity College, an affiliated college of the University of Toronto, and therefore not directly under the Board of Governors' jurisdiction.

Colonel George Drew, leader of the opposition, reinforced the minister's concern. Then suddenly he introduced Underhill's name into the discussion by quoting to the legislature the controversial last paragraph of Underhill's speech to the Canadian Institute of International Affairs, made four years earlier but recently published in *Canada Looks Abroad* (London 1938), in which he had declared that the poppies which grow in Flanders fields no longer had any interest for the people of Canada. 'Shame! Shame!' shouted Premier Mitchell Hepburn, as he thumped his desk indignantly. Drew continued: 'Now the time has come to stop and to stop permanently statements of that kind by a man who either in or out of the educational institution is speaking to the public as a member of that institution.' Such beliefs were corrupting the minds of youth and thus jeopardizing the future of democracy, he pointed out. Government ought to have the right to demand that 'in the schools they shall teach what we know as British democracy and shall not do anything to assist subversive elements which are seeking to destroy these ideals in which we believe.' 'I am disappointed,' Hepburn responded, 'that the University Board of Governors has not up to now disciplined Underhill in a manner befitting the crime he has committed. It smacks of rank sedition.'

It was at this point that Colonel Hunter introduced a motion of dismissal. The minister of education advised that before putting the motion to a vote he consult with the university authorities. Drew agreed, claiming he wanted only to express the government's disapproval of these professorial outbursts. Hunter consented too, although he claimed to have heard and read enough of Underhill to be convinced 'that the action should be taken.' The debate ended with Premier Hepburn's assurance that if the proper authorities did nothing 'to bring these men into line,' the government would step in. He implied that this would meet with public approval by reading a telegram from the Newmarket Lions Club which urged that university grants be further reduced by the province 'until the governing body weeds out men who parade themselves before the public as traitors to the public and who poison the minds of Ontario's finest young men and women.'

The outburst in the House was part of the general hysteria that erupted any time that an individual criticized the imperial connection, especially if that individual was a university professor who was not expected to have disloyal thoughts, or at least not to express them publicly.[2] The tension was especially intense as war loomed over the horizon. Underhill claimed that an outsider could not appreciate how far the war hysteria had gone in Ontario.[3]

There was, as well, a degree of political showmanship in the attack. It was not that the politicians did not believe what they said, but that they said it emphatically and emotionally because they were using the opportunity to attack indirectly their opponents. In this case the opponents were twofold: the Mackenzie King Liberal government which, both Hepburn and Drew could agree, was despicable when it came to its attitude towards Britain; and the University of Toronto administrators, who were not getting along with politicians probably because some, like President Cody, had been politicians themselves and had necessarily acquired political enemies in the process. Underhill had gathered from gossip that the attack on him was a convenient means 'to get at Cody by making his position so uncomfortable that he will be forced to resign.'[4]

The quotation itself was a poor example for Drew to choose. While it expressed Underhill's sentiments and views precisely and was a strongly worded and most offensive statement to 'right thinking Canadians,'[5] it was nevertheless written over four years earlier as a private document for general discussion only. Furthermore, the excerpt quoted from *Canada Looks Abroad* was taken out of context and therefore magnified out of proportion.

The Board of Governors, forewarned of the discontent in the House, met the very same day under the initiative of Dr H.A. Bruce, leader of George McCullagh's Leadership League and former lieutenant-governor of Ontario. The board instructed the president to ascertain from Underhill whether the controversial quote was an accurate statement, when it was written, whether he consented to its publication, and if he still upheld these views. Cody acted immediately. He wrote Underhill the following day, Friday, demanding that he appear in the president's office at eleven o'clock sharp on Saturday morning.[6] Underhill missed the appointment because he and his family were vacationing, blissfully ignorant of the whole affair, and probably, he recalled, 'crossing the Thousand Island bridge into New York State about the time that Hepburn and Drew stated their foaming at the mouth scene.'[7] But he arrived back to the furore on Monday night.

In the interval Cody met with Chester Martin, head of the history department to elicit his opinion of the crisis. Martin recalled wearily that this was the fourth occasion during his headship that he had had to discuss Underhill's conduct with the president. On all occasions there was never a question of Underhill's loyalty to the department or to the university in what he taught. It was always over his manner of discussing public questions outside the curriculum of the university. Each time he was led to understand that Underhill would avoid future speeches, only to find him reneging. This latest statement Martin found 'indefensible and unworthy of a scholar in Mr. Underhill's position,' but he pointed out to the president that it could not be construed as a recent outburst. He also appealed to the president to use 'restraint and discretion.'[8]

Cody was hardly restrained or discreet – nor was Underhill – when they met on Tuesday morning. The president accused Underhill of being 'a trouble-maker who was costing the University untold sums of money (this business came just in the midst of troubles about our estimates).' If Underhill wanted to keep his job, Cody warned that he had better co-operate by writing a letter explaining the circumstances surrounding the quotation, apologizing for its phrasing, and promising not to offend in the future.[9] That afternoon Underhill composed his letter. He explained that it was unfair to represent words of his written considerably earlier as his present position, although he admitted that he still held these views and that he had no prior knowledge of its recent publication (a view upheld by R.A. MacKay, the editor of the book, in a cable to Cody). As for the specific statement on the poppies of Flanders fields, it should not be construed 'as a reflection upon the Canadian soldiers who fought on the Western front during the Great War. After all, I am one of those soldiers myself.' Instead, it conveyed his strong conviction that Canadians should avoid repeating the mass murder of 60 000 in another European war. He agreed that some of the sentences in the passage were 'phrased in such a way as to be offensive to a good many people, and I regret very much having expressed myself in this way.' He got around Cody's insistence of a future promise by pointing out that he still kept his previous promise of two years earlier to avoid undesirable publicity. The best proof was the recent attack on him for a statement taken out of context and written before he made his promise. 'I think you might take the fact that I have behaved myself reasonably well in these recent years as a guarantee that I can be trusted when I say that I shall do my best in future to behave as reasonable men would expect a professor to behave.'[10] It was a moderate and honest statement, and not nearly as offensive as it could have been, given the underhanded way in which his name had come into the controversy.

Others expressed for Underhill the indignation that he felt. Alan Plaunt, of the Canadian Radio League and a friend of both Underhill and Drew, wrote the latter to express alarm at Drew's inappropriate outburst. Such attacks, hurled 'at defenceless citizens under cover of political privilege.' were more of a threat to democracy than the statements of a few innocent and concerned professors, Plaunt argued. The serious issue at stake was the denial to professors of the traditional British right to speak and write on public questions according to their conscience. Even more dangerous was a new principle implied in the speeches by the politicians that 'no educational institution receiving funds from the government should harbour opinions dissimilar from those of the majority of the legislature' – an outright fascist doctrine which threatened a university's autonomy. What peculiar concept of democracy did Drew have, Plaunt queried?

Drew replied with a definition that showed just how divergent the two men's views were. Democracy was the right of publicly elected individuals to fire a public employee who was undermining the values upon which that institution survived, in the same way that a congregation could dismiss a minister who ridiculed the religion upon which the church was founded. It was a strange analogy, and one that completely overlooked the concept of academic freedom which was Plaunt's main point. Still, it was a popular belief in the 1920s and 1930s: that the men who paid the piper had the right to call the tune. Drew went on to argue that his concept of democracy would best be preserved 'on a simple acceptance of the fact that we are British than if our youth are instructed by parlour pinks who preach Empire disunity from the cloistered protection of jobs which gave them all too much free time.'[11]

Meanwhile, faculty members sprang into action. Some resented the political pressure being put on the university and were alarmed at the possible repercussions for academic freedom. Samuel Beatty, dean of the Faculty of Arts, and Harold Innis gathered together the heads of the Arts departments in the University of Toronto and University College to issue a statement to the president which expressed faculty sentiment. They agreed unanimously that Underhill's statement was 'ill-advised and offensive' and suggested, as a solution, the establishment of a small committee of academics to deal with the case. The hope was to internalize the controversy and get it, along with similar cases in the future, out of the political realm where the university's autonomy was threatened. Beatty and Innis delivered the statement personally, and warned the president that he would be in for a hard time from his staff if Underhill were fired.[12] Student pressure was also applied in the form of a petition to the president, with 1014 signatures, which defended the right of professors to free speech. In the classroom, neither Underhill nor Grube had attempted to promote his private beliefs among the students, the petition noted. The number of signatures would have been larger, the organizers pointed out, if it were not so late in the academic year. The small number of signatures should not, however, be construed as student indifference to the issue.[13] It was the first time that faculty and students had rallied together to protect the autonomy of the university; in this respect it was clearly a first step towards academic freedom. More discouraging was the response of the Toronto newspapers to the incident. None rallied to the defence of academic freedom in its editorial; only *Saturday Night* came out in Underhill's favour.

By Wednesday the situation was looking better. Cody was in good spirits for the special board meeting that afternoon. He had with him a statement of support from the faculty and students, along with a written apology from Underhill and an outline of Underhill's military record to present to the board. He presented his report which contained liberal quotations from the letters received from Underhill, Martin, and the senior professors, and an important section on Underhill's war record – information that surprised many governors. A deputation, consisting of Dean Beatty and Professors Martin, Kennedy, and Innis, appeared in person before the board to elaborate on their written statements. Then Underhill appeared and made a statement 'as to the spirit and method of his teaching' in which he declared that he put all sides of a question before the students, warned them of his own bias, and allowed them freedom to form their own conclusions.[14]

Underhill expected fireworks at the meeting, but was pleasantly surprised. He reported to friends that Howard Ferguson, 'of all people, was operating with his usual smoothness to prevent any trouble.' Only 'that old reprobate Sir William Mulock and Doctor Bruce who is head of George McCullagh's Leadership League' gave him any trouble.[15] The board deferred further consideration to a subsequent meeting when the president would have time to prepare a paper embodying all the facts. Underhill assumed this delay was long enough for the Ontario legislature to adjourn, thus ending the need for immediate action. One week later Colonel Hunter withdrew his resolution, with assurance from the minister of education that the university was acting on the incident.[16]

The president presented his final report on 22 June, well after the heat of the incident had subsided. He gave a brief history of the events to date, a summary of the various views presented, and a final section on the importance of academic freedom. Cody argued that a professor may have the 'legal right to express views which might jeopardise the wider interests of his institution and his colleagues, but the possessing of this legal right suggests the question whether he has a moral right to do so.' Thus a university administrator might be in a position of defending the right of free speech of an individual whose views he disagreed with. He stressed the difficulty of balancing the intellectual freedom of the university 'against all tyranny and assault,' and of ensuring responsibility on the part of its instructors to seek the truth and to express it in a form marked by 'dignity, good taste and the decent restraints of scholarship.' It was as strong an appeal for academic freedom as could be expected at the time. The board was persuaded to take no further action on the case.[17]

In the mean time, Underhill, feeling cocky about his latest victory (although he admitted the strain had ruined both his sleep and his appetite and even adversely affected his golf), wrote a letter to the editor of *Saturday Night* to complain of 'misrepresentation' in an article on the controversy, in which it was reported that Underhill had been 'promoted in the field' to the imperial army. 'My commission was solely the result of pull exercised on my behalf by some kind Oxford friends.' It was whimsical remarks like that that provoked the authorities and convinced at least one board member that the recalcitrant professor had not 'turned a new leaf' as promised.[18]

The storm passed, and Underhill settled down to a summer of relaxation and research on Edward Blake. Then in September the inevitable happened. War broke out in Europe on 1 September; ten days later Canada was involved. Underhill saw some of his ablest students abandon their studies to join the fight. He witnessed the dissension in CCF and LSR ranks over the issue of involvement or isolationism. Most shocking of all was his realization, by the spring of 1940, that allied strength was a myth. Hitler had a stronger hold on Europe than he ever realized. By the summer of 1940 Nazi troops had swept through Denmark, Norway, the Low Countries, and France. Only Britain remained in Western Europe as a bulwark to Nazi domination, and already the Battle of Britain was on, with a massive and sustained attack on the British Isles. Out of concern, the 'disloyal' Underhill applied in June to the Department of Immigration to take care of two British refugee children, Elizabeth and Robert Wilson, who were part of a plan to billet British children in homes in commonwealth countries.[19]

What impact would the war have on Canada? That was Underhill's main concern in his writings; it was also the main subject of discussion at the Couchiching Conference on 16 August 1940. At the very time that the meetings were getting under way, Prime Minister Mackenzie King was consulting with President Franklin Roosevelt about the feasibility of establishing a Permanent Joint Board to plan a common defence of North America against a possible Nazi attack. Two days later, on Sunday, 18 August 1940, it became a reality with the signing of the Ogdensburg Agreement.[20]

There was much to discuss among the academics, newspapermen, politicians, labour leaders, and civil servants who met on those tense days on the shores of Lake Couchiching. Underhill participated on the last day of the conference, Friday, 23 August, in a panel discussion on the subject 'A United American Front,' a prophetic and timely topic. Norman J. McLean, brother of J.S. McLean of Canada Packers, chaired the session. Two of the panelists were Americans: Clark Foreman, public works commissioner from Washington, and J.F. Greene of the Foreign Policy Association of New York. The two Canadians were C.E. Silcox, a Toronto clergyman, and Professor Underhill. R.E.G. Davis, secretary of the conference, had purposely selected Silcox and also requested that he speak last to counteract Underhill's anticipated controversial views.[21] Underhill spoke for twenty minutes. No official record of the speech was kept, so that the only sources of information are his rough notes, newspaper reports written from brief notes, and a draft of the speech which Underhill made ten days later. The gist of his argument was that the Ogdensburg Agreement inaugurated a new era in Canadian relations with the United States and Great Britain: 'We in Canada are now committed to two loyalties, the old one to the British connection involving our backing up of Britain, and the new one to North America involving common action with the States to protect our geographical security in our North American home ... We can no longer depend on the power of Britain and France standing between us and whatever may develop on the continent of Europe. And so we can no longer put all our eggs in the British basket ... Let it be noted that this new step in our policy does not necessitate a breach with our old connection. As I said at the beginning we have now two loyalties to be followed in practice when we plan our defence policies.'[22]

Nearly everyone present who heard the speech and commented on it at the time agreed that it was a temperate, reasonable, and, for Underhill, low-key address. People who traditionally disagreed violently with him admitted, in the words of one of his critics, that 'I have never heard Underhill when I felt that he carried his audience with him better and when he antagonized such a small proportion. There was nothing in the address which could in any reasonable way be interpreted as an undermining of Canada's war effort.'[23] To those present, Underhill's speech had caused no concern. They were surprised, therefore, at the agitation it aroused in public.

The controversy erupted from the press reports which did not necessarily misquote but clearly did distort the message by highlighting certain phrases, such as 'all our eggs in the British basket' or 'the relative importance of Britain is going to sink no matter what happens,' which, when taken out of context, appeared more provocative. Particularly exaggerated were the reports in the Orillia *Packet and Times* and the Toronto *Telegram*, both always ready to make trouble for Underhill, which implied that Underhill's speech was treason by advocating the abandonment of the British cause in the hour of her greatest danger. As one perceptive individual correctly noted: 'I am confident that if anyone other than Underhill had made the speech he did, there would have been none of the violent criticism which has been indulged in in a couple of quarters. It is a case of undue readiness to believe the worst because of an unfavourable disposition toward him.'[24]

Cody's home telephone began ringing Saturday night and continued all day Sunday as irate citizens logged complaints against the Toronto professor. The president was exasperated at the prospect of another fight with the board and the politicians to save this man who hadn't enough sense to keep quiet for his own good. He took the initiative to cable Underhill at Geneva Park: 'Have received vigorous protest regarding report of your address in yesterday's *Telegram*. Kindly send me full statement of what you said Friday morning. I had understood you were not making public speeches at present.' Underhill never received the telegram, having left for his cottage in the Muskokas at the end of the session. Davis received the telegram and immediately appealed to E.J. Tarr, president of Monarch Life Assurance Co and a friend of the president, who was present at the session, to cable Cody in defence of Underhill's position.[25]

Some disgruntled individuals expressed their disgust through political channels in hopes of more effective action. The Right Honourable Arthur Meighen wrote Ernest Lapointe, minister of justice in the Liberal government, to insist that the federal government intern Underhill for slanderous remarks that could only discourage recruiting. J.J. Addy, secretary of the British Empire Association, forwarded a copy of a resolution passed by the association to the attorney-general of Ontario, Gordon Conant, protesting against 'the state subsidized University of Toronto retaining on its staff any person uttering such a disloyal twiddle-twaddle,' and insisted that this 'subversive' professor be investigated under 'the Treachery Act,'[26] whatever that might be.

Underhill anticipated trouble and tried to head it off. He wrote the president from Muskoka on 1 September and enclosed a copy of a letter he had just sent to the *Star* reprimanding the paper for its slanderous editorial. He assured Cody that his remarks had none of 'the undesirable qualities which the Toronto editors [*Star* and *Telegram*] have so characteristically uncovered.' Cody was not placated. He still insisted on 'a full statement from you of what you did say.' Underhill complied the following day, 4 September, with as exact a reproduction as possible, assuring the president: 'I haven't consciously watered down in my typescript anything that I may have said verbally.'[27]

By this time, the forces committed to ousting Underhill from the university were mobilized. Duncan McArthur, the recently appointed minister of education for the Ontario government, asked Attorney-General Conant to assign an inspector to investigate Underhill's past, to discover the circumstances surrounding the Couchiching speech, and to survey his present activities with the prospect of prosecuting him under Regulation 39 of the Defence of Canada Regulations. The top man was selected, Inspector Alex Wilson, head of the 'anti-sabotage-subversive squad.' For two weeks he had someone survey the Underhill house while he searched out information on Underhill's life and interviewed a wide range of people who had been present at or involved in organizing the Couchiching Conference. He presented his final report to Conant on 16 September. His brief sketch of Underhill's life, although full of factual errors, was illuminating on the Couchiching issue. He pointed out the difficulty of proving Underhill's guilt without an official report of the speech, and emphasized the widespread agreement on the moderate tone of the address. In the end, he recommended no action be taken against Underhill, since the circumstances were 'not strong enough to warrant the institution of proceedings under the Defence of Canada Regulations.' Two days later, Conant relayed the report and recommendation to McArthur.[28]

The Board of Governors met to discuss the recent crisis on Thursday, 12 September. Just prior to the meeting the president conducted an unpleasant interview with Underhill, accusing him of breaking his promise not to speak in public. Underhill snapped back that he had promised only 'to behave as reasonable men would expect a professor to behave' and that his latest speech did not violate that promise. He pressed the president to point to sentences in his Couchiching address that were disloyal or improper. Cody replied that particular utterances did not matter, that it was his 'constant making trouble for the University.'[29]

At the board meeting Cody reviewed the previous dispute with Underhill, presented Underhill's draft of the speech and his letter of refutation to the *Star*, and read some of the correspondence he had received. Then followed a free-wheeling discussion as to what action should, and could, be taken. The chancellor, Mulock, moved that the president recommend that Underhill's connection with the university be severed, after full consideration of his conduct and utterances for the last thirteen years. The secretary of the board recorded unanimous agreement. Further discussion followed. In the end the members agreed to withdraw the motion and to make a final decision at an adjourned meeting on Monday. In the three-day interim, the president was to prepare a report, and the chairman, Bruce Macdonald, was to consult with the university lawyer, Hamilton Cassels, as to the possibility of dismissing, and the procedure to follow to dismiss, Underhill.[30]

It was a busy weekend for Underhill and his supporters. Underhill informed of the Monday meeting, rushed a letter to Alan Plaunt in Ottawa appealing for help from that end. C.E. Silcox, Norman McLean, Malcolm Wallace (chairman of the Couchiching Conference organizing committee), B.K. Sandwell, and J.B. Brebner all wrote to Cody on the weekend, confirming Underhill's moderate language and reasonable analysis in the Couchiching speech. Brebner, Silcox, and Wallace warned of the damage to Canadian-American relations should Underhill be dismissed for pro-American sentiments. Silcox informed Cody that he was in close touch with the situation in the United States and that 'any undue publicity about the matter might have a very unfavourable reaction and simply provide ammunition for the die-hard isolationists ... [S]ome powerful papers in the States would jump at an opportunity to make the most of any attack on Frank.'[31]

Canon Cody had another quiet Sunday disrupted as he met with J.S. McLean of Canada Packers and J.M. Macdonnell, president of the National Trust Company; the two men were probably asked by Underhill, as friends, to defend his case. Underhill believed that the business tycoons on the board, of which there was a majority, would be more likely persuaded by the arguments of their peers than by academics. He was convinced that it was the 'strenuous action' of his business friends, ironically, that saved him. 'They have both been magnificent, and this is the second time they have come to my help.'[32]

Monday's board meeting was crucial. The president's report was ready, and Cassels had reported back to the chairman. The lawyer advised against an attempt to dismiss Underhill over the Couchiching speech, since there was insufficient evidence. As to earlier statements which 'might have justified his dismissal at the time they were made,' he claimed they could not legally be considered now as constituting grounds for dismissal. The best the authorities could do was to notify Underhill that his employment was terminated, or to inform him that 'his services were no longer needed and to pay him the amount of salary to that date.'[33] The meeting itself was anticlimactic. The president reported: 'After careful inquiry I find that there is no stenographic report of his speech and of the subsequent discussions, nor is there other satisfactory evidence to support the published account of what he said. I therefore recommend that no action be taken in respect thereof.' The members of the board agreed. The chairman made a public statement immediately afterwards that as far as the board was concerned 'the incident was closed.'[34]

The incident may have been closed but not the attempt to dismiss Underhill. Pressure continued to mount. One source was the Toronto *Telegram*. For a solid week the paper devoted at least one editorial to denouncing Underhill. The editorial of 20 September expressed dissatisfaction with the governors at the University of Toronto for refusing to discipline Underhill for his Couchiching speech. The paper also renewed the controversy of April 1939. Underhill was going to correct the editor on some factual errors in his account, but decided to keep quiet. He informed Cody: 'This whole business has been so unpleasant for the University as well as myself that I must obviously avoid the public platform for some time, and so I give you this undertaking not to make public speeches outside of the University for the next year.' The promise was made on the urging of Dean Beatty and other colleagues 'who thought it would ease matters a little with the authorities,' Underhill recalled later.[35] Malcolm Wallace blasted the editor of the

Telegram for Underhill. 'Surely it is a lamentable thing,' he noted, 'that in a day big with crisis we should squander our energies in belabouring those of our fellow citizens whose opinions we do not entirely approve of.' A colleague in the history department, Donald Creighton, also wished 'that the *Tely* lay off, and that something comes up which distracts its attention. The thing most to be feared is another crisis in the legislature.' Carlton McNaught, a friend in the LSR, linked the two, the *Telegram* and the politicians, particularly Drew and perhaps Hepburn, together in a conspiracy to 'force the matter before the Legislature.' This was based on suspicion more than on fact. Underhill believed the same and was already preparing ammunition for a possible counterattack against the politicians by collecting speeches by members of the Legislature that expressed isolationist and anti-British or pro-American sentiments.[36]

Thursday, 26 September, was the next regular monthly meeting of the Board of Governors. Not surprisingly, Underhill's case continued to be discussed. During the heated debate Balmer Neilly, a Varsity graduate, former president of the Alumni Association, and mining engineer, presented a motion that the board not re-engage Underhill. Further discussion followed, with Chief Justice Hugh Rose claiming the resolution out of order, since only the president could recommend dismissal. Neilly would not be deterred. At a board meeting of 10 October he reintroduced his motion, and backed it up with an impassioned speech. He was sick and tired of the delays and indecisiveness that only gave Underhill further opportunities to offend 'the prestige and good name of our University.' Neilly sneered that 'he has developed to a high art his ability to carry an audience with him on a basis of suggestive rather than direct criticism, and when, in its enthusiasm, the audience crashes over the precipice, he remains on top, to smile and explain and perchance regret that his remarks were erroneously quoted and misunderstood.' This professor 'was making mockery out of the Board with his endless promises couched in slimy terms.' Why delay further? The speech, however, did not convince the majority of the board members. The meeting ended with another demand for a presidential report.[37]

Canon Cody was caught in a dilemma. Only he could recommend to the board a professor's dismissal and he wanted to leave the issue until the end of the academic year, in hopes that the problem would solve itself. Neilly and other board members were insisting on action before Christmas, for fear of another undesirable situation erupting. Cody had to agree. He had given Underhill numerous reprieves in the past without effect. No sooner would one crisis die down than this radical professor would be embroiled in another. Each time Underhill managed to slip out of the controversy unscathed and almost invigorated for the next fight. Cody felt that Underhill was unappreciative of his efforts to save him. Carleton Stanley, now president of Dalhousie University, told Underhill that Cody had 'complained wearily of what he had to go through on your account, and thought that if you knew his weariness you would say nothing till the war is over.' Even some of Underhill's friends felt that he was not 'particularly grateful,' that he 'did not seem to care whether they [did] anything or not.'[38] When would it end? If Underhill was not stopped now, how far would he go? What further embarrassments would he cause the university?

Cody made his report at a special board meeting on 19 December. It showed a decidedly negative attitude, absent in previous reports, towards Underhill. He began by insisting that the point at issue was not academic freedom 'in the proper sense of the term.' Even if it were seen as such, however, the blame for curbing that freedom would be Underhill's. Underhill had failed frequently 'to realize the responsibility of his privileged and dignified position as a teacher and the loyalty that is due to his institution and his colleagues.' The real issue, however, was thirteen years of abusive comments and broken promises on Underhill's part. Often it was not even what he had said so much as the way he said it. His views and the way he expressed them were offensive to respectable people. The university was bearing the brunt of the attacks through misunderstanding and hostility from the public. The substance of Cody's report was summed up in his closing remarks: 'Since November 24, 1938, Professor Underhill's utterances have been discussed by the Board of Governors on seven separate occasions, including two special meetings. An inordinate amount of time has been devoted to his conduct during the tenure of his professorship. No other member of our teaching staff has called for reproofs and warnings. These indicate that the Board has not adopted a general policy of restraint of freedom of speech, but is doubtful of his discretion and has no great confidence in his willingness or his ability to carry out his promises of silence or amendment. There is always the fear that he will again make some statement in such a form that public indignation will be aroused and further injury done to the good name and the usefulness of the university.' Thus Cody moved that 'without reference to specific details of the writings or utterances of Professor Frank H. Underhill and viewing his record as a whole, I believe it would be better for the University that Professor Underhill's services should be dispensed with and I so recommend.'[39]

The die was cast. All that remained was to decide procedure. Some members, including Chancellor Mulock, Chief Justice Rose, Leighton McCarthy, and Dr Anderson, tried in vain to delay further. Other members felt it advisable to postpone action until after the board had notified the provincial government of its decision 'in order to ascertain its opinion.' This proposal was agreed. The chairman of the Board of Governors, Bruce Macdonald, along with McCarthy, Ferguson, and Neilly, formed a deputation to meet the minister of education at his home on Friday, 27 December at 11 AM. The board would meet later the same day to hear the government's views.[40]

There is, unfortunately, no record of the discussion at McArthur's home nor any lengthy report of the delegates' account to the board. It is clear, however, from the brief notes made by the secretary of the board at that meeting that the government heartily agreed with the board's decision and in fact threatened to act itself when the House reconvened in February if the board failed to act immediately. With this political support behind it, the board chose a committee of three – the chairman, the president, and Leighton McCarthy – to execute its decision. Later, it was decided to replace the president by the chancellor, since the president, who had final say, had to appear impartial in the affair. It was this special committee that met with Underhill in the Board Room on 2 January 1941, and began another intense debate on the case.[41]

Underhill kept a detailed account of the meeting. Chancellor Mulock opened proceedings with a statement that ' "public opinion as expressed in the newspapers and elsewhere" made it necessary that I should leave the University, and that the Board considered that my continued presence on the staff was doing harm to the University.' At no time during the interview, Underhill recalled, was a new cause mentioned or a fresh action of his given as a reason 'why they should decide to get rid of me *now* rather than last September.' He was promised the money from his pension fund plus a year's salary if he agreed to leave. The three delegates recommended that Underhill go away and think about their 'offer,' consult with his friends, and let them know his decision before the board met the following Thursday, 9 January.[42]

He arrived home shocked, dismayed, and angry. The first thing he did was to cancel arrangements to billet two more British refugee children who were expected any day. 'They were coming from the custody of Lady Gooderham, of all people!' he informed Plaunt. Then he got in touch with his lawyer – none other than Leopold Macaulay, the high-ranking Ontario Conservative politician in Underhill's riding of York South and an arch-rival of Hepburn's, and thus a valuable source of inside information. (Underhill had an instinct to cultivate acquaintances with influential people.) Macaulay supplied Underhill with an abstract of the relevant sections of the University Act and textbook references and case notes dealing with the status of university professors and their employment. He pointed out that the Board of Governors was seeking to enforce Underhill's retirement 'under circumstances which would render it almost impossible to obtain employment at any University in Canada. While they may have the legal right to do so by a strict interpretation of The University Act, such forced retirement or dismissal would, in my opinion, constitute a grave injustice not only to yourself but to the University of Toronto.'[43] It was encouragement for Underhill to fight on.

He phoned Beatty, Innis, Wallace, and Martin to inform them of recent developments. That weekend a group of concerned colleagues formed a commitee to support Underhill if he refused to resign. 'On their unanimous advice,'

Underhill reported a couple of days later, 'I decided not to resign, my own inclinations having been in that direction from the moment of my interview.' Beatty agreed to see the president on Monday when the latter returned to the city. He found Cody adamant against Underhill, claiming that the Couchiching affair had not been closed but only postponed. 'The most the President would concede was that he would meet a deputation from the staff on Tuesday afternoon,' Beatty reported. Beatty was looking 'glummer than I have ever seen him and glummer than I ever hope to see him again,' Underhill noted at the time. Cody also stated that most of the staff would not oppose Underhill's disappearance, 'only a few from University College,' according to Beatty.[44]

Chester Martin was very annoyed that the board had taken action against a member of his department without first consulting him. 'I cannot contemplate without despair this bankruptcy of all confidence and co-operation in dealing with his matter,' he wrote. He was so upset that he left his bed (where he was confined with the flu) to see Cody, only to be 'the recipient of a bad-tempered outburst from the President' because of his letter of protest.[45]

The faculty deputation that met President Cody for three hours on the Tuesday consisted of twenty of the most influential professors in the university. President Cody kept some brief notes on the line of argument that each of the delegates took. Professors G. Norwood, Griffith Taylor, and Brett were concerned about knowing the 'precise charge against Underhill,' while Professors Ralph Flenley and George Brown of the history department wondered if outside influences were pressing the president to act as he did. Professor Charles Cochrane and Dean Samuel Beatty came out strongly against the president, calling the whole incident 'indiscreet and irresponsible' and certain to hinder the spontaneity of the staff. Innis stressed the unsuitable publicity that the dismissal of Underhill would bring to the university, especially among labour groups. Professor W.R. Taylor agreed, claiming that labour groups were 'watching the university concerning Underhill.' Principal Malcolm Wallace spoke about the possible disunity resulting from the incident, both inside the university and outside, with Canada's relations vis-à-vis the United States and Britain. He also stressed Underhill's good reputation as a teacher. Professor Bertie Wilkinson felt more information was needed before any action was taken, and Professor Hardolph Wasteneys disagreed with the method used to handle the case; it did not show the true ideal of a university. Two delegates supported President Cody. Professor W.P.M. Kennedy of Law saw trouble for the University of Toronto if Underhill remained. He believed that common sense was the basis of academic freedom, and that Underhill had failed to use discretion. Dr J.H. Elliott agreed to stand by President Cody's decision, whatever it might be. Professors F.C. Jeanneret, G.L. Duff, R.McGregor Dawson, and C.A. Ashley were present but did not speak.

Cody replied that the issue was neither Underhill's teaching nor freedom of speech but rather the welfare of the university. The board had decided in September that Underhill was a detriment to that welfare, and therefore had to be dismissed. If universities failed to have a policy to get rid of unsatisfactory members of faculty, the task would be assumed by the government, a far worse situation.[46] Canon Cody was 'considerably shaken' by the hard line of the professorial delegation; he had obviously underestimated faculty support for Underhill. Innis tried to cushion the shock by assuring the president by letter that the faculty's comments 'were intended to express a feeling, which I am sure you sensed to the full, among all members of the staff of general affection for you.' But he also made it clear that he was behind Underhill all the way, and he gave a new reason for his support. He attributed Underhill's rebellious nature to his involvement in the Great War. 'It is possibly necessary to remember that any returned man who has faced the continued dangers of modern warfare has a point of view fundamentally different from anyone who has not. Again and again have we told each other or repeated to ourselves, nothing can hurt us after this. The psychic perils of civilization mean nothing to us.' Innis was probably revealing more about his reaction to war, having been wounded at Vimy Ridge, than Underhill's, but he was convinced enough to be willing to risk losing his own academic position to save his colleague's.[47]

Once again, students rallied around their popular professor. The third- and fourth-year modern history students submitted a petition to Cody on 9 January, the day of the official board meeting, that showed the highest respect for Underhill's teaching: 'The very keynote of his teaching is to inspire each and everyone of us to think for ourselves. We consider this to be the worthiest aim of any Universiy and such an ideal to be the very foundation of Freedom itself. We pay this tribute to F.H. Underhill gladly, as students who admire and respect him, knowing him to be a thorough scholar and a stimulating, tolerant teacher.' A graduate petition, circulated by a former Underhill student, Ken Bryden, 'on the advice of certain members of the University staff,' expressed the same ideas and sentiment. A number of students who were unable to sign a petition wrote directly to Cody or participated in a telephone campaign to the president's office on Underhill's behalf. Adding to student support were numerous letters and telegrams from university alumni, and former students and friends of Underhill's, to the point where Cody admitted to being 'surprised at the fervor which had arisen from all across Canada ... to help the good old man.'[48]

While Cody was being bombarded with Underhill 'fan mail' and telephone calls, Underhill was doing his best to apply even more persuasive pressure. He wrote on Monday, 6 January, to his associate, Hugh L. Keenleyside, a high-ranking member of the Department of External Affairs and secretary of the Permanent Joint Board of Defence, to explain the case and to appeal for help. Underhill's version went as follows: 'The pressure really comes from Hepburn who has been seen in vain by both Howard Ferguson and the President. The younger members of the Board are of course Hepburn's gunmen. His using of his power over the annual University grant is an abuse of power and completely undermines the intention of the University Act of 1906, which was to divorce the University from political influences.'[49] Keenleyside did not delay. The next day he sent a memorandum to the prime minister and secretary of state for external affairs, Mackenzie King, in hopes that he might intervene on Underhill's behalf. 'The effect of such a scandal at this critical time, both on public opinion in Canada and in the United States, would be most unfortunate,' he reminded King. 'Underhill is very well known in some circles in the United States and the liberal press there will not fail to publicize his case. This will be seized upon by the isolationists, the anti-British and pro-German elements, and Canada will be depicted as a centre of imperialistic reaction.' Keenleyside conveyed the same message in a telegram to Cody, in a letter to Senator Norman Lambert, in letters to Leslie Thomson and O.M. Biggar of the Department of Munitions and Supply, and in a message to his immediate superior, O.D. Skelton, the undersecretary of state for external affairs, who also tried, without success, to persuade the prime minister, as an alumnus of the university, to intervene.[50] Mackenzie King was sympathetic, but apparently not willing to take a step which might be interpreted as intervening in a provincial matter, especially against his old enemy, Hepburn, the two men having disagreed on almost everything since the time of the Rowell-Sirois commission that had proposed an altered view of dominion-provincial relations.

At this point Jack Pickersgill, a secretary in the Prime Minister's Office in Ottawa, who was following the case with interest and concern, met C.G. 'Chubby' Power, the associate minister of national defence, while lunching with another Liberal M.P., Brooke Claxton. Pickersgill knew of Power's friendly relations with Hepburn and his strong support for freedom of speech and civil liberties, and believed he might be the best person to pressure Hepburn. With Claxton's encouragement he broached the subject with Power and found him 'thoroughly receptive, though he never heard of Underhill or his problem.' Pickersgill then recalled: 'Later that day, Power called me, and, in a thick husky voice said: 'Jack, I called Mitch about your friend Longbottom. That isn't the right name but he [Mitch] knew who I meant and said he would try to do something.' I realized that Power was on one of his periodic drinking bouts, and assumed Hepburn would ignore the call.'[51] Such was not the case. Hepburn summoned Harry Nixon, his deputy prime minister, into his office and 'asked him to telephone President Cody, and urge him to have the Board refrain from action against Underhill.' This is substantiated by a note in the agenda book for the board meeting of 9 January that 'McCarthy, the Acting Prime Minister of Ontario, and Dr. McArthur requested deferring the case.' Underhill attributed this sudden turnabout on Hepburn's part to political pressure from Ottawa, 'since I can't believe that Cody was lying to everybody to whom he has talked during the past few months about pressure from Queen's Park.' Keenleyside had also noted on a copy of Cody's reply to his telegram which Keenleyside sent to Underhill that Mr Hepburn had sent a telegram 'stating that high authority in your Department had asked us to delay any action in regard to Prof. Underhill.' Keenleyside informed Underhill that this reference to his department was likely a mistake on Hepburn's part and 'probably refers to Power.'[52] Power's telephone call, then, proved most effective in easing the political pressure from Queen's Park on Cody and the board.

Meanwhile, on Wednesday, 8 January, the day before the board meeting, Macdonald, chairman of the board, phoned Underhill to say that the committee who had met him on the previous Thursday would be in the Board Room again on Thursday afternoon to talk further with him if he wished to see them. Underhill informed Macdonald that he had decided to decline to resign and was sending him a letter to that effect. 'Oh,' Macdonald said, 'It isn't a question of your declining to resign, but of whether you will accept the opportunity which we offer you.'[53] Responding to this remarkable turn of events, Underhill composed his letter to the chairman of the board that afternoon, explaining why he refused to resign. He denied a number of allegations that from hearsay he thought might be the reasons why he was being pressured to leave. The only official explanation given, he reminded the chairman, was 'public opinion ... not a very specific reason for so serious an action,' especially since there had been no further public opinion since last September, when the board had decided not to take any action. So he demanded in writing 'an exact formulation of the charge or charges'[54] against him with the right to respond to them.

There is no indication that Underhill's letter was discussed at Thursday's board meeting, but there was plenty to talk about concerning the *cause célèbre* at that important meeting behind closed doors at Simcoe Hall. It is impossible, however, to know exactly what did transpire because the members of the board decided that 'what happens at the Board [meeting] is secret and not disclosed today,' which was translated in the official minutes as 'further discussion of the Chancellor's motion regarding Professor Underhill was postponed.' The few notes in the agenda book indicate that the president read for discussion Keenleyside's telegram, that Chief Justice Rose made a damning indictment of the case against Underhill and tried to get it postponed, and that the chairman polled the board members to see 'how many were in favour of dispensing of Underhill's services.' A majority were still in favour; they were only hesitant about acting at this critical and controversial time.[55]

Their hesitation to act more decisively was due in part to the successful pressure applied from Ottawa. The board instructed Cody to telegraph Prime Minister Mackenzie King in his capacity as secretary of state for external affairs to ascertain whether Keenleyside's telegram should 'be construed as the personal opinion of the sender, or a statement of the official attitude of the Department of External Affairs ... I am sure that you will understand the position of the Board of Governors in this matter, since if the telegram records the official opinion of your department, it must necessarily carry much weight.'[56]

Premier Hepburn was forced to come out from behind the scene when Carlton McNaught published a statement in the *Toronto Star* on 10 January declaring that the real reason for the board's trying to get rid of Underhill was 'pressure from a political source.' Hepburn assumed the reference was to himself, and phoned McNaught to dispel the accusation. 'There was no suggestion made of cutting the grant to the university, or anything like that, made by me,' Hepburn assured McNaught. 'If there was any political pressure in the matter it was from the other side ... The fact is that when I heard of some such move being taken, I went to the university authorities, as did George McCullagh, and urged them not to persist in the move. Indeed, I would regard it as unwise at the present time and in view of Canadian-American relations, if actions were to be taken against him for his views in that connection.' Clifford Sifton, owner of the *Winnipeg Free Press*, wisely attributed Hepburn's fervent denial as the best evidence of his guilt.[57]

The next morning, Nixon, acting minister of education (McArthur was ill), reported to the *Globe and Mail* that the government would treat the university estimates equitably, regardless of what the governors decided about Underhill. The case was entirely a matter for university authorities in which the government would not intervene. Cody supported the political cover-up, which led Underhill to conclude that there was 'a remarkable paucity of truth-telling on the part of most of the authorities involved.'[58]

By mid-January Underhill was confident that he had weathered another storm. He was being retained, he commented jokingly, 'in order that the British Empire may win this war.' Earlier he was not so sure. On 4 January, for example, he had written to President Herbert Davis of Smith College, New York, about the possibility of a teaching position. All that seemed in the past now. The support from colleagues, students, and friends in the past two weeks had been tremendous. That and the 'poetic justice' of Cody's illness after the case were about the only consolation he could find in the sordid affair. The confrontation left him drained and embittered. He was depressed with the university in general. He advised his best graduate students to go to the United States for their higher degrees. He dearly wanted a year's leave of absence, but he doubted his chances, since members of the board 'must be pretty sore on me just now after being made to look so bad in public.'[59]

Little did he know how sore they continued to be. At the regular board meeting of 23 January it was decided to defer action against Underhill until the first meeting in June, but definitely not to close the case. There was a further delay in early June so that the governors could consult with Nixon. Then on 26 June bitter governors led by Howard Ferguson moved that Underhill's 'services be dispensed with. This resolution is not to be construed as any personal reflection upon the President.' The chairman asked the president if he wished to speak to the motion. Cody said that he had consulted with government officials and senior members of staff and wished now to withdraw his earlier recommendation of dismissal in favour of one recommending that 'no action be now taken to dismiss' Underhill. The chancellor reminded the board members that no action could be taken without the president's consent. A vote was taken on Ferguson's motion anyway, with a majority of those present still voting in favour of Underhill's dismissal. Nothing further on procedure appeared to have been decided.[60]

There the matter rested during the summer months. Underhill heard rumours that there was still a group of board members agitating for his dismissal and he was afraid to leave Toronto for a summer vacation at his Muskoka cottage. At the first board meeting in September the case was deferred. At the 25 September session Osler argued that the case should have been dealt with in June. Neilly wanted to know why the wishes of the board had not been carried out. The chancellor recommended letting matters rest; the majority of the members consented. So ended, finally, the Underhill case.[61]

By this time Underhill claimed that he was willing 'to keep quiet and out of trouble. This is unheroic, but I am now past fifty years of age.'[62] It was more than age, however, that kept Underhill out of further trouble. By this time, ironically, he had become his own worst critic of his socialistic and anti-imperialistic views.

11

Revisionism in
the War Years

'We who were hoping to see society reconstructed so as to make possible a humane civilization, see it caught up in a general absorbing war effort.'[1] The sense of pessimism and defeat conveyed by that sentence permeated Underhill's speech to the Toronto branch of the LSR on 10 November 1939, the eve of the twenty-first anniversary of the Armistice. For two months the country had been at war. Radicals were without a spiritual home, their liberal beliefs in the essential goodness and rationality of man and in a better world after the socialist millennium mocked by the death of another generation in a battle, ironically, to save the world. What should be the response of socialists? They could escape, he argued, by deceiving themselves into believing that it was a holy war or by turning to their private lives – both of which were irresponsible acts. Or they could work towards a better social order in the postwar era. All need not be lost, a chastened Underhill asserted, so long as some good could come out of the destruction. It was a rallying cry to his socialist colleagues not to despair but to act responsibly by setting about to formulate meaningful war and peace aims.

The speech had been preceded by two months of debate among LSR members on the meaning of the war for the socialist cause, Canada, and the world. Underhill favoured neutrality. 'The capitalists will use us,' he warned the CCF National Executive during an emergency meeting in Ottawa on 6 September 1939. 'We must keep out.'[2] Neither socialism nor Canadian nationalism would be advanced by joining another European war. 'Canada, Europe and Hitler,' the title of one of Underhill's *Forum* articles,[3] indicated his order of priority in dealing with the war. First Canadians had to know what they were fighting for. If it was simply to defeat Hitler then it was a futile exercise, for Hitler was a symptom of a deeper malaise that stemmed from dissatisfaction with the terms of the last peace treaty which had put ideological aspirations above economic concerns. It was Keynesian thought revised for a Canadian audience.

What Underhill proposed in the way of war and peace aims was a 'United States of Europe,' a suggestion that anticipated Winston Churchill's popular idea of a united Western Europe. 'No one of the national states of Europe west of the U.S.S.R.,' he observed in October 1939, 'is of sufficient size to be economically self-sufficient in any sense. Unless they can all be started together in some form of co-operation towards raising in common their standards of living, they will continue to cultivate their historic hatreds and eventually return again in desperation to their age-long European process of mass-murder.'[4] Such views were consistent with his socialist beliefs. A united Europe, he hoped, would be the first step towards a federation of socialist states which might eventually bring peace to this war-stricken area of the world. Others felt differently. Eric Havelock, vice-president of the LSR, and Joe Parkinson argued that fascism was the number one enemy of democracy. To be obsessed with national concerns blinded an individual to more serious international forces which affected Canada as much as Europe. It was not a question of following Britain's lead but of taking the initiative in helping to check the menace of totalitarianism.[5]

The LSR members reached a compromise in an official letter drafted by Underhill and sent to Prime Minister Mackenzie King on 6 September. They avoided taking a stand for or against joining the war effort. Instead, they pointed out the danger for Canadians of going to war without a clear understanding of their purpose for doing so. The letter read in part: 'There is no question that the victory of Nazi Germany would mean the destruction of spiritual values which are vitally important to the progressive advance of mankind. But unless the governments fighting against the Nazis have a clear idea of the order which they wish to see emerge after the war, and a fixed determination to strive for that order, it is unlikely that the war will lead to anything but destruction and chaos, while the liberties we are now asked to defend will be destroyed in the process.'[6] Four days later, Canada was at war. The LSR's appeal for clarity went unheeded.

Underhill scrutinized the Speech from the Throne that brought Canada into the war to discover the implications for Canadian autonomy. Did the resolution commit the Canadian people to war against Germany, or did it simply make provisions for effective military steps, Canada already being in the war by an act of His Majesty? The wording was ambiguous. Underhill took great delight in pointing out this vagueness to Jack Pickersgill, Mackenzie King's private secretary, at a party in Toronto in mid-September. 'Yes, you are exactly right, Frank,' Pickersgill replied with a smile. 'I drafted that resolution, and I drafted it so that it would be left uncertain in the mind of anyone who looked at the grammar of it fairly closely.'[7] Underhill was disheartened; his fight throughout the thirties to clarify Canada's position vis-à-vis Britain's in case of war had been dismissed as insignificant in one grand sweep.

The debate in the LSR reached a climax at a meeting of the editorial board of the

Canadian Forum on Saturday, 23 September. Havelock and Parkinson resigned from the board to protest against Underhill's negative views of the war in his articles. If this was the league's policy, as reflected in their official journal, then these two men wanted no part of it. Other board members worried about the repercussions for themselves and the journal of having Underhill's and Grube's names on the masthead, given their unpopularity at Queen's Park. No one seemed to know what the league's position in the *Forum* should be. Maybe it should cease publication. Grube, as managing editor, imposed order at this point, and suggested that they go ahead with the October issue. Then he and Underhill would meet with Scott, Forsey, and Marsh from Montreal to discuss the *Forum*'s fate. Underhill was most accommodating at the joint meeting. He was unhappy about withdrawing his name from the masthead, seeing it as a retreat at a time when bold action was needed, but agreed with the group's decision to remove all names except Lou Morris as business manager and Eleanor Godfrey as managing editor. He also consented to be political editor again, since he believed that the *Forum* could play a useful role in discussing Allied war and peace aims.[8]

In early March 1940 Underhill gave the fifth lecture in a series 'Canada in Peace and War' sponsored by the departments of modern history and political economy at the University of Toronto and later published under that title by the Canadian Institute of International Affairs.[9] Those in the packed audience in Convocation Hall who knew Underhill's views must have been surprised at his low-keyed address with a notable absence of animus towards British imperialists and Canadian colonialists. In dealing with political developments of the prewar and war periods, he pointed out with unusual objectivity the two opposing concepts of imperial federation and national independence as pursued by Borden and Laurier, respectively. If there was any hero in the story, it was Borden. His policy of national greatness through imperial solidarity was based on a realistic perspective of the inevitable position of Canada when war broke out. Canadians had at least a modicum of influence they would not have had under Laurier's policy of Canadian autonomy, even though they would still have been pressured into a military contribution to save the empire. Borden's weakness was his failure to continue to pursue these 'national advancements' after the war. 'The Imperial War Cabinet never developed into an Imperial Peace Cabinet.' Canada returned to the Laurier position under Mackenzie King in the 1920s and 1930s, only to be pressured into another British war, this time without any effective voice. It was a chastened Underhill who realized that all his efforts and those of the Mackenzie King government to keep Canada out of another war at Britain's side had been in vain. In the end, Canadian isolationists were less successful in achieving greater autonomy for Canada than were Canadian imperialists, who at least had succeeded during World War I in getting the nation a voice in deciding the future of the war of which they were a part. It was a noble admission of error on his part, so obvious in light of his steady and strong isolationist views of the thirties. Underhill came to appreciate that it was not only 'with every change of Government that Canada is made into a nation over again,' as John Willison had noted, but 'with every world war.'

Shock and doubt were Underhill's reactions to the defeat of France on 10 May 1940. 'The astonishing overthrow of the allied armed forces in Belgium and France has made all predictions as to the course of the war (except, presumably, the predictions of Hitler's experts) look so foolish that it seems rather useless for commentators to do anything but wait and see what new efforts the Führer may launch against Britain.' He had rationalized the Nazi sweep through Denmark and Norway the previous month, in the realization that France and Britain could block further advance. He never once doubted that the Allies would emerge victorious; the mighty British navy and the powerful French army were invincible.[10] Now, Britain stood alone in Europe against an indomitable Nazi force. The Western nations faced a greater horror than war itself in the serious prospect of a postwar world dominated by totalitarianism. How wrong he had been! Underhill retracted a number of his previous views; it was a case of overreacting to a situation which he had failed to anticipate. He now agreed that the first concern of the Allies had to be 'the military defeat of the Nazi and fascist armed forces.' Canada had a role to play. He still objected to sending Canadian troops overseas, not because the war was of little concern to Canadians but because Canada had only 'poorly trained and equipped troops.' 'Two or three divisions, more or less, make little difference in the gigantic clash of armies in France.' With glaring inconsistency, he publicly chastised Prime Minister Mackenzie King for failing 'to concentrate the national effort since last September or increasing Canadian production. If we had some planes and tanks to send overseas now we should feel a great deal happier.' He even warned Canadians of a possible German attack – an idea that he had dismissed as absurd a year earlier. The country would need to ally with the United States for protection; he anticipated that spring the signing of the Ogdensburg Agreement in mid-August.[11]

During the summer of 1940, as Germany bombed Britain daily in the Battle of Britain, Underhill was rethinking his views about the war. Assumptions which he had accepted without question in the thirties no longer seemed so self-evident. He found that the best way to work through a problem or to generate new ideas was to read. He read eclectically on the meaning of the war, from philosophical treatises to propaganda literature, and from scholarly studies to popular magazines, in an effort to detect a pattern in the seeming chaos. He concluded, along with Francis Williams, the Fabian socialist, that the war was the military component of a social and intellectual revolution that would decide whether democracy or totalitarianism would be supreme in the world.[12] The battle between socialism and capitalism was insignificant compared to this more fundamental and irreconcilable struggle between democracy and totalitarianism. Underhill realized that he and his socialist colleagues had been so busy fighting British capitalists and imperialists of the last war that they were blinded to the new power struggles in the present war. Democracy was on trial. And since democracy was an offshoot of liberal ideology, then liberalism was under attack. Liberal-socialists in the interwar years had failed to bring in the new millennium. They had, in fact, contributed to war by refusing to confront the existence of power politics as a real force in national and international events. The naïvety of liberals in the interwar years concerning power politics was the thesis of E.H. Carr's *The Twenty Years Crisis: 1919–1939* (London 1946), a book that Underhill strongly recommended as essential reading for liberals of any persuasion.[13]

Power politics was the deciding factor of world development. In a self-revealing statement, Underhill wrote: 'Living as we do in an age when great shifts of power are taking place we are more conscious now than we were before 1914 or even in 1919 of the fact that all politics is power politics.'[14] It was evident in the struggle in Europe, where daily the world waited for the results of the power play occurring there; it was equally evident in the shift in the centre of power in the Western Hemisphere from Britain to the United States, as reflected in the Ogdensburg Agreement. Underhill grew impatient with liberals who continued to develop utopian schemes of world federation for the postwar era that overlooked the existence of power politics. Francis Hankin received the biting edge of Underhill's sharp criticism in a note on a manuscript on postwar reconstruction submitted for Underhill's appraisal. '[It] has the defect of all writings by liberals that it doesn't consider thoroughly enough the issue of power. (See Carr on The Twenty Years Crisis). Society is made up of individuals and groups struggling for power, and this struggle is inherent in the facts of human nature and in the limited amount of distributable goods on this planet. You cannot dismiss this struggle by fine words about "equity" ... or with nice constructions of state controls – for the ultimate question is which group is going to control the state machinery.'[15]

Furthermore, power could no longer simply be equated with capitalism. It was the capitalist nations, ironically, which were fighting to save democracy against the more advanced 'socialist' states of Germany and Russia with their state-regulated economies and their centralized governments. Was there a contradiction between socialism and democracy? Underhill denied that there was, so long as socialism was based on liberal ideas, as was Fabian socialism. Still, there were inherent dangers in socialism. There was the danger of putting the means to achieve democracy above the ideal of a democratic state: to value strong leadership, centralized control, and the curtailment of immediate freedom as ends in themselves rather than as means to achieve the higher ideal of democracy. Underhill was struck by James Burnham's argument in *The Managerial Revolution* (New York 1941) that state socialism was leading not to greater democracy but to a managerial society as elitist and authoritarian as the capitalist society it was expected to replace. And Burnham was an American Trotskyite![16]

Underhill's revisionist thinking made him critical of colleagues and friends who seemed unable to see the situation from his new perspective or unwilling to be concerned about what was happening in the world. His speech to the LSR national convention in Montreal on 8 and 9 June 1941, 'A Summary of the Whole Socialist Position,' 'contained so many opposing ideas that one would not have known (had he never heard Mr. Underhill in action before) just whether he was an enemy alien, a tired radical or an agent provocateur,'[17] the bewildered secretary recorded. He was a tormented and an uncertain individual trying to find meaning in an insane world.

The pessimistic speech was the last thing that LSR members needed. They had met in an effort to revive the organization, which was dying a slow death. Underhill felt the organization was in danger of being trapped in old categories of thought from the thirties which were inappropriate in the changing world of the war and the postwar eras, the very rigidity of thought that the organization had criticized in its opponents during the Depression. The league should be disbanded, since it was 'dragging on a listless life' anyway, to be replaced by a new dynamic group of individuals who would be able to look on postwar developments with different assumptions. He wrote to the inner circle of founding members in the spring of 1941 to get their reaction. Frank Scott agreed to abolishing the league, but he doubted the wisdom of beginning a new organization. 'I am concerned over the small amount of permanent and weighty writing which our group has done, in which we could really make a lasting impression on the younger group of Canadians ... We have dissipated our efforts.' Underhill agreed with Scott's reasoning only to a degree. The LSR had been too limited in its scope and too narrow in its focus. By concentrating on national concerns, its members had overlooked larger philosophical questions relating to democracy, liberalism, and socialism. Could not a group of intellectuals deal with these issues and, in so doing, continue to make a valuable contribution to educating the Canadian public?[18] In the end, however, the league disbanded in 1942 without being replaced by a new organization of intellectuals.

Underhill also tried to stir debate among his academic colleagues. On 23 May he participated in a panel discussion with the Abbé Maheux and R.A. MacKay at the Canadian Historical Association's annual meeting on Arthur Lower's recent controversial article 'The Social Sciences in the Post-War World.' Underhill agreed entirely with Lower's thesis that the crisis of the modern world made it imperative for the social scientist to become involved in current affairs and to draw conclusions about values in his society. He had made that point five years earlier, only to be reprimanded at that time. Now the idea was more acceptable, he noted, because of the contribution of social scientists to the Rowell-Sirois Commission established in 1937 to examine dominion-provincial relations, and because of the dangerous effect of the war on the values of Western civilization. He wished his colleagues felt the same way. Once again, as during the Depression era, Underhill chastised his colleagues, particularly historians, for their indifference to the radical changes going on around them. He accused them of using history to retreat from rather than contribute to the present intellectual revolution. In an effort to rectify this situation Underhill volunteered to chair the program committee for next year's meeting. He aimed to generate more debate on current issues through more 'relevant' papers. He began by asking H.N. Fieldhouse, a University of Manitoba historian, to give a paper on 'The Failure of the Historian.' He also decided to make intellectual history the unifying theme of the conference in keeping with his beliefs that the current world crisis was intellectual, not economic in nature. He contributed a paper on 'The Political Ideas of the Upper Canadian Reformers 1867–78' which, although not exactly 'relevant,' did nevertheless deal with the ideas of an earlier era that was undergoing a similar 'crisis of liberalism.'[19]

Meanwhile, active politics beckoned the scholar once again. After the poor showing of the Conservative party in the 1940 federal election a group of Conservative Toronto businessmen resurrected Arthur Meighen as the next leader. He needed a seat in parliament and a 'safe' riding was chosen – York South. Since the Liberals decided against running a candidate for fear of splitting the left vote, the only other candidate running was Joseph Noseworthy, CCF, a local school teacher.[20]

Underhill's dislike for Meighen was matched by his admiration for Nose-worthy. He agreed to write Noseworthy's campaign speeches and to speak on his behalf at local rallies.[21] The Underhill home was opened up for CCF meetings for both Noseworthy and Ted Jolliffe, Ontario CCF leader, while Underhill also wrote anonymously a scathing article, 'Meighen Redivivus,' in the January issue of the *Forum*. He tried to discredit Meighen as a possible national leader by showing him to be the political mouthpiece of a group of Toronto magnates 'led and directed by a little group of Ontario mining millionaires' who were detested in every other area of the country. 'Like George McCullagh, like Mitch Hepburn, like all those frustrated Toronto megalomaniacs, he is itching to coerce somebody to impose on the rest of Canada the Toronto way of running a war. But somehow or other the rest of Canada has never thought much of the Toronto way of doing things.' The attack was too much for Eugene Forsey. As a friend and admirer of Meighen, he rejoined in a letter to the editor in which he set the record straight on some factual errors in the article particularly concerning the *cause célèbre* of the Constitutional Crisis of 1926. Underhill dismissed these minor inaccuracies as trivia that did not add up to any serious challenge to the main indictment of Meighen for his unfavourable record on social legislation or on the war issue. Then Underhill turned the attack on Forsey, accusing his friend of being politically naïve. The debate between the two men continued into the April issue and then in private correspondence after that.[22] By this time, however, the final judgment had been made, for Meighen went down to defeat. The evening of 9 February 1942 was one of celebration in the Underhill home on Walmer Road.

The mood of celebration was foreshortened, however, with the death of J.S. Woodsworth in March. The 'prophet in politics' had been seriously ill for some time and the end was expected, but his passing left a void. He was the most respected and honest politician that Underhill had known. In an editorial of tribute he reminded CCFers that Woodsworth's greatness lay in his ability to keep the CCF a movement and to prevent it 'from degenerating into a mere party manoeuvring for office.' Underhill admitted that he and other CCFers 'used to complain behind his back that he was too much of a missionary and not enough of an organizer, but this country still needs missionaries more than it needs organizers.'[23] Underhill joined with a group of CCF parliamentarians to form a committee to decide on a fitting memorial to this great Canadian.

During the late thirties, Underhill had been looking for some serious and substantial subject in Canadian history, and he soon had in mind a new project: a biography of Edward Blake, the enigmatic intellectual who led the Liberal party between 1879 and 1887 and who split with his successor, Laurier, on the reciprocity issue. Underhill had abandoned his earlier proposed biography of George Brown because of the lack of material on his personal life. Blake seemed a more promising individual to write about in this respect; there were Blake Papers in the library of the University of Toronto, and Underhill knew Hume Blake, the grandson, who could provide assistance. In fact, it was Hume Blake who had asked him to study his grandfather, when he had to abandon such a project himself because of the responsibility of administering the family estate. Edward Blake seemed a good subject for a biography – an intellectual, a Liberal, and a relatively unknown politician. What Underhill wanted to do was to use Blake's life and political thought on such issues as the tariff, the building of the railway, the national policy, and constitutional reform as a means to get at a much larger and more interesting study of 'the quintessence of Canadian liberalism' in the late nineteenth century. It was Blake the intellectual rather than Blake the politician that intrigued him. The study would be as much intellectual history as biography. So he started in enthusiastically to examine the Blake Papers – no mean task given Blake's deplorable handwriting[24] – to read Hansard and newspaper reports of Blake's speeches, and to study the politics of the period. Out of that initial research period Underhill published four articles on Blake in 1938 and 1939. Two more were published later.[25]

The main theme in these historical articles was Blake the Canadian nationalist.

In keeping with his own strong nationalist and isolationist position in the 1930s, Underhill stressed, possibly overemphasized, Blake's efforts for Canadian autonomy when discussing this politician's views on Unrestricted Reciprocity, the Supreme Court Act, the National Policy, and Canadian-British and Canadian-American relations. Nationalism was the 'quintessence of Canadian Liberalism' in the late nineteenth century. Unfortunately this nationalism, premised on a spirit of liberal democracy and liberal humanitarianism, was losing out to a sinister, materialistic, and aggressive nationalism – a popular theme in Underhill's later historical writings.

Underhill was anxious to devote a substantial amount of time to Blake, and in the fall of 1941 began making inquiries about a Guggenheim award, given annually by the American philanthropist Simon Guggenheim to outstanding scholars. He proposed to use the time to finish his biography of Blake, which he intended to be part of a larger 'thorough and comprehensive study of the intellectual origins of Upper Canadian radicalism from the days of Gourlay and Mackenzie to the days of Brown, Blake, Mills and Cameron.'[26] He admitted to the selection committee that he still had a lot to do: he had to examine private papers in the Public Archives of Canada, numerous newspapers for the period, and Blake's legal and constitutional work. He felt, however, that he would complete this research in the summer of 1942 and would be ready to write during the academic year of 1942–3 if awarded a fellowship. He would spend the year in the United States where he 'could get more work done away from all local associations in Toronto' which lured him from the writing of history. He had no specific place in mind, so long as he had access to a good library with adequate books on Canadian history and politics.

His referees listed on his application were A.R.M. Lower of United College, Winnipeg; Chester Martin, head of the history department, Toronto; Fred Landon of the University of Western Ontario; Bartlet Brebner of Columbia University; Percy Corbett and Frank Scott from the Faculty of Law, McGill University; and E.K. Brown of the Department of English at Cornell, who had helped him with his research on Goldwin Smith.[27] It was a distinguished list, but one obvious name was missing – Harold Innis, the Canadian scholar who was best known in American academic circles. Henry Moe, fellowship secretary, consulted Innis about Underhill's scholarly abilities. Moe paraphrased Innis's reply as follows: 'I gather that you do not consider Underhill as good a scholar, *qua* scholar, as you do Lower of Winnipeg who is the same age – but that, considered as a *writer*, Underhill has a lot of quality.' It was a fair comparison. Innis also informed Moe of the unpleasant dispute between Underhill and the university authorities, and he later attributed Underhill's success in winning a Guggenheim as compensation for this episode.[28]

On 21 March Underhill received word that he had been granted a Guggenheim

Fellowship for one year commencing September 1942. He had decided to go to New York on the invitation of Brebner at Columbia University.[29] On 17 September 1942 Ruth and Frank crossed the border, destined for New York City. His initial impressions of the city and of Columbia University were characteristically negative: the city was big, dirty, and noisy; the university large and impersonal. He regretted not going to a quieter New England university, such as Harvard or Yale, which would have been more appealing to his temperament. There were few opportunities to meet other academics for stimulating discussion even though Brebner had arranged for him to have an office in the library. He put in his spare time walking around the city and visiting the numerous art galleries, where he came to appreciate modern art. He went on a buying spree of expensive woodcut prints of quiet American pastoral and rustic scenes to add to the collection that he had begun in the late thirties. On many evenings the Underhills attended symphonies, concerts, theatre, and museums, or they could dine out at moderately priced restaurants. When Betty, who was in her first year of science at the University of Toronto, joined them for the Christmas holidays, the three did a whirlwind tour of the city with 'an orgy of theatre going.' He was 'letting loose' after the constraints of his year in Toronto, and he saw the year as a 'reward' for his 'struggles.'[30]

Underhill spent part of his Guggenheim year working on Blake, but a lot of time reading current writings of American historians and political scientists, especially on the subject of the function of political parties in a North American democracy. The interest was in keeping with his questioning of the impact of the war on liberal democracy. He attempted to apply the ideas of these American theorists to Canadian party history in his paper 'The Canadian Party System in Transition' delivered at the Canadian Political Science Association's annual meeting in May. It was an important paper in which he presented some new thoughts on the subject.

He began by assuming that the chief function of political parties in North America had been to act as 'brokers' of competing interest groups rather than to formulate any clear-cut philosophy or program. But instead of going on to deride this purpose, he argued that it was essential in a democracy. 'A democracy is simply a society in which all interest groups have an equal chance to present their claims for benefits from the gains of civilization and to get them adjusted.'[31] In North America the two traditional, loose conglomerate parties best fulfilled this task. This was particularly true in the United States where the Democratic party under F.D. Roosevelt offered a New Deal program that appealed to diverse interest groups within the party. He buttressed his case by quoting from two of the latest American studies which defended the brokerage nature of North American parties: Pendleton Herring, *The Politics of Democracy* (New York 1940), and Alfred Bingham, *The Techniques of Democracy* (New York 1942).

In Canada, the situation was slightly different. The Liberal party, the Canadian equivalent of the American Democratic party, had no 'national purpose' under its leader in the 1930s, Mackenzie King, with the result that third parties arose to represent the interest groups excluded from the two traditional parties – farmers and labourers. He noted: 'It is a paradox of the two-party system that it works best when there are more than two parties, for the challenge of new parties preserves flexibility in the old ones.' Still, the ideal was a two-party system, but one in which parties were divided on the left and the right of the political spectrum while still able to attract a multiplicity of interest groups. Such parties needed to be visionary yet practical, principled yet flexible.

George Ferguson was the commentator on the paper.[32] He assumed that it was the same old Underhill presenting the same old message of the 'two old greedy and cynical and highly capitalistic parties' being challenged by the young and dynamic CCF party. He failed to detect Underhill's admiration for the brokerage function of North American parties, or the surreptitious praise for the Liberals as the wielders of national unity, or the open-ended conclusion as to where the new and dynamic party of the future might emerge. Ferguson assumed that Underhill expected the CCF to be that party, yet Underhill had cautiously avoided making such a claim. Furthermore, he had asserted that the function of third parties was 'to formulate issues before the major parties were ready to take them up, to agitate and educate, to present new points of view, and to leave the great responsibility of adjusting conflicts and working out a national policy to the major parties.' His reading of the Rowell-Sirois *Report*, from which he quoted extensively, and his sensitivity to the divisions and hostility between the two founding races during the tense war years, led Underhill to appreciate the importance of maintaining national unity as performed by the traditional parties.[33] He was aware of the danger to democracy in a nation where the majority attempted to impose its will on the minority. Consensus, not unanimity, was a hallmark of democracy, and a united nation was the first step to a socially reconstructed Canada. A more tolerant attitude to French Canadians marked his writings in the 1940s and 1950s, in contrast with his earlier views of the 1920s and 1930s. It was not the same Underhill of the 1930s preaching the same message, but an unsure and sober individual challenging his beliefs in light of changing times and willing to see the virtue in the existing political system. It was the beginning of a gradual move back to the Liberalism that he had abandoned in the Depression years.

Clearly one of Underhill's strengths was his willingness and ability to change his views in light of changing times. To some people this was a sign of weakness; but to Underhill it was an indication of his willingness to approach a subject with an open mind, even though he appeared, ironically, to be closed-minded about it in light of his trenchant argument for his particular point of view.

After the Canadian Political Science Association meeting the Underhills left New York City to spend the summer months in Hanover, New Hampshire, where Betty joined them for an enjoyable and relaxing summer.[34] Dartmouth College had an excellent Canadiana collection, and the small-town atmosphere and serene countryside appealed to Underhill's aesthetic taste. He found solace in these peaceful surroundings and in the intellectual milieu of the New England states. Here was the finest of puritan America, and he was realizing how puritan he was.[35] The high culture and elitist position of New Englanders, particularly at the Ivy League universities, seemed to him the good life, Plato's *Republic* in reality. He wished that he had had the opportunity to teach at Harvard, Yale, or Princeton; what a contrast to Toronto, which seemed to inherit the worst of puritanism. Still, he was puritan enough to feel uneasy in such comfortable surroundings; the situation brought back memories of Oxford days.

On their way back to Toronto in early September, the Underhill family stopped in Ithaca, New York, where Underhill met with C.W. de Kiewiet, history professor at Rochester, to sketch out a proposal for an edited book on the correspondence between Lord Dufferin, governor-general of Canada from 1872 to 1878, and the Earl of Carnarvon, secretary of state for the colonies from 1874 to 1878.[36] The project would take ten years to complete, largely because of Underhill's procrastination in getting his part of the manuscript together.

Overall, he found his Guggenheim year a rewarding experience. He had made some personal contacts which would prove useful in arranging future trips to the United States to teach summer school. He had gained tremendous insights into American politics and public opinion, and could now talk with greater authority on the similarities and differences between Americans and Canadians. Such comparisons, in fact, became a favourite subject in most of his articles during the following year. He envisioned himself as an interpreter of opinions between the two nations, helping each to overcome the ignorance and distrust of the other, and agreed to act as a Canadian commentator for a new monthly journal, *The Frontiers of Democracy*.[37] He wished his Guggenheim year had been as rewarding for his work on Blake. Instead, he had to report to the Guggenheim Committee that he had not even come close to his projected target of a completed manuscript. 'Finding myself in good libraries I'm afraid I spent too much time reading stuff that wasn't available in Canada and refreshing myself on a good deal of Canadian history in the background of my subject.' Yet he admitted that this was only a symptom. The real problem was 'making Edward Blake come to life.' That 'had me baffled for a great deal of my year.' When his friend, Forsey, suggested that he consider using psychoanalysis on Blake, Underhill replied curtly: 'I should think that Blake's attitude to the governor-general and to his office was the national expression of the strong feeling of nationalism which was raised in many Canadians in the first decade of Confederation ... [N]ationalism of this kind was a pretty common phenomena in the nineteenth century, and I think it needs a more subtle and complex explanation than an excess of patria protestas in the upbringing of 19th century children.'[38]

Underhill rationalized the problem by arguing that he lacked the ingredients of diaries, personal letters, and memorabilia necessary to understand the inner workings of Blake's mind. He was expressing indirectly his own frustration of working on Blake when, in a review of Ronald Longley's recently published biography of Francis Hincks, he wrote: 'In Canada the letters which our public men have left behind seem to have been confined for the most part strictly to business, i.e., to the political business of manipulating groups of men; and three or four hundred pages of this is apt to become pretty dreary stuff ... In fact, after being immersed in the study of Canadian politics for any length of time, one is almost inevitably led to wonder whether most Canadian public men ever had any interests wider than the eternal business of manoeuvring and manipulating, whether they were capable of a philosophy or a religion.'[39]

At the root of the problem was Underhill's disillusionment with Blake as a subject of historical research. This nineteenth-century politician was not the great 'intellectual in politics' that he had assumed. Blake was motivated by practical interests like every other Canadian politician. He lacked political ideas, or at best his ideas were practical and parochial rather than philosophical and universal. Underhill concluded that Blake, like the Canadian liberalism of his era, became introspective because he had no connection with the wider intellectual currents of British and American thinking. 'On the whole developments in the outer world formed only a rather shadowy background to the Canadian scene. The attention of Canadian politicians was mainly directed to their own local problems; and it was primarily from domestic conditions that both Liberals and Conservatives derived their principles of action.' Blake could not be the proper subject for a study of Canadian liberalism, and Underhill's real interest in the man was the light that he could shed on the Canadian liberal mind in the late nineteenth century. Deep inside he doubted that he would have the enthusiasm or interest to complete the Blake biography, although he tried to convince himself otherwise until the time of his death. The tragedy was not his failure to finish the biography but rather his determination to stay so long with a subject that ultimately did not excite him.[40]

In the fall of 1943 Underhill returned to Toronto and to a full schedule of activities – teaching, speaking engagements, meetings, and writing essays and journal articles. It was an exciting time in Canadian politics with the CCF party picking up strength nationally and becoming the official opposition in the Ontario legislature in the August election, winning thirty-four seats. Underhill should have been elated but he was not. He had an uneasy feeling about the party; CCFers seemed caught up in their own rhetoric, talking about long-term goals and detailed programs to usher in the new socialist state. They seemed short on definite and immediate proposals for change. 'We are tending far too much to talk about the general principle of planning, rather than to make concrete plans,' he complained to his friend, Carlton McNaught. 'Socialism of itself will not solve anything unless it is administered by men who come into office prepared for particular emergencies which are likely to arise, and with a wide imaginative conception of the sort of creative projects that can be put into action within five years.' A reconstruction of the educational system, a universal health program, better housing, and a more efficient transportation system were a few of the projects he had in mind. 'We are in danger of letting the socialist cause seem one that appeals only to doctrinaires or that is interested chiefly in imposing authoritarian controls ... I am worried ... about the problem of freedom in a community in which the state has become the nearly universal employer, and I'd just as lief have us approach that problem gradually.'[41] He distrusted abstract theories, grandiose schemes, and utopian dreams as unrealistic and undemocratic. Only totalitarian states had fixed goals and detailed long-term plans, he reasoned, because their leaders never had to appeal to the people. The redeeming quality of a democracy was its ability to alter its way as the needs of the people changed.

He found justification for his uneasiness in a celebration party that he attended for the Ontario CCF at the King Edward Hotel soon after his return to Toronto. As he sat at the back of the hall listening to the party chiefs, Ted Garland and Ted Jolliffe, extol the virtues of the party's position, a strange feeling came over him. These men really believed that they were about to be elected to lead the province into the Promised Land. 'It was a victory of the forces of the Lord over the forces of wickedness,'[42] he recalled. He was coming to suspect a party whose members believed that they had a right to govern on the basis of their virtue alone. When politics became messianic, it became dangerous. Here was a concrete example of his inherent fear that socialists could be as intoxicated by success and power as could any other individuals, and that, worst of all, they would be in a better position to wield that power, if elected, through the collective policies they advocated. Soviet Russia was Nazi Germany immediately came to his mind.

Underhill's critical view of the CCF brought him into conflict with party stalwarts. A disagreement arose between him and George Grube, president of the Board of Directors of the *Canadian Forum* and provincial secretary of the Ontario CCF, and David Lewis, national secretary of the CCF, over the relationship of the *Forum* to the CCF party. Now Underhill had come around to accept Hugh Dent's position, which he had strongly opposed in 1932–3, that the *Forum* should present a variety of viewpoints. This meant publishing articles that questioned the nature of socialism as well as those that were critical of the CCF party. Such diversification of opinion was healthy in a democracy, and besides, it stimulated debate on controversial subjects. He did not believe that just because the party was on the verge of political success it should not be challenged. In fact, that was all the more reason to force the party executive to clarify its position on important national and international issues.

Grube and Lewis thought otherwise. At a time when the CCF was on an upswing in Ontario and across Canada there was need for solidarity, not dissension, in the ranks. '[T]he CCF has entered a period of very severe struggle with the capitalist parties on the one hand and the Communist party on the other,' Lewis wrote to the executive of the *Forum*. 'The present stage of struggle is of a nature where our opposition is not likely to be delicate or particularly scrupulous. Such a situation places upon us it seems to me an even stronger obligation to watch carefully every step than at any other time.' What initiated the letter was an article in the June issue by E.A. Beder, a CCF supporter, in which he had pointed out the tremendous obstacles to world peace for socialists. Lewis had no objection to the content, but he disliked the pessimistic and defeatist attitude. 'It is one thing to point to the grave dangers which must be overcome; it is another thing to describe them in a tone which suggests that they cannot be overcome.'

The reprimand was really meant for Underhill, who was far more pessimistic and vocal than Beder. In a private letter to Grube, Lewis reinforced Grube's 'uneasiness about the tendency on the part of McNaught and Underhill to use phrases which cause discomfort ... It might be a good idea for Carl and Frank to practice writing their pet phrases down for their own satisfaction and, having done so, re-write the sentence for an objective purpose.' Lewis maintained that the *Forum*, as the 'only non-Communist progressive journal in Canada,' and the only possible national paper for the party, could not 'afford the luxury of "subjective editing."' Its popularity required of the editorial committee that it consider 'the political consequences of what appears in the paper.'[43]

Ill health plagued Underhill for much of 1944. It was the result of his ulcer troubles that had developed in the late thirties, and had been exacerbated as a result of the tension from his threatened dismissal from the university and his confrontation with socialist friends. The year had begun well, so well in fact that he overextended himself with the heaviest commitment of public lectures, speeches, and meetings since the mid-thirties. In addition, he was revising lecture notes in light of new material collected from his extensive reading in the United States. He ended up in the early spring exhausted. He had come to dread early spring as a low time in his activity when mental and physical exhaustion from teaching and speaking publicly made him susceptible to flu and ulcer problems. Then he would become depressed as he was unable to complete his teaching term satisfactorily and was forced to cut back on speaking engagements and writing.

This time his sickness had started with sinus trouble, followed by a severe attack of duodenal ulcer. He was hospitalized for a week in early July and ordered by the doctor to relax and avoid tense situations for the rest of the summer. That meant no public engagements or extensive writing. Compounding the problem was his worrying about his unfulfilled promises. He felt depressed every time he thought about the Blake project. He had returned from his Guggenheim year determined to work on it while the material was fresh in his mind; he had not touched it all year.

Now, when he had time to work on it, he was too sick to do so. Then there was his promise to de Kiewiet to write the introduction to the Dufferin-Carnarvon letters; that, too, would have to wait.

Weighing him down further was the strain of caring for his aged and invalid parents who needed around-the-clock attention. They had moved in with Ruth and Frank upon the Underhill's return to Toronto from their Guggenheim year, when both parents were too ill to care for themselves. Frequently Ruth would stay up nights attending to them, and Frank would take responsibility during the day as much as possible. The couple had little privacy or time alone together, and they found the obligation put a great deal of strain on their relationship and curbed their social life. Betty recalled in later life coming home and finding her father crouched in a corner of their upstairs sunroom, drinking his afternoon tea away from his mother in order to have a few moments to himself. But there was no question of his parents going into a nursing home. They had supported him throughout his schooling and during his troubles at the university; the least he could do was to care for them in old age. His parents would live with them for the remainder of their lives, his father passing away in 1946 and his mother in 1953. These were very trying times for Ruth and Frank, and the added stress took its toll.[44]

Out of frustration he lashed out at friends and colleagues, often over insignificant matters that irritated him. He wrote to the secretary of the Canadian Institute of International Affairs to complain about the 'propaganda' in *International Affairs*. 'Occasionally it does print a good analytical and informative article, but most of its stuff is just the correct, orthodox, Oxford accent, old-school-tie talk at which the more genteel of British imperialists are so expert that they can reel it off in their sleep. Its book review section is especially atrocious.' It was typical Underhill criticism, but it had a cutting, almost malicious, edge to it which was uncharacteristic. He lit into the CCF executive for deleting some minor words and phrases from his February address for the publication *Planning for Freedom*. Colleagues in the history department found him moodier and more irritable than usual.[45]

His ill health extended into the fall, and he went through the motions of teaching. But he was not going to let sickness get in the way of one important commitment: the address at a fund-raising dinner in honour of J.S. Woodsworth at the King Edward Hotel on 7 October. He had been unable to help raise funds for the Woodsworth Memorial Fund during the summer, and this speech would be his contribution to this outstanding Canadian. He spent September researching Woodsworth's life and composing the speech.

That evening, 150 friends and admirers listened to as fine a tribute to J.S. Woodsworth as could be heard anywhere. It was Underhill at his best, lucid and perceptive, but not in his typical fashion. The speech was in the form of a 'sermon' with moral and spiritual uplifting and a depth of sincerity; it was sober without a trace of flippancy or even humour. Clearly he was talking about a man – a friend –

who had moved him deeply. He spoke of the moral courage, sympathy for the underdog, passion for clarity, and intellectual pioneering of this 'untypical Canadian.' Underhill spent little time discussing Woodsworth's activities as leader of the CCF party, emphasizing instead his work as a 'consulting sociologist' in his All People's Mission, his years as a longshoreman, his activities in the Winnipeg General Strike, and his association with the Progressive movement. The emphasis was intentional, for the moral of the 'sermon' was that Woodsworth was fundamentally a missionary and the CCF, which he founded, was a movement. In closing, Underhill reinforced this message for the benefit of the party stalwarts in the audience: 'The C.C.F. is still what Mr. Woodsworth left it, a movement devoted to the social and economic change in the interests of the great mass of the plain common people. Let us resolve to keep it a movement and to save it from sinking into being merely a party intent on collecting votes. And one of the best ways to do that is to foster through this Woodsworth Foundation a vigorous programme of imaginative social study and research, so that Woodsworth House may become a source of the same kind of inspiration as radiated from J.S. Woodsworth's successive offices of church minister, social worker and member of Parliament.'[46] The speech was an immediate inspiration; over $1700 was raised that evening to help establish an Ontario Woodsworth Memorial Foundation.

In January 1945 Underhill gave another memorable lecture, this time to the Literary Society of University College on John Morley, the most brilliant of the young Liberal intellectuals in the Gladstone era who was concerned with the threat to liberty in an age of equality. The speech reflected Underhill's growing concern with the nature of liberalism in the postwar era. The popularity of the lecture lay in Underhill's ability to relate Morley's views to those of present-day liberals who, in the immediate postwar era, were experiencing a period of unrest and uncertainty similar to that in Morley's time. Morley's greatness was his faith in the ideals of liberalism – rationality, progress, and human perfectibility – in an age when liberalism was coming to an end in the power politics of the Bismarckian era of the late nineteenth century. Today, Underhill noted in comparison, liberals were again called upon to defend their beliefs in an age of cynicism and doubt. Morley still had a message for the present age: 'Sooner or later when our generation has had its fill of Machiavelli, we shall have to find our way back to that faith which uplifted men in the age of reason. We shall have to rediscover the truth that the most important fact about man is that he is a rational creature. And when we have made that rediscovery we shall no doubt begin to behave again like rational creatures. For we shall then be aware once more of the responsibility that rests upon men who are the heirs of eighteenth-century Enlightenment and of nineteenth-century Victorian Liberalism.'[47] The challenge was more personal than anyone in the audience probably realized. He was the John Morley of his generation of Canadians searching for the meaning of liberalism in the new postwar world.

12

Liberalism in the Postwar Era

Two themes dominated Underhill's life in the first decade of the postwar years. The first was his apotheosis as an inspiring and dedicated university teacher. The second was his re-evaluation of liberalism and his resulting gradual dissociation from socialism.

Underhill had his best years of teaching just prior to the war and particularly in the postwar era. He loved teaching the veterans who took advantage of free tuition to swarm to campuses across the country. Here were men driven to succeed not only by their war experiences but by the dark cloud of the Depression that still hung over them. Sceptical, pragmatic yet idealistic, demanding a better and more 'relevant' education than the students who immediately preceded them, they invigorated Underhill and encouraged him on to even greater heights in his teaching as he responded to the challenge.

He had by this time perfected his teaching technique.[1] He taught the courses he wanted to teach – modern British and Canadian history – as courses on the history of political and social thought. In his British history courses, for example, he spent more time, especially in his seminars and tutorials, on the writings of Jeremy Bentham, John Stuart Mill, and the Fabians than he did on political events or constitutional developments. He continually shortened the time period covered, allowing him to dwell longer on the modern period where, through a more intense absorption in the writings of the period, he and his students could savour the age that they were studying. His lectures were models of the genre: well organized, lucid, witty, provocative, and informative. Each dealt with a single theme or topic which Underhill explored in depth, drawing on his wealth of factual information, bringing in appropriate quotations from the sources, and referring to the most recent literature. They had a 'sand-blasting' effect, as though the listener was hearing the very latest information and interpretation of the subject. He presented his lectures in a rather high-pitched voice, not eloquent or dynamic, but authoritative, clear, and pleasant to listen to. Some twenty years later, S.F. Wise recalled in writing to Underhill 'the anticipation [students] felt before each of your lectures on 19th century British history, given, you'll remember, in Hart House theatre. It wasn't just that you put us in touch with a body of ideas of great importance, but the sense you gave of the relationship between ideas and social and political change – a sense strengthened by our awareness of your own concern with the world we were living in.'[2]

In each of his lectures he presented a definite viewpoint, which aroused emotions in his students. Students frequently responded to his liberal-socialist interpretations either with applause and cheers if they liked his outrageous, witty, and bombastic statements, or with jeers and even occasionally by walking out in disgust if they disagreed. One lecture which always elicited a strong response, he recalled in later life, was one of his favourite lectures on Queen Victoria, full of comical references to 'the dear old lady.' There was a good deal of the actor, the court jester, the celebrity, in Underhill; he enjoyed playing to his audience, to enhance and to enliven his informative and scholarly lectures. But while the professor had strong and definite opinions, he judiciously introduced the opposite viewpoint in both his lectures and his seminars. A few students have recalled that they acquired as much of an appreciation and understanding of British conservatism as of British liberalism from Underhill's British history courses. In fact, Maurice Careless recalls that he and a couple of others in a course on modern Britain formed a club, 'The Young Reactionaries,' with their own chant:

Onward, onward young reactionaries,
One step forward, three steps back.

To those students who shared his enthusiasm for history, politics, and ideas, Underhill could do no wrong. They still today describe in superlatives his teaching technique right down to the minutest detail of his idiosyncrasies – the smile that came over his face when he was about to 'get a good one off'; his nervous laugh and bobbing head; the pencil in his vest pocket that he used to check off a point in his lecture notes; the constant fumbling with his tie – or some penetrating remark that he had made in one of his lectures. His popularity, however, went beyond these converts to affect a generation of Toronto students, many of whom took his courses or sat in on his lectures as an 'extra' course rather than as one required for a particular degree. Douglas Fisher recalls that Underhill 'often had several hundred attend a class with an official enrolment of 75 to 80.'

Yet his real strength as a teacher came in the seminar. Prodding students to think deeper about a subject, encouraging discussion, arousing debate, asking penetrating questions to develop a rudimentary idea, listening attentively to responses, and, most of all, exciting them about ideas: these were Underhill's qualities as a seminar instructor. Great emphasis was put on original documentary sources or texts, and Underhill's insightful comments on particular passages and his depth of understanding amazed his students. His approach was warm but not uncritical – he did not suffer fools easily – and his seminar was conducted in a relaxed yet invigorating atmosphere. His seminars often had a waiting list. One student recalled that she first signed up for Underhill's course and then worried about arranging the rest of her timetable around it.[3]

On at least one occasion, however, Underhill broke down under the pressure. The seminar discussion was on Mackenzie King and conscription. Douglas Fisher, subsequently a CCF–NDP member of parliament and a political commentator, raised the question of King's wisdom in refusing to introduce immediate conscription. Underhill insisted that King was right, and refused to back down. The veterans in the class replied that if Underhill had seen the 'guts of war' in the battlefields he would think differently. The majority of the students participating in the discussion opposed him. In tears of rage, he walked out of the seminar unable to deal with the issue any further.[4]

His responsibilities as a teacher went beyond the classroom. He treated students as mature adults with ideas of their own, meeting them informally outside the classroom. Feeling perhaps more at ease with them than with his colleagues, he had them to his office for afternoon tea and invited those closest to him for dinner parties or social gatherings at his home. Students were also included in social functions that he arranged for visiting academics to the department or the university. Any occasion was an opportunity to broaden a student's intellectual horizons. These were hallmarks of a man who loved students; teaching, he claimed in later life, 'is the best life in the world.'[5]

Underhill's election in 1946 as the president of the Canadian Historical Association marked a high point in his professional career, an honour as well as a recognition of his contribution through his teaching and his historical essays. He used the occasion of his 1946 presidential address to make a major statement on Canada and liberalism in the mid-twentieth century. No longer could Canadians assume that liberalism would survive and grow in their country as it had in the past: 'The freedom which our Victorian ancestors thought was slowly broadening down from precedent to precedent seemed to become more and more unreal under the concentrated pressure of capitalistic big business or of the massive bureaucratic state.'[6] To Underhill, Canada's challenge in the mid-twentieth century was to preserve liberalism in a world confronting 'a crisis of liberalism.'

Canadians were ill-prepared to confront this crisis because they lacked an intellectual tradition. The explanation was historical: the weakness of a radical tradition in Canadian history, a point he had first made in the 1920s. Canada's first great democratic upheaval, the rebellion of 1837–8, was a failure; Canadian liberalism in the late nineteenth century remained British and respectable, instead of becoming American and radical; social reform movements at the turn of the century remained on the fringe of politics, disorganized, apolitical, and ineffective against the domination of big business. Why? The ultimate reason was Canada's early rejection of the Age of Enlightenment, the mainspring of liberalism. 'In Catholic French Canada the doctrines of the rights of man and of Liberty Equality Fraternity were rejected from the start, and to this day they have never penetrated, save surreptitiously or spasmodically. The mental climate of English Canada in its formative years was determined by men who were fleeing from the practical application of the doctrines that all men are born equal and are endowed by their Creator with certain unalienable rights among which are life liberty and the pursuit of happiness.' In its rudimentary form Underhill's hypothesis anticipated Louis Hartz's great theory in *Liberalism in America*, although the conclusions of the two men were significantly different.

The presidential address was pure Underhill, with much to reflect upon: the lack of an intellectual tradition in Canada; the rejection of the ideas of the Enlightenment; the illiberal nature of Canadian history; the need for a new historical perspective; and the significance of liberalism within Canada and within Western civilization. Yet he developed none of these ideas at any great length, throwing them out at random and in a rambling fashion to germinate as they might. Once again, however, as in his 1927 CHA paper, he anticipated the direction of historical writing for the next generation: the emphasis on intellectual over economic history. The speech was typical of Underhill in another respect: there were scant words of praise for what Canadian historians had accomplished in the past. He did acknowledge the prolific writing of the economic historians of the 1930s, but only to point out the weakness of their impersonal history with its 'ghostly ballet of bloodless economic categories.' He berated his fellow historians, much to their annoyance, undoubtedly, for not doing enough and for pursuing the wrong approach to the subject. They should have been doing intellectual history, and they should have been more interested in the history of countries other than their own, even though he was the one who had appealed for more Canadian history in the 1930s. It was the culprit accusing the innocent.

The speech was also an *apologia pro vita sua* of the time: a rationale for his failure to finish his intellectual biography of Blake, and an explanation for the failure of Canadian liberal-socialist intellectuals, like himself, to have much of an impact on Canadian political life. Canadian intellectuals were working against great odds in their attempt to inject ideas into Canadian life. The speech also indicated the thrust of Underhill's thinking for at least the next decade: his search for Canadian liberalism within the context of British and American liberal tradition.

One of the immediate effects of the speech was Underhill's decision to teach a fourth-year seminar on 'The Liberal Tradition in Canada.' The idea was Frank

Knox's, an economist at Queen's, who suggested to Underhill, while congratulating him on his address, that he ought to be running a seminar on the liberal tradition. 'So I changed my fourth year Canadian history seminar and my graduate seminar to the liberal tradition so it became a study of liberal ideas,' Underhill recalled. 'And it worked much better than anything I'd done before.'[7] Indeed, it soon became his most popular course.

Underhill's search for the meaning of liberalism led him to question socialism too. He became more conscious than ever that the only meaningful socialism was one based on liberal-democratic values. He emphasized this in his important two-part *Forum* article on 'Fabians and Fabianism' in early 1946. The article formed a sequel, over a decade later, to his 'Bentham and Benthamism' piece. In both studies he placed the particular 'ism' in its historical context to show it as part of the continuous British liberal-socialist-democratic tradition. 'Fabian socialism ... in its essential character is simply a logical development of the search for the greatest happiness of the greatest number which Bentham and his circle carried on within individualistic categories.' Fabianism had continued to remain liberal by altering its program as the needs and circumstances of society changed. Its strength lay in its flexibility and practicality, in its refusal to be tied down to an ideology in a constantly changing world, just as he believed Canadian socialism had done in its formative stage in the 1930s.

The articles on the 'Fabians' marked a slight departure by the author of the Regina Manifesto from his earlier political allegiances. He believed that the LSR derived its inspiration and guidance from the Fabians, and it was these liberal-democratic values that lay at the roots of the CCF movement. However, Underhill was no longer certain in 1946 that the CCF party continued to adhere to those principles. He feared that the party had lost its 'principles' in its quest for political power. It had also become rigid and dogmatic, the prisoner of antiquated theories and policies, applicable perhaps in the Depression years but not in the postwar era. 'We need to do some serious re-thinking about the relationship of our type of socialism to the liberal tradition which has been the most precious inheritance of the history of the last few centuries.'[8] His ideological rift with the party leaders widened in the months to follow. The forum where this vicious debate and infighting occurred was, ironically, Ontario Woodsworth House.

The house, purchased by the Woodsworth Foundation in the winter of 1944–5, was a three-storey mansion on Jarvis Street in downtown Toronto. It soon proved too large for the foundation's activities, and the committee decided to rent space 'to organizations in sympathy with the general aims and purposes of the Foundation.' The CCF Ontario section leased the second floor, and the *Canadian Forum* the coach-house at the rear. The centre became a clubhouse for 'all those who were interested in the spread of socialism in Canada.'

Always an activist, Underhill became involved in the Woodsworth Foundation as its first vice-president and educational director.[9] The latter position required him to organize a series of public lectures of interest to socialists, to order books and journals on socialism for the library, and to arrange the publication of pamphlets. He envisioned Woodsworth House as an updated version of the LSR, even appealing to the same men – Eugene Forsey and Frank Scott, for example – to write pamphlets for the organization. But significant differences existed. He wanted an independence for Woodsworth House from the party, permitting it, if necessary, to question and criticize the nature and meaning of the socialism that the party espoused.

During the initial organizational period two political elections had been held that affected the development of Woodsworth House. On 4 June 1945 an Ontario electorate returned a Conservative government; one week later, the Canadian populace re-elected a Liberal government.[10] The CCF fared poorly in both elections, a blow to their great expectations after their recent electoral successes in Ontario and Saskatchewan. The Ontario CCF Steering Committee attributed the poor standings to the anti-socialist propaganda and the smear tactics of their political opponents. To counteract, all sympathetic socialist organizations should consolidate their efforts, Woodsworth House becoming the centre for this campaign. Underhill led a group of dissenters who opposed this viewpoint. The CCF did poorly in the elections because the party leaders failed to present a case convincingly enough to disprove the opponents' accusations. The intellectuals in the CCF could provide this educational work if they stopped running for political offices. The value of Woodsworth House would be to provide this work, but only if it remained an educational centre and resisted becoming a propaganda centre for the CCF party.[11]

Underhill frequently asked his socialist colleagues how liberal-democratic their form of socialism was in practice. In a speech on 'Socialism and Liberty' at Woodsworth House on 24 November 1946, for example, he argued that CCFers were concerned more with planning than with freedom. 'Planning will be done by people who like managing other people,'[12] he cautioned. Socialists needed constantly to be reminded of those two old liberal proverbs: eternal vigilance is the price of freedom; all power corrupts and absolute power corrupts absolutely. There were two simple tests for socialists to judge their faith in liberty: one was to reread Edward Bellamy's *Looking Backward* with the experience of Russia and Germany in mind and to judge how appealing they still found the book; the other was to examine their views on 'Soviet Democracy' to see if they still believed Russia to be 'a society of workers and peasants ever marching on to ever new democratic victories.' A democratic society, he said, needed more checks and balances on power.

A spirited discussion followed the speech, encouraging Underhill to express the same ideas in the *Canadian Forum*. Interestingly, Underhill waited close to a year before presenting his views in 'Random Remarks on Socialism and Freedom' in the August 1947 issue. One newspaper pointed out that 'the champions of Free Enterprise' were making 'capital' out of the article, by pointing out that one of the founding fathers of Canadian socialism had succeeded better than anyone else at knocking 'the bottom out of the c.c.f.'s socialist program.' Another newspaper accused him of 'turning turtle' and labelled him the 'Prodigal Son Returned.'[13]

Underhill naïvely believed that the article would 'generate more intelligent discussion about the problems of a general socialist policy.' Instead, it created confrontation and ill-feeling. Frank Scott wrote to scold Underhill for his rash action which could only harm the ccf. George Grube complained publicly in a rebuttal in the next issue of the *Canadian Forum*. Accepting Underhill's premise of the need for perpetual vigilance against the threat of state power, Grube argued that a democratic socialist government could best foster and preserve that freedom.[14]

Undaunted by these counter-attacks, Underhill continued to press his socialist colleagues. In an introductory lecture to a series on 'Prophets, Critics and Isms' at Woodsworth House in the fall of 1948, Underhill argued almost with glee that even British political parties had moved together ideologically. They were like two stage-coaches that splashed each other with mud as they went along the highway, both going in the same direction and to the same destination. In an effort to provoke a response he claimed that if he were in England today he would vote for the Conservative party. Then he poked fun at the antiquated ideology of the Canadian ccf and denounced third parties as detrimental to the existence of an ideal two-party system. ccfers were 'fools,' he claimed, and 'may just as well be Conservatives or Liberals.'

A number of those present failed to see the humour or the logic in Underhill's speech. 'I had hoped to stimulate discussion, but I only succeeded in stimulating denunciation and invective,'[15] he noted in a prefatory remark to his second lecture. Bernard Loeb, a friend and a past president of Woodsworth House, censured him for his negative views: Underhill ridiculed optimists and scorned idealists as innocent fools, he complained, and equated optimists and idealists with anyone who expressed a viewpoint different from his own 'realistic' one. 'What are you?' he asked in exasperation, 'Are you a Conservative, a Liberal or a Sozialist [sic], or are you just a member of the middle class with no political opinion, an opportunist [?]'[16] He was a critic, fulfilling his moral obligation to make people think, even if it meant being attacked by friends and colleagues. In his mind intellectual honesty, meaningful debate, and the search for truth were higher goals than social acceptance. It was the same mission that had always inspired him, and he pursued it with the same relentless zeal, emotionalism, and determination as in the 1930s. Only the enemy had changed from 'greedy capitalists' to 'power-hungry socialists.'

The final confrontation that Underhill and his followers waged against the CCF party hierarchy occurred in the fall and winter of 1951–2 over the role of Woodsworth House. In September 1951 Underhill volunteered to publish through Woodsworth House a *CCF Newsletter* to educate party members through editorial comments on current events, standard CCF policy, and the general socialist ideology. His opening article in the first issue of the *Newsletter* established the theme and approach of later editorials: 'Canadian socialists have concentrated far too much on economic questions and have too easily convinced themselves, if not their neighbors, that if we could only change the economic system we should all live happily ever afterwards ... Have we any concrete policy on education, apart from making it more freely available to poorer students? What do we proposed to do about fostering literature and the arts and sciences? How do we proposed to tackle the problems of modern mass-communications – the daily press, the popular magazines, the movies, radio, television, etc.?' The reaction to the *Newsletter* was predictable. Non-party sympathizers praised Underhill as a harbinger of the future direction of socialism; party supporters criticized him as the saboteur of an already vulnerable party. As one commentator noted: 'It is hard to believe that its [the *Newsletter's*] incredibly bad timing was not deliberately planned to sabotage the chances of CCF candidates in the forthcoming provincial election.'[17]

The bitter antagonism between the two groups surfaced in February 1952 at the annual meeting.[18] The uncertain financial state of Woodsworth House left the executive unable to pay its plumbing bill, and the account had been referred to a collecting agency. The educational group blamed the party, with its low rental fee, for the financial crisis. Party sympathizers blamed the foundation with its overextended educational program. The executive felt that they must sell the house and find less expensive accommodation elsewhere. Their opponents viewed this decision as a deliberate attempt to end the party's affiliation with Woodsworth House. Both sides sought to ensure that their candidates got elected to the executive. In the membership drive preceding the meeting the party outdrew the Underhill group, as the party, through the initiative of Charles Millard, a Canadian director of the United Steelworkers of America and an active member of Woodsworth House, could rely on the trade unions.[19] Dr H. Wilkinson, the president of the foundation, referred in his report to the deliberate 'power drive' by CCF officials to increase 'their' membership in Woodsworth House. David Lewis then requested an amendment to the president's report, demanding that the foundation engage in more research 'which will advance the idea of co-operative Commonwealth in Canada and ... serve as ammunition to the socialist move-ment ... ' He moved that 'neither Woodsworth House nor any of the property con-nected with it shall be sold or otherwise disposed of, without consent of the CCF Ontario Section.'[20] To foundation members, such a motion would concede that the CCF dominated the supposedly non-partisan institution. As Loeb, now behind the Underhill group, stated: 'If the organization has to consult a political party and get permission from it to dispose of its assets, it is not independent any more.' In the end, the CCF party members won. The majority of the candidates elected that night were active CCF members: David Lewis, Reid Scott, Marion Bryden, Gwenyth Grube, and William Newcombe. A few of the old guard remained, but clearly the party was in control.

Underhill sat in the front row at the meeting but did not speak because of ill-health.[21] In the April issue of the *Canadian Forum* he published his response: Ontario CCF party members had conducted a 'purge' of the foundation 'with an unscrupulous thoroughness that the Communists themselves could hardly have bettered.' He went on to criticize the party in general: 'The CCF in Ontario has ceased for all practical purposes to be a missionary party concentrating on winning more and more converts, and it is slowly sinking into a sect whose leaders seem mainly interested in maintaining at all costs their own authority within the sect.'[22] The Woodsworth House controversy embittered its antagonists for a lifetime. Underhill never forgave David Lewis for his part in the dispute and vowed never to vote for a party of which Lewis was the leader; Lewis in turn denounced Underhill, and reiterated his account of the dispute in his autobiography.[23] In future, Underhill interpreted all of Lewis's political actions in terms of power politics. In 1962, for example, Underhill wrote to fellow historian Gordon Rothney, who was expressing his own reservations about the CCF party: 'Personally, I think that the main threat to the New Party is Dave Lewis who will be the real power whoever the nominal leader may be. He is by instinct a communist commissar, and he hopes to have all the machine of the trade unionists to wield his purposes.'[24] Underhill continued his affiliation with the CCF, especially with the national party, and he continued to vote CCF, federally at least as long as Lewis was not leader. But his heart had left the party.

Such confrontations bothered him. He liked arguing, not fighting. Not surprisingly, this period of transition in his thinking and confrontation with close friends and colleagues affected his personal health. In January 1949 he was hospitalized for a severe duodenal ulcer; he missed classes for over a month and was only able to go through the motions of teaching for the remainder of the term. One year later he was hospitalized again, with severe haemorrhaging of his ulcer. An immediate operation was imperative. Two of Underhill's students made an appeal in his classes for blood donors, and many lined up to volunteer their help. After the operation, Underhill telephoned each donor to thank him or her for saving his life.[25] Then again in the spring of 1953 he had another haemorrhage, no doubt partly brought on by the Woodsworth House controversy.

Underlying Underhill's attacks on the CCF lay an uneasiness, almost a paranoia, about communism, comparable to his deep distrust of imperialism in the 1930s. His search for 'communistic' tendencies within the CCF could be viewed as a moderate Canadian version of the 'Red Scare' in the United States during the periods when suspected communists were ferreted out for public prosecution. While Underhill decried the emotional and exaggerated attacks on the CCF by such anti-communistic extremists as B.A. 'Bert' Trestrail, he fully accepted their basic concern with the authoritarian tendencies in CCF circles. In this Cold War era, Underhill insisted that Canada get actively involved in helping to police the world. In a world divided between two superpowers, there were only two choices: to side with the Americans or to join forces with the Russians who stood for everything inimical to democracy and freedom. He stood by the Americans. At a time when many Canadian intellectuals were criticizing American foreign policy as being a new form of imperialism, Underhill accepted implicitly the arguments of American 'hawks.' In his postwar writings on international affairs we find an underlying assumption that American foreign policy was right and morally justified. The Americans had to fight fire with fire. If the Americans did not check Soviet expansion in Europe or Asia, then communism would spread through military force throughout the world, until ultimately Americans would have to fight for freedom on the doorstep of North America.[26]

The communist coup in Czechoslovakia revealed once again Russian intentions to dominate the world: 'By this time only shameless party-liners and incurable innocents of the Henry Wallace type can profess to believe the communist version of the coup which has changed Czechoslovakia into a one-party totalitarian state.'[27] Czechoslovakia was only the next in a succession of European states that would fall into the Soviet sphere of power before the American effort to build a healthier economy in Western Europe had been effective. The non-communist world had to stand up to the Soviets militarily, in a way that it had failed to do against the Nazis a decade earlier. The fall of China to communism in 1949, and the expansion in 1950 of communist-controlled North Korea into the non-communist south, terrified Underhill. He interpreted the war as a decoy by the Russians to get the Americans involved in a war in Asia, where they were most vulnerable, permitting Russia to strike more effectively in Western Europe. He praised the quick American response to the Korean crisis as a corrective to the 'disgraceful series of backdowns before brutal aggression which make the decade of the 1930's such a painful memory.'[28] His only regrets were that the Americans had not been more aggressive, and that the Western nations had not rallied behind the Americans in a display of unanimity.

Such views brought Underhill into conflict with CCF colleagues, including his former student and friend Kenneth McNaught, the son of Carlton McNaught. In a debate on CCF foreign policy in the *Canadian Forum*, McNaught (writing under the pseudonym of S.W. Bradford in fear of Underhill's reaction) criticized the party for its pro-American foreign policy. Did the CCF have an alternative to the Liberals' foreign policy? Had Canadians, he argued, achieved national emancipation from the British in the last century, only to become an American colony or satellite in the next?

McNaught's arguments – even his tone and style – brought Underhill back to his 'foolhardy days' in the 1930s.[29] If CCFers could be accused of innocently swallowing the hawkish arguments of the Americans, then 'Bradford' and his left-wing associates had imbibed excessively in simplistic propaganda of radical British Labourites. How could Mr Bradford realistically believe that the West could 'co-operate with Russia on the atomic bomb, on Korea, on disarmament, or on any other major issue, on any basis which differs from complete capitulation to Russian terms'? Only military force would stop the aggressive, expansionist Russian empire, the world's greatest threat to democratic liberalism.

Underhill's attitude towards William Lyon Mackenzie King became more conciliatory, as was obvious in a series of articles he began in 1944 and which continued until King's death in 1950. Underhill felt the articles to be a sufficiently important reflection of his views to have all five of them included, despite repetition, in his anthology *In Search of Canadian Liberalism*.[30] If read consecutively, they reveal an evolution in Underhill's thinking from a position of grudging respect in 1944 to enthusiastic support by 1950.

In his initial piece of September 1944 Underhill emphasized King's failure to provide leadership in the most pressing areas of concern in the interwar years: labour reform, social services, and constitutional reform. The credit for Mackenzie King's political success, Underhill argued, belonged to his inept political opponents and his indifferent political followers; King 'towered up like a mountain in the House of Commons because of the flatness of the landscape opposite him.'

> Just consider the list of Conservative leaders in his day. First, there was Meighen, the lean and hungry Cassius, the bitter fanatic who lost votes all across the country every time he won a debate in the House ... Then there was the preposterous Bennett of the booming voice and the beetling brows, the lord of the iron heel. Mr. King had only to sit back quietly in opposition for five years and let Bennett hang himself. Then there was the lightweight Manion, followed quickly by the old muzzle-loading blunderbuss from New Brunswick. And now, when Mr. Bracken was beginning to make Mr. King nervous by never committing himself to anything except pious abstract platitudes such as might have come from the author of *Industry and Humanity* himself, and just when the strains of a long war seemed to make it certain that even a government of archangels could not

survive the next election, along come the two Georges [Drew and McCullagh] from Toronto. They have equipped themselves with a battle-cry that is sure to turn everyone outside Ontario against them; and Mr. King must be beginning to think that once again his old ally, Providence, is on his side.

King also proved a master-mind at obscuring issues, the best formula for political success in Canada.

Two years later Underhill admitted that King had met the needs of the Canadian people better than any of his critics were willing to admit. In explaining King's political success, Underhill noted his ability 'to take advantage of the fundamental pattern in which the Canadian people vote' – that the other eight provinces combined against Ontario. King's success lay in his failure politically in his own province of Ontario: 'He came into his own, and his own received him not.' Here was a backhanded, grudging compliment to King's political astuteness. The other explanation of his success, he added, was the tendency to accept middle-of-the-road parties in North America at a time when such parties elsewhere were being crushed between the old conservatism on the one side and the new proletarian movements on the other.

By the time of King's retirement from politics in 1948, Underhill could actually speak in positive terms of his political success. In two national accomplishments – national unity and national autonomy – King had the stature of a Macdonald or a Laurier. 'Mr. King is the leader who divides us least,' Underhill concluded in summing up the man's career. Now he appreciated just how difficult a task that was in a nation as deeply divided as Canada. Under King, the Liberal party contained a wide variety of interest groups whose needs were being fulfilled. 'The essence of a national party which is capable of government in Canada is that it should have a substantial following from all the main groups and sections of the country – geographical, racial, religious, and economic – and especially that it should unite enough of the French and English within its ranks to make possible a stable and continuous administration of the country for a decade or a generation.' Mackenzie King had to his credit another liberal national policy: he led us from colony to nation. He completed the mission, initiated by Laurier, 'of an independent Canada within a British Commonwealth which is no longer an exclusive association, which has no central organs for making military or economic policy, and which tends more and more to merge itself into the larger more comprehensive Atlantic Community ... '

The final article, written on the eve of Mackenzie King's death in the summer of 1950, praised the prime minister for his political astuteness. King had defeated politically all his opponents, from the Dafoe-Crerar-Hudson group, through the Progressives to the CCF, not to mention the Conservatives. This liberal understood power politics. His success could, and should be, a lesson to members of the CCF party as they pondered their political future. With this appeal, Underhill had come full circle from his desire in the 1930s for Mackenzie King and his Liberal party to take lessons from the new CCF party.

Underhill offered no explanation to those bewildered by his about-face in his political position. The unexpressed assumption was that views changed as circumstances altered, and only a poor thinker left his opinions firm and set. In this respect Underhill was more the political commentator than the objective historian. Still, the two roles were not mutually exclusive. Evident in these 'contemporary' articles were the ideas and interpretations which would influence a generation of historical writings on Mackenzie King. To what extent Underhill directly influenced such writings is difficult to say; that his views had weight among his students goes without saying.

Underhill's uncritical views of King seemed by some to be flattery for the ulterior motive of personal gain. It was common knowledge that a search was on for an official biographer of the late prime minister. Underhill was clearly interested, but to impute personal motives to Underhill's revisionist views of King is to do injustice to Underhill. He expressed opinions because he genuinely believed them or wanted to generate debate, not because he wanted to advance his personal position. His moral scruples and self-effacing ways were evident in his letter of application to Fred McGregor, head of the selection committee:

> While I realize that you are still only exploring the situation and are not making offers to anyone, I think I ought to say that I'd be willing to be considered as a possible biographer of Mr. King. The objections are that you might not think me sufficiently sympathetic and that you might have doubts whether I'd come through with a complete work in any reasonable time. As to the first, I fancy I am as good a liberal (with a small 'l') as the most other possible choices, though of course you know well enough what some of my criticisms of Mr King have been. It is about the second point that I'm most conscious of being vulnerable, and I'm not particularly proud of my record as a writer so far. But the subject appeals to me and I'll do my best.
>
> It is impossible to keep on talking about oneself without seeming unbearably conceited. So this is just to ask you not to rule me out altogether from your considerations; and if you have already done so, to apologize for thrusting myself forward.[31]

In the end Underhill lost out in the competition because, in the words of Norman Robertson, clerk of the Privy Council at the time and a Mackenzie King literary executor, 'he hasn't published very much, and has earned the academic reproach of being a better starter than finisher.'[32]

13

Curator of the
Liberal Tradition

The early 1950s moved slowly for Underhill. His ulcer problems sapped him of energy and at times of enthusiasm. His unfinished work bothered him. It had been so long since he had worked on Blake that he himself wondered if he would ever finish the study. Even the Dufferin-Carnarvon correspondence dragged on, to the great annoyance of his co-editor, de Kiewiet, who wrote a letter of exasperation in February 1953 blaming Underhill for the endless delay in completing the manuscript, already ten years in the making. Underhill pleaded patience, that ill-health had thwarted his efforts at sustained work.[1] In his writings he reiterated his standard views on politics of the 1940s: the inability of the CCF to become anything more than a splinter group (because of its refusal to alter its program to reflect the new concerns of the postwar era); the Canadian pattern of voting for a different provincial party from the federal party in office; the lack of clear issues and ideological differences between the major parties; the need for some form of proportional representation; and the success of the Liberals as the party that 'divided us least.'

The professor, soon-to-retire, also felt very pessimistic. The optimism that had sustained him in the thirties had been found wanting. He attributed his pessimism to 'the times.' In a closing speech to the 1953 Couchiching Conference he contrasted the atmosphere surrounding the conferences of the 1930s with that of the present: 'In the early days what was looked for in our discussions was uplift, millenial [sic] inspiration, the assurance that there was a solution for all problems just around the corner. This week what has impressed me most is the atmosphere of what I call realistic pessimism or pessimistic realism.'[2]

Underhill's best writings in the early 1950s articulate this pessimistic mood, and explain its origins in the intellectual history of modern Western civilization. His interest in the 'pessimistic spirit of the age' attracted him to examine Arnold Toynbee's *A Study of History* (London 1948).[3] He had recently been elected to the

Royal Society of Canada, and chose Toynbee's massive work as the subject of his address at the meeting in June 1949: 'It is a commonplace now that during the past generation or more our Western world has been going through an anti-rationalist, anti-scientific, anti-liberal, anti-democratic reaction.' Toynbee, as a classics scholar in Oxford in the pre-1914 era, was ill-prepared for the shock of the Great War and the postwar depression that spawned Spengler's *The Decline of the West*; in reaction, he looked beyond the secular world into the metaphysical realm for the purpose of history. As a 'metahistorian,' seeking to find 'a supraterrestrial society, a City of God,' Toynbee moralized rather than judged objectively the modern age of Western civilization. More like the St Augustine than the Thucydides of the modern West, Toynbee saw the 'forces of evil' at work in society. The essay showed Underhill at his best. He explained the complexities of Toynbee's works. The talk revealed his skill as a historian too – particularly his ability to get at the essence of a difficult subject and present that thesis in a clear and concise way. Having been a contemporary of Toynbee's at Balliol, he had gone through a similar period of doubt and disillusionment in his own thinking.

The awareness of imminent retirement contributed to Underhill's depression. Initially he had hoped to continue teaching at the University of Toronto on one-year appointments with the Board of Governor's approval, but that was not to be. The year of his official retirement, 1954, coincided with a period of substantial change in the history department. Chester Martin had retired in 1952 and now Ralph Flenley, the department head and only other member of the department who was a contemporary of Underhill, was slated to follow. Underhill gave the farewell address at Flenley's retirement dinner: 'I don't mind admitting that I'm going to be rather lonesome from now on,' he confessed. He recalled the early days when Flenley, Martin, and himself were junior members of the department first established by George Wrong. In his opinion Wrong's single most important contribution to the department was his emphasis on teaching. In a self-revealing and prophetic statement, Underhill noted: 'Now, of course, we all know that the atmosphere of the big complex, modern university is not such as to encourage the serious teacher – in spite of the pious words of university administrators to the contrary. The men who win honors and promotions, the departments who achieve big appropriations and the wide publicity are not those who emphasize teaching. Teaching is a process which can only be vital when intimate and informal personal relationships grow up between individual teachers and individual students; and this requires devotion, concentration, patience on the part of the teacher, and uses up time, temper, nervous energy. For all of which the only credit that accrues to the teacher is that which is stored up in the memories of students.'[4]

  With Flenley's retirement, the search for a new chairman began. Two men were the main contenders: Underhill and Creighton. Underhill allowed his name to stand, even though he could remain in the department only on yearly contracts. The fact that the two men were arch-rivals made the selection task very difficult. It is hard to understand the intricacies and complexities of the dispute and hostility that arose between these two titans in the history department of the University of Toronto in the 1950s. A legacy of stories, myths, innuendoes, and even slanderous statements remains from the dispute to distort and conceal the issue itself. In personality the two men were similar in a number of ways, yet significantly different in others: both were high-strung, easily irritated, prone to quick temper, and apt to get on each other's nerves. They could both be morose at times, although Creighton had a more pronounced reputation for this than Underhill. Both had a dry sense of humour and wit: with Underhill it tended to be light and flippant, at times caustic; with Creighton, it was ponderous and severe, at times vindictive. Each could be strong-willed to the point of being headstrong and unreasonable on a principle or point about which he felt strongly. Two prima donnas who desired recognition both vied for recognition among students and colleagues, each in his own way. With Underhill, it became a sense of loyalty and almost hero worship with some students; with Creighton, it was more of a quiet respect for a man who engendered awe and often fear in students. Creighton resented the comfortable financial position that Underhill had enjoyed as a full professor during the Depression, years in which he worked as a struggling lecturer. He also resented Underhill's tremendous popularity with students, his public recognition, and his influence in the department – all of which Creighton felt were vastly out of proportion to Underhill's scholarly activities.[5] Underhill admired and envied Creighton's success as a scholar and writer of history. Ideologically, they emerged in the postwar period as complete opposites: Underhill, the liberal, an admirer of Mackenzie King, a defender of the United States in the Cold War, and a critic of the British influence in Canadian history; Creighton, the conservative, a vehement critic of King and Liberal politicians in general, staunchly anti-American, and an admirer of the virtues of the British tradition in Canadian history. By the mid-fifties the hostilities between the two men became so great that both found it difficult to be together in the same department. When Creighton got the chairmanship, Underhill felt the slight.[6] If he had remained in the department for long under Creighton's chairmanship, the tension would only have escalated to an unbearable point. Fortunately, in the fall of 1955, Underhill was offered the position of curator of Laurier House in Ottawa.

As a fitting testimony to Underhill's long association with the Department of History, a farewell dinner was held. Creighton had agreed to make the arrangements, but when he failed to follow through, Sydney Hermant, a former student, and Edgar McInnis, a long-time member of the department and then director of the Canadian Institute of International Affairs, took the initiative. Originally scheduled to be a departmental dinner only, Underhill requested a larger dinner of some seventy-five friends and associates. The date chosen was the evening of 30 January and the place the Albany Club, 'a pointed comment on my recent tendencies in the conservative direction,' Underhill remarked.[7] His farewell address, entitled 'Valedictory,' was 'only an excuse to talk about myself.' There were two curious features of his life, he pointed out: he had never received a promotion since he had been hired a full professor in 1914; and he was not a self-made man, since the direction of his life had been a series of accidents as opposed to conscious decisions on his part. Only twice in his life had he made a decision or taken the initiative on his own: in 1915, when the joined the army, and in 1922, when he proposed to his wife. Then he talked about his political activities and his teaching. 'The teaching I enjoyed the most of all,' he admitted, and he compared himself to 'an intellectual wetnurse assisting in the birth of ideas in the minds of students.' The best I can wish the younger generation is that they may have as much fun as I in playing with political ideas,' he concluded. 'A wonderful speech – the best farewell address I have listened to in my forty-three years on the University staff,' commented F.C. Jeanneret, principal of University College.[8]

Underhill had mixed feelings at the time of his retirement. He was sad to be leaving teaching, a career that he had loved. Yet now he could devote his time to writing. He had three major projects in mind: foremost, to complete his Blake biography; to do a history of Canadian liberal thought; and to edit an anthology of his writings. He certainly had few regrets about leaving the city of Toronto. He later compared his reaction to Toronto to that of an earlier rebel, William Lyon Mackenzie – the city brought out the worst in both of them.[9] Most of all, the move to Ottawa was a new beginning.

It was Kaye Lamb, dominion archivist under whose jurisdiction the house-cum-museum came, who was responsible for making the curator's job an honorary writer-in-residence position. When J.E. Hardy, Mackenzie King's house steward, was about to retire as curator of Laurier House in 1954, Lamb suggested to J.W. Pickersgill, minister of citizenship and immigration, that the curatorship be converted into a 'post for a "visiting professor."' Pickersgill agreed and got the necessary legislation through cabinet. There the matter rested until the summer of 1955, when a search for a possible candidate for the position began. Lamb consulted Pearson, secretary of state for external affairs, and the two agreed that Underhill was the best person and that he could use the time to finish his long-awaited study of Edward Blake. Underhill was enthusiastic about the position when Pearson offered it to him unofficially in early August, particularly if it could be a two- or three-year appointment to make it worthwhile to sever his connection with the University of Toronto. Pearson agreed to a three-year appointment at an annual salary of $6600.[10]

Underhill began as curator and honorary writer-in-residence at Laurier House in

October 1955. His administrative duties were light – minor supervision of the commissionaires and responsibility for the Mackenzie King Papers lodged in the house; otherwise Laurier House was a convenient place to work in a modest office on the top floor, once an anteroom to Mackenzie King's study. He was expected to commit himself to his Blake biography, and he did begin to pursue further research and draft out chapters of the manuscript. But much of the time he spent meeting old friends and former students who dropped by to visit him, and carrying on an active life of public speaking, radio broadcasting, and writing newspaper and journal articles. At the age of sixty-seven he had no intention of slowing down; he was enjoying the position of senior scholar, increasingly being called upon to discuss current or past events as a popular after-dinner speaker or a provocative commentator.

One other scholar shared the House with Underhill: MacGregor Dawson, who was writing the first volume of the official biography of Mackenzie King. The two men had tea together on a regular basis, when they shared thoughts, information, and interpretations of the King era.[11] Underhill had no part in Dawson's writing of the volume, but it would be no exaggeration to say that the book reflected a good deal of Underhill's views of the man.

The Laurier House position coincided with a period of illness for Underhill. In the spring of his first year he suffered the first of a series of strokes that would weaken him physically.[12] He was forced to go on a low cholesterol diet. That, along with his bland diet for his ulcer, severely limited what he could eat. His doctor also ordered him to take long periods of rest away from his work. This initiated a period of renewed visits to Muskoka, where he would spend his summer vacation with his family. In a way it was like old times, but much had changed in the interval. Their daughter, Betty, had married Mordern Harfenist, and the couple had three children. Underhill enjoyed the role of grandfather and was devoted to his grandchildren. Not surprisingly, he encouraged them to read by constantly buying them books. Since the Harfenists lived in New York, Ruth and Frank made regular trips south to visit them.[13]

Illness was one reason for the slow progress of his work on Blake; the enigma of the subject was the other reason. During his years at Laurier House Underhill began another intense search for people with potential Blake family information, worked out the Blake family tree, drafted chapters of the manuscript, and wrote those chapters that interested him the most on Blake's ideas.[14] He also gave a paper on Edward Blake at Carleton in the spring of 1956 as part of the series 'Our Living Tradition.' It was a masterful summary of Blake's life, his political ideas, and the historical context of late nineteenth-century Canada in a most informative and entertaining speech, but it added nothing new that he had not already said in his earlier Blake writings. It was evident that the subject still eluded him. And his pessimistic conclusion seemed to prognosticate the outcome of his study: 'Blake spent most of his career in Canada fighting for a liberalism that was a minority cause. He left Canadian public life just when, in purely domestic politics, the liberal tide was beginning to flow ... What an ending to a career which had begun in such hope! What a contrast to those early years of the 1870's when Edward Blake had been, as Goldwin Smith put it, "the child of promise and the morning star" of advanced Canadian liberalism! By the time of his death in 1912 his name was largely forgotten in Canada. He had been a failure. But surely modern Canadian Liberals, in their present years of success, should acknowledge how much they owe to this noble failure.'[15]

When the curatorship of Laurier House terminated on 15 October 1959, having had one additional year of grace to the three-year contract, there was still no biography of Blake, not even close to a completed manuscript. Underhill was saddened to realize how long the project had dragged on, with embarrassing questions from colleagues as to when they might see the book in print.

Underhill's period without a 'job' was brief. By the beginning of 1960 he was hired for one year as a consultant for a history of the National Research Council. Moreover, from the time of his arrival in Ottawa, he had a close association with Carleton College, eventually to become Carleton University. His first contact came in April 1956 when James Gibson, dean of the college, invited him to become a member of Senate, a position he readily accepted. The next year Underhill helped to organize at Carleton an Ottawa chapter of the Canadian Political Science Association, consisting of about two hundred members, mostly civil servants and Carleton faculty, who met three or four times a year for a general meeting and regular study groups.[16] In September 1964 Carleton offered him a part-time appointment as visiting professor of political science, a position he held for three years until ill-health forced him to give it up, at which time the university made him professor emeritus of political science.[17] He taught a course in Canadian political thought, which drew heavily on the writings of American and British political thinkers too. It was a popular course for students, who enjoyed the opportunity to be taught by 'the dean of Canadian history.' Underhill revelled in the intellectual stimulation of discussing and debating politics with students during the formative period in their intellectual maturity. His wife was convinced that his teaching at Carleton 'added years to his life.'[18] In appreciation for all that Carleton gave him, he willed his personal library to the university, where a separate 'Underhill Library' was established under the aegis of the history department.

Underhill enjoyed the years in Ottawa. He liked being in the city that was the pulse of the nation's politics, although he prided himself for never stepping inside the Parliament Buildings during his years in the capital. In the first years in Ottawa they rented an attractive house at 116 Springfield Road in Rockcliffe Park, an exclusive area of the city reserved mainly for Ottawa's mandarins. Then in 1967 they moved to the inner city, where they rented a duplex with all facilities on the main floor (since Frank was not supposed to climb a lot of stairs) in an older house at 266 Maclaren Street. The apartment was small, with little room for his books and file drawers which had to be stored in the basement; his periodical rack, the envy of any small library with room for over fifty periodicals, had to go in the living-room. It took awhile for them to adjust, but they made it feel like home until they were uprooted again in the early 1970s just before Frank's death. Many enjoyable evenings were spent reading a book while listening to classical music in the background. In his later years Underhill acquired a substantial record collection, especially of his favourite composer, Beethoven.

One of the major themes in Underhill's writings in the fifties and sixties was Canadian, American, and British relations. It was a popular topic of the day, and Underhill had little to add to an appreciation of the historical nature of the relationship. His contribution was a conceptual one. He made two key points in his speeches on the subject. First, that the North Atlantic triangular relationship worked best for Canada if it were an isosceles triangle, with the British and the American angles of equal strength. In the British century from 1839 to 1939 that had meant strengthening the American angle; in the American century beginning in 1939 it would mean strengthening the British angle. Since neither Britain or the British commonwealth alone was powerful enough to offset the American influence, Canada could only restore the balance by seeking a larger Western European union. Such a triangular relationship was important in enabling Canada to play a meaningful role in the world. As he later explained: 'We had to make sure that we were included, that is, that the relationship was in the nature of a triangle. Otherwise we should have remained an insignificant dependent colony of Britain or become an insignificant dependent satellite of the United States.' Second, he argued for Canadians to emphasize the positive aspects of American influence if they were to continue to play an important role in this triangular relationship. They could begin by ceasing to think of American cultural penetration as 'alien,' an insidious form of American imperialism, and begin to see it as simply a twentieth-century phenomenon. 'The United States has gone further into the twentieth century than the rest of us – that is all,' he pointed out to the Ontario Liberal Association at their 1957 spring meeting. 'But we are all drifting towards this homogenized culture, this uniform conformist society. Canada has gone furthest next to the u.s. because we live next door to the Americans.' Rather than lament this inevitable integration, why not take advantage of it, he argued, to create in Canada 'a better American way of life than the Americans have. A better *American* way of life, not just a better way of life.'[19]

Closely related to the topic of Canadian-American relations was the broader and equally pressing subject of Canadian identity. Inevitably, the issue of identity hinged on the question of what features distinguished Canada from the United

States. While most analysts emphasized Canada's British nature, northern location, and distinctive historical evolution, Underhill dismissed these obvious differences as anachronistic symbols of Canadian nationalism in the twentieth century. The Canadian identity in the twentieth century had to be its North American nature. Nationalism and continentalism were compatible 'isms,' or, more specifically, Canada should become more American in its identity. This viewpoint inevitably brought him into conflict with his fellow historians. The occasion for one confrontation was a review of W.L. Morton's *The Canadian Identity* in the *Globe and Mail*. He compared Morton, in his vehement denunciation of everything American, to Cardinal Newman, in his distaste for everything modern. 'Just as Newman in Oxford in the 1840s, confronting with horror the monster of Liberalism, set himself with his companions in the Oxford Movement to save his society from the modernism of the nineteenth century, so Morton in Winnipeg is launching a Manitoba Movement to save his society from the Americanism (i.e., the modernism) of the twentieth century.'[20] Yet, Underhill noted, the America that Morton was trying to save us from was already a part of the Canadian psyche and the Canadian way of life.

At times Underhill felt that the Canadian obsession with American dominance was detracting Canadians from appreciating one of the unique features of their identity: its bilingual and bicultural nature. He claimed in his speech on 'The Future of Canadian Thought' to the Prairie Conference on National Problems in Saskatoon on 11 September 1964 that amicable English- and French-Canadian relations in one federal union had been the uppermost concern of the Fathers of Confederation. One hundred years later this wish was still unfulfilled. He urged each side to understand and appreciate the other position. English Canadians could begin by reading the Tremblay Report of 1956, *Le Devoir*, recent works by the French-Canadian historian Michel Brunet, and the speeches of the leading nationalist intellectuals in contemporary Quebec. Ironically, in the process of outlining the demands of the French Canadians as set forth in these recent writings, Underhill revealed his own lack of appreciation, or at least lack of empathy, for the French-Canadian position. 'I think it is time,' he informed his audience, 'that some English Canadian intellectuals told their French opposite numbers that these proposals of theirs are intolerable to us, as they now have been telling us that the existing Confederation which we have found reasonably comfortable, is intolerable to them.'[21] There were shades of his long-departed hero George Brown and of his rural Ontario upbringing in the speech. As Arthur Lower once remarked: 'George Brown and *The Globe* and Upper Canada – Ontario – have never since been far away from him.'[22] Underhill's liberalism was magnanimous with regards to the rights and freedom of the individual; it was, like that of many English-Canadian liberals of his era, less than magnanimous with regards to minority rights in a majoritarian democracy.

The closest Underhill came to setting down in a coherent and sustained way his thoughts on Canadian history as they related to the issue of the Canadian identity was in his six half-hour radio lectures on CBC in the fall of 1963 entitled 'The Image of Confederation.' The opportunity to give the lectures came in January of that year when Bernard Trotter of CBC Public Affairs invited Underhill to give that year's Massey Lectures, an annual series begun in 1961 in honour of Vincent Massey, former governor-general of Canada. Realizing the magnitude of the undertaking, Underhill feared that he had insufficient time and nothing new to say to meet the challenge; but it was too good an invitation to turn down. Already by the end of January his creative mind was at work, sketching out in general terms what he would eventually do: a capsule intellectual history of Canada since Confederation through an analysis of the 'image of Confederation' in the minds of its leading intellectuals. He had even decided chapter divisions.[23] He knew what he wanted to say from his various public lectures on the subject; he had only to pull the material together, make it coherent, and add a new twist in the presentation.

The lectures were a concise, cogent, and brilliant synthesis of the ideas of Canada's political thinkers – at least Canadian liberal thinkers. Beginning with the Fathers of Confederation, he showed how a liberal-democratic concept of nationalism as evidenced in the Confederation Debates and the romantic political writings of the Canada First movement lost out to an aggressive, racist, Bismarckian-type of nationalism in the late nineteenth century. These two forms of nationalism vied for dominance in the debate between the Canadian imperialists and Goldwin Smith, between Wilfrid Laurier and Henri Bourassa, and in the present between English-Canadian and French-Canadian nationalists. These brief but amazingly comprehensive lectures encapsulated Underhill's ideas on a number of subjects that interested him in Canadian history: the role of ideas in Canadian development; the success of the biracial party for Canadian unity; the modus vivendi of French- and English-Canadian relations; the various forms of Canadian nationalism, from imperialism and continentalism to independence, and their influence on the evolution of Canadian history; the influence of power politics in deciding Canada's role in world events such as the Boer War and the two world wars; the shift from the British to the American century of dependence after World War II; Canada's place in the North Atlantic triangle; the role of big business in political party make-up; the need for a modern intellectual nationalist movement, 'more sophisticated and more effective than the Canada First Movement of the 1870s'; and the search for a modern national purpose that would be 'a moral equivalent of the CPR.' In characteristic fashion, none of these varied themes was developed at length; they remain only as a reminder of his unique imprint on the writing of Canadian history.

The lectures were an immediate success. Letters of congratulation and praise came to Underhill from attentive listeners; when the book was published by the

CBC it sold over 6000 copies in two years, a remarkably high figure for that type of book.[24]

'Conservatism, Liberalism, Socialism – What Do They Mean in Canada?' was the tile of a lengthy address Underhill gave to inaugurate a lecture series at the University of Western Ontario in the fall of 1962;[25] it also aptly summed up a second major theme in Underhill's writings in the fifties and sixties: the meaning of these 'isms' as ideologies and as party philosophies in Canada. It was a theme that had always interested him, and one on which he held a consistent outlook despite appearances to the contrary. The consistency came in his search for the fundamental democratic roots of liberalism as embodied in a faith in individual freedom, social justice, and human potential for good. At times Underhill seriously questioned and doubted these beliefs, only to return to them with deeper conviction of their essential soundness as philosophical principles of life. Both conservatism and socialism had been tried and found wanting; only liberalism was able to withstand the test of time and crises in his estimation. This was the conclusion that he had come to in the early years of his life, and it was the same conclusion that he came to in the final years when once again he re-evaluated the strengths and weaknesses of liberalism.

The fundamental distinction between a liberal and a conservative was a different perception of human nature. 'A liberal has a faith in human nature. That may be a very naive faith and as time goes on he may become more skeptical about that faith of his, but still it remains. The conservative has a doubt about human virtues. A conservative believes in Original Sin; the liberal doesn't.'[26] He admitted that liberals were on the defensive in the mid-twentieth century. Everything conspired against such a faith from the devastating destruction of two world wars, to scientific evidence of man's irrational nature, to modern man's willingness to be controlled by totalitarian forces be they political, social, or cultural, the latter in the form of mass media. Underhill aptly summarized the weaknesses of liberalism in his Dunning Trust lecture at Queen's in January 1955:

Liberalism is in essence a Utopian faith with a confidence in the possibilities of human nature. But our modern psychologists have uncovered deep subconscious instinctive drives in us which pervert our reason; our theologians have achieved a renaissance of Original Sin; and we have had to witness in the last generation outbursts of the demonic element in human nature whose existence we had forgotten. We have learnt to our cost the terrible potentialities of man's inhumanity to man. We have had borne in upon us how fragile is our civilization. Our life seems to be one continuous process of preparing for, fighting or recovering from war. Religious thinkers, moreover, tell us that this sickness of our civilization is directly due to its liberalism, to western man's belief that he could solve his problems by reliance upon himself alone without having recourse to supernatural help.[27]

The modern liberal had to admit to these inherent weaknesses of his ideology; he had to be a 'pessimistic liberal.'

Yet Underhill always returned to a faith in that liberalism that he questioned. Although he plumbed the depths of despair, he always surfaced with a renewed faith in the essential goodness and potential of man that he claimed underlay liberalism. In his Dunning Trust lecture, for example, he concluded optimistically that the Western World was on the eve of a new liberal era which only required an intellectual leadership to bring it to fruition. He appealed to Queen's students to provide that leadership. In his Royal Society of Canada presidential address on 'The Revival of Conservatism in North America,' he ended on his familiar optimistic note: 'In spite of the brave new conservative world that I see coming, I still keep up some hopes. Just when everybody has been successfully adjusted socially, some innocent young savage will find his way one day into the stacks of some university library. And he will accidentally come across the writings of John Stuart Mill or Bertrand Russell or Uncle Charlie Beard or of some younger rebel like C. Wright Mills. At that moment a liberal political movement will start all over again.'[28]

While emphasizing the differences between liberal and conservative ideologies, Underhill stressed the similarities of socialism and liberalism, so long as socialism was within the British liberal-democratic tradition. Socialists, he argued, adhered to the same fundamental beliefs and wanted ultimately the same objectives as liberals; they differed only in the means to achieve those objectives. Even here the gap was closing as society was moving towards a system which was a mixture of public and private enterprise. Underhill therefore supported the CCF's decision in 1956 to abandon its extreme program of the Regina Manifesto to adopt the more moderate Winnipeg Declaration of Principles. 'No one would dream of claiming that Liberals and Conservatives must remain monolithic unalterable entities frozen in the form given to them by Gladstone and Disraeli ... Why not, then, admit that Socialists also can modify their views in the course of time without betraying their principles or deserting their traditions?'[29] Such a view was justification for Underhill's insistence of keeping a foot in both the Liberal and CCF camps. The ideal political system in Canada lay somewhere between these two political movements. Just where, though, he was not sure. The 'New Frontier' had still to be discovered.

The quest for the meaning of liberalism was the main theme in his collected essays, *In Search of Canadian Liberalism*. The book had been five years in the making because of Underhill's difficulty in deciding what to include or, more precisely, what to exclude. He finished the introduction on 26 November 1959, his seventieth birthday. That was the date he requested at the end of it, but further delays necessitated the later date of July 1960.[30] The introduction gave a capsule view of his intellectual journey, an explanation of his shifts in thought, and his own critique of the volume – as penetrating as any review.

The book was a fine tribute to Underhill. The essays ranged from his earliest publication in 1927 to his recent Queen's convocation address in the spring of 1959. No attempt was made to edit out of the articles controversial sections or to exclude essays from the volume that reflected a viewpoint to which he no longer adhered. In fact, he included an essay on isolationism precisely because he had written so much on the subject in the 1930s, even though he now disagreed completely with his earlier position. One weakness of the book was the lack of adequate representation of his sprightly, witty, and iconoclastic *Forum* writings of the 1930s, simply because they were outdated in their reference to specific events or people. The result was a book that reflected the moderate, sober, and urbane Underhill more than the rebel. It was easy to forget when reading the articles that Underhill had been an active participant in the CCF and a founding father of the LSR. He had wanted to include his original draft of the Regina Manifesto but was unable to locate a copy. Another weakness was in the organization in three parts without a concern for chronology. Such an approach made it difficult for the reader to appreciate the evolution of his thoughts in his search for Canadian liberalism. Finally, the deliberate exclusion of his Blake articles, in anticipation of the biography, is regrettable in light of his failure to complete the project.

Still, his sprightly style and his critical and penetrating mind were evident throughout the book. As one reviewer noted: 'The book contains some very good invective, worth preserving. It will also reward former students of Mr. Underhill in search of vintage Underhillisms.' Underhill received his own reward for the book as the recipient of the Governor General's Award for non-fiction which included a cash prize of $1000. Norman Smith commented on the Canada Council's wisdom in making the award: 'If a country can have enough wit and wisdom to grant so august an honour as the Governor General's Award for Literature to a quiver full of arrows such as these, then there must surely be hope for us [Canadians].'[31]

Underhill dedicated *In Search of Canadian Liberalism* to 'Mike Pearson.' Some people attributed the move to political ambitions, particularly to get himself a senatorship. When the rumour to that effect circulated a year or so later, Underhill wrote Pearson to assure him that he was not interested: 'I don't think I would make a very good Senator.'[32] The dedication reflected Underhill's moderate political stance and revealed his enthusiasm at that time for Pearson's potential in turning the Liberal party to the liberalism for which Underhill had been searching.

His faith in Pearson's potential was evident in a letter of congratulation he had written to his friend upon assuming the leadership of the party in January 1958. 'You are the only person I can see who is likely to be able to turn the Liberal party in a liberal direction which is what I hope you intend to do ... by setting up some sort of a brain trust from university men to advise you and by making a point of calling informally at university faculty clubs and lunching with selected members. Also you should start some conferences for the younger people, as Vincent Massey did years ago at Port Hope. And you might plan eventually for a Liberal Yellow Book on the English model.' The Liberals needed to be on the left, constantly trying to win support from the CCF, he pointed out. Then in a typical jocular fashion, Underhill claimed the Liberals could begin by trying to win him over to the party; in a postscript he reminded Pearson that 'at the next election, I shall be voting CCF.' Pearson thanked him for his advice but told him 'to stop making such silly statements about voting for the C.C.F. in the next election.'[33]

His faith in Pearson's ability did not, however, check his usual critical nature. In the fall of 1960 Underhill was one of 150 selected participants for 'The Study Conference on National Problems' at Queen's University. Strictly speaking, the conference was not a Liberal party affair but rather a policy seminar to discuss the direction that liberalism (the ideology) and the Liberal party should take – preferably together. Some Liberals boasted of Underhill's presence on the program as evidence of 'the prodigal son' returned. If so, he was a more rebellious man than the youth who had left the Liberal household some thirty years earlier. As Pearson noted in his *Memoirs*: Underhill's presence was the best assurance that the conference was autonomous from the party and that 'the virtue of the Liberal Party would not be exaggerated.' Underhill warned Mitchell Sharp, the conference organizer, that he was 'almost certain to say something that will not be approved by official Liberals.'[34] His banquet address was a free-wheeling attack on the weaknesses of Canadian liberalism and the Liberal party. 'I don't know anything about defence, export and import trade, monetary and fiscal policy, collective bargaining, wheat, social security, state medicine, urban rehabilitation or all the other technical questions with which this conference has been concerning itself,' he pointed out by way of introduction. 'My specialty is general invective.' He proceeded to complain about everything regarding the conference, from the topics discussed to the ones that were not discussed and should have been. He concluded with a classic analogy of himself to another free spirit: 'I feel like Huckleberry Finn. I've no home to go to. And, like Huck, I reckon I got to light out for the territory. For the past twenty-five years or so I been floating down the political Mississippi on the CCF raft. And now, this week, my Aunt Sally Sharp, she's caught up to me, and she's wanting to adopt me in a good Liberal home, and civilize me, and I can't stand it. I been there before.'[35]

14

The Apotheosis of the Critic

As Underhill gradually became more fully retired, his role as intellectual critic came to be fully appreciated and recognized as something useful in itself – an ongoing process. Indeed, one of the themes which dominated his own writings in the sixties was the role of the university in Canada and, more broadly, the function of the intellectual in Canadian political life. In the twenties and thirties he had appealed to academics to get involved in political controversy. Their failure to do so, he believed, was the reason for the ineffectiveness of political reform movements in Canada compared to Britain and the United States. By the fifties and sixties he could talk optimistically about the involvement of academics in the political sphere. In a review of *Social Purpose for Canada*, a book published by the University League for Social Reform (a 1960s equivalent of the LSR), Underhill noted: 'By this time the right of university professors to take part in controversial politics, and the propriety of their doing so, seem no longer to be questioned in public. Since the 1930's, in fact, professors in the social sciences and humanities have been growing more and more vocal in public affairs. They write controversial books and articles and letters to the newspapers, they deliver controversial speeches. They serve on royal commissions and they advise governments. They work on party committees and they attend party conventions ... All this means that we have come a long way since the 1930's in achieving in our politics some more direct communication between the university community and the mass democracy outside. Both our Canadian universities and our Canadian political parties are becoming more mature.'[1] Universities and society at large had become more tolerant of academic dissent, and he believed that he had contributed to that growing tolerance by his involvement in the political controversies of the thirties and his threatened dismissal in 1940–1.

But inevitably he had new concerns to express. He feared that these politicized professors and students were not elevating the quality of Canadian political life.

Too many of the intellectual elite were getting involved only in the 'parochial aspects' of party politics or in winning positions of political power for themselves. 'Parties need intellectuals to do fundamental thinking for them, but intellectuals cannot do fruitful thinking if they are preoccupied with winning power for themselves within the party,' he warned in a review of Walter Young's *The Anatomy of a Party: The National CCF* (Toronto 1969).[2]

He had in mind an elevated role for the intellectual elite in Canada. 'The mark of the intellectual is that he is in search of truth rather than of power,'[3] Underhill cautioned. He should be interested in raising the quality of political life by going beyond party politics to devise party philosophies and ideologies. In political terms, this meant moving the party to that ideal medium between party and movement; parties needed to achieve concrete political changes without losing their principles and respectability. The models he had in mind were, as always, the British Fabian Society and its alliance with the British Labour party and the association of intellectuals with the American Democratic party, first under F.D. Roosevelt and later under John F. Kennedy.

Why did such political elites exist in Britain and the United States and not in Canada? Earlier he had explained the Canadian weakness as a lack of an effective intellectual radical political tradition. Even into the fifties and sixties he would frequently use that argument. Now he was more apt to blame the universities. They were failing to produce 'young men and women with disciplined, critical inquisitive minds ... who are accustomed to objective, rational methods of enquiry, who have acquired the Socratic faith that the unexamined life is not worth living.'[4] This pessimistic conclusion was more challenging than sad. For Underhill's whole life had been a crusade to raise the level of political consciousness among the Canadian university students and to elevate political debate among politicians and the general public. It was not in his nature to be satisfied. He could, however, look back proudly on a job well done; he had played the role of the intellectual critic effectively, and he had enjoyed all but its most unpleasant scenes.

Underhill had lived a full and active life. And he was, in the twilight years of his life, receiving his share of recognition and honours. (He preferred to see such honours as evidence only of his respectability and therefore ineffectiveness as a critic.) He received honorary degrees from six universities – Queen's, Carleton, Toronto, Saskatchewan, Manitoba, and York – and became professor emeritus of political science at Carleton and professor emeritus of history at Toronto. He was also awarded the coveted Tyrrell Medal at the Royal Society meeting in 1967 for his outstanding contribution to history. J.M.S. Careless read the citation which proclaimed Underhill's right to the award on the basis less that he has written history in Canada than that he has taught it; less that he has added to its wealth of detail than that he has penetrated its whole meaning; less that he has filled up pages of print – though he has filled many – than that he has fostered ideas, and people with ideas, to stir the flaccid mind of Canada ...

Above all, however, Frank Underhill deserves citation for the Tyrrell Medal because his work has been in the best sense inspirational. By his habit of mind, his intense commitment, and his intellectual energy, he has inspired history and historians in Canada – scholars, public men, citizens, in varied activities of life. He might be called, with incomplete truth, a latter-day Goldwin Smith or a Canadian Bernard Shaw – but the fact that so many Canadians of so many opinions, in so many fields, would recognize him fully and warmly as 'F.H.U.' is all the claim that he needs to merit this acknowledgement today.[5]

That same year he received a Canada Council medal and in the following year a Medal of Service in recognition of his outstanding contribution to his native country.

His speeches and discussions in his last years were usually retrospective and were welcomed without qualification. At his last appearance at the Canadian Historical Association in the spring of 1970, which was held in Winnipeg, he appeared in a session with Arthur Lower on 'The West in Retrospect.' His speech was superb: warm, personal, anecdotal, sincere, and witty. He began, tongue in cheek, by claiming no right to be on a program intended to honour the centennial celebration of the founding of the province of Manitoba; he had never studied or written about the province's history. He chose instead to talk about a subject that he did feel comfortable discussing: his personal recollections of living in the West. He recalled his early memories of J.W. Dafoe and J.S. Woodsworth, his years as a professor at the University of Saskatchewan, and his political education through his involvement in the Progressive movement and later in the CCF. Yet today, he pointed out, this same dynamic West was in political disrepute. The legacy of these earlier populist movements was Diefenbakerism. What had gone wrong? He confessed to his audience that he was no longer certain about anything. Then with a gleam in his eye, he ended his speech with his characteristic ray of hope: 'As for me, while I've wobbled somewhat in my political affiliation in Canadian politics over the last generation, I shall be voting again for Mr. Trudeau. In American politics I have never wobbled; ever since 1936 I have been voting the straight Democratic ticket, and I expect to continue doing so. I am an old man now, but in our Canadian national politics I rather wish I could hang on long enough to be able to vote for Ed Schreyer.' A year later, the CHA executive made him an Honorary Life Member of the association.[6]

Another form of academic recognition was a Festschrift to be published in his honour. It was, however, somewhat disappointing. Though the editor, Norman Penlington, had been one of Underhill's students, too few of the contributors were. Furthermore, the book was badly delayed and, apart from the Underhill bibliography and an essay on Underhill's *Forum* writings of the thirties, the contributions were not well received.[7]

Underhill was also sought out for interviews. On his seventy-ninth birthday he was interviewed by Douglas Collins on CBC television. Collins dwelt mainly on Underhill's shifts in political support and his altered views over time, thus forcing him to explain and justify the apparent contradictions. He admitted to these changes and confessed to being wrong on a number of issues, but underlying the shifts was a consistent search for 'the good life,' the ideal liberal society. He revealed the pleasure he had in the search, and regretted no part of it. The interview seemed to be a prelude to the big celebration for his eightieth birthday. On the eve of that birthday, the CBC did an hour-long tribute. Various friends, colleagues, and public figures – Walter Stewart, Morley Callaghan, Eugene Forsey, Douglas Fisher, W.L. Morton, Frank Scott, M.J. Coldwell, and William Kilbourn – talked about the significant contribution that Underhill had made to Canadian life. They recalled Underhill the recalcitrant spirit, the man of wit and bombast, the iconoclast, the court jester, the gadfly, and the indomitable individualist.[8]

The next day was his birthday party. The organizers had given Underhill free rein as to whom he wanted to invite and the list had steadily grown to the point where the 125 guests could not be accommodated at Carleton and the party was moved to the Rideau Club. Underhill had laboured hard over his speech. In the weeks leading up to the celebration he sat quietly in his armchair reflecting on what he wanted to say and the people he wanted to acknowledge, collected bits of information from various articles which contained appropriate quotations or relevant material on his life history, jotted down on scraps of paper ideas that came to him, and wrote out at least two drafts of the speech.

The party was a wonderful success. Everyone appeared relaxed, and Underhill had an opportunity to talk with most of the guests present. The four introductory speakers were witty and their remarks penetrating. Underhill was in fine form. His speech was very long, to the point where Ruth worried that the audience would tire of listening, but no one else took notice of the length; they were too absorbed in listening to his light-hearted journey through his past.[9] 'Sometimes the melody of an evening does not just linger on but dances and dances through the mind with persistent gaiety and spice. The complimentary dinner given Frank Underhill last week on his 80th birthday was such a time.' That was Norman Smith's impression of the evening as reported in the Ottawa *Journal*. Peter C. Newman described the celebration as 'a moving and a very Canadian occasion, with 100 or so of his friends gathered to pay tribute to the most influential thinker this country has so far produced.' Christopher Young compared Underhill's speech to 'a wise man's journey ... without the slightest trace of vanity or self-esteem.'[10]

In the last two years of his life, Underhill was still active. In addition to his appearance at the CHA he spent a weekend at York University with colleagues and students on the occasion of receiving an honorary degree. But he was increasingly unwell, feeling exhausted by the slghtest exertion and needing long periods of rest.[11] The fatal stroke came on a Monday. He was rushed to the hospital and remained in intensive care until Thursday morning, when he died peacefully; it was 16 September 1971.[12]

His life ended as it had been lived: with Underhill ready to embark on new adventures. He and Ruth had just moved in late summer into a new high-rise apartment. They would have celebrated their fiftieth anniversary that year. It had been difficult to uproot themselves so late in life and adjust to a new place. Yet the move was symbolic of Underhill: he was always uprooting himself, intellectually at least, and embarking on new adventures. He still had his books to give him comfort and joy. Only a few days before the stroke he had arranged his 'favourite' books, those that had 'made [his] mind' and those written by his students, on a special shelf close to his armchair where he enjoyed reading. He had made a new list of books to order and journals to subscribe to or renew. He was ready to begin again.

The simple, unassuming, almost plain service was, as he had requested, at a nearby funeral home. There were no flowers and, since he was cremated, no burial afterwards. A eulogy was given by LSR associate Joe Parkinson, and the Reverend King Gordon conducted the service. Gordon reminded the mourners that in the sorrow of the moment could be found a joy: those present were fortunate to have known, and to have been touched by, this man. He quoted from an editorial tribute that, he said, Underhill would have agreed with: 'Let there be no wry charity in what is said of Frank Underhill. This was a man who never tried to wrap up his meaning, who despised insincerity, a dissenter by temperament, his conformity only to intellectual honesty.'[13]

There were numerous personal letters of condolence and tribute. The *Toronto Star* described him as 'one of Canada's most prominent historians and political theorists ... a man of massive intellect.' Lester Pearson would remember Underhill as 'an old and dear friend ... who cut through sham and prejudice to seek the truth and serve the general good.' The *Winnipeg Free Press* recalled his excellent qualities as a teacher: 'stimulating, provoking, making fun but at the same time opening innumerable windows for the students who crowded his classes.' Two of those students wrote tributes to their favourite teacher. Blair Neatby, in an obituary in the *Canadian Historical Review*, wrote: 'His success as a teacher can be explained in part by his respect for those who shared his interest in political analysis. He responded to a trite comment, not by challenging but by developing it and giving the impression that the comment had initiated his own observations and insights. He could be a sharp and incisive critic, but he was always gentle in conversation ... For many of his students and colleagues, however, the most vivid memories will be of evenings at the Underhills, of the hospitality at Walmer Road and elsewhere, and of the cosmopolitan circle of friends which Frank and Ruth Underhill attracted.' Douglas Fisher ended his column on 'The Legacy of Frank Underhill' with the comment: 'His impact on politics is over except as it lives as example in the memory of those who were taught by him and who pass it on.'[14]

One final tribute was a poem by George Johnston in a commemorative issue of the *Canadian Forum*:[15]

F.H. Underhill, 1889–1971

Who knows
by what right one is happy
    speaks wise,
honest and sharp-tongued to
    his world,
unhopeful that it may come
    unsnarled.

We saw
you small upon a platform
    yet so
that every corner quickened
    with what
your eye laid open and
    your wit,

    now gone;
our comfort, to remember
    a man
stubbornly the same, stubbornly
    himself

    and our
Frank, who marked, for all his
    candour
easier than we deserve. As
    we know
the last mark will be harder.
    Adieu.

Frank Underhill was a man of contrasts. In his private life he was a quiet, shy, almost retiring individual. He was a committed husband, devoted father and grandfather, and a sincere friend. He considered friendships to be of great importance, and he treasured them for a lifetime. In the words of one of his friends, he was 'a nice and kind man.' In the university classroom, he enjoyed teaching students and was genuinely interested in their intellectual growth. Students found him to be a friend as much as an instructor, willing to step down from his pedestal to be concerned about them as individuals. Yet his public image was that of an *enfant terrible*. He projected in his writings an image of himself as an outspoken, critical, and fiery person. A number of people have commented on how surprised they were to meet this mild-mannered man after reading his sharp and critical essays in the *Canadian Forum*. The contrast stemmed from his deep conviction that his mission in life was to act as an intellectual provocateur, constantly forcing Canadians to think – often against their will and in ways that they resisted – about ideas and issues that he believed should concern them.

The role was not always rewarding. He failed to write a magnum opus or even to produce a single definitive study of any major theme or topic in Canadian history. He is not remembered as a champion of any particular cause, or the exponent or defender of a political theory or ideology. He never received the accolades usually bestowed on a party man. And he never felt at home in any particular social or intellectual environment. Still he did what he enjoyed doing. He liked the role of the polemicist, the intellectual gadfly. He revelled in the joy of making those in authority uncomfortable, constantly needling them to justify their position or defend their point of view. His critical nature made him a popular and well-respected teacher. He challenged students to think critically about their beliefs and those of society at large to an extent that few teachers have succeeded in doing. Equally, more than any other Canadian intellectual of his generation, he provided the political ideas that stimulated the thinking of the Canadian intellectual elite of his time. He had that edge of perception and that breadth of knowledge that enabled him to look at issues with fresh insight and with a different perspective, and he had the ability to present his ideas clearly and cogently to others. His writings – sprightly in style and iconoclastic in thrust – unlocked the stereotypes of perception and liberated the thinking of a generation of Canadians.

There were evident results too. As a historian he made his contributions to the profession. They were not in the form of an outstanding work or an earth-shattering new interpretation of Canadian history, but he knew the right critical questions to ask of the past and in so doing greatly advanced the study of Canadian history. He had an intuitive sense of where Canadian history was going or should be going, and he helped to guide the writing of that history for his and subsequent generations. He was a major figure in the reassessment of the Canadian 'Whig' school of history with its emphasis on constitutional history at a time when few historians seemed capable of or interested in diverging from the standard approach. He could be rightly considered Canada's first intellectual historian, presenting the themes that would preoccupy those who pursued the subject in depth. He formulated the brokerage theory of Canadian political parties as puppets of powerful interest groups – an interpretation which has yet to be superseded. Finally, as an inspiring teacher, he animated his 'dull as ditchwater' subject for his students as few professors could and thus inspired a generation of younger historians to write the books that he was unable to do.

In his writings on contemporary subjects, he had an equally impressive record. For one thing, he presented a perspective on controversial subjects which, although not always correct, was a healthy alternative to the prevailing viewpoint at a time when Canadian attitudes were intolerant and entrenched. In a period when most professors were unwilling to speak out for 'lost causes,' he took a stand on what he believed to be right to the point of almost losing his academic position; in so doing, he played an important part in advancing the right of academics to participate in political controversy. In more specific terms, he assisted in the intellectual birth of the CCF party and helped to keep alive and in good health one of the few quality critical journals in Canada, the *Canadian Forum*, through the difficult years of the 1930s. From a wider perspective, he was a 'clearing-house' of ideas from Britain and the United States. In presenting these ideas within the Canadian context, he elevated and enriched the debate of Canadian issues and thus helped to move Canada intellectually into the twentieth century.

His writings have also greatly advanced our understanding of the nature of Canadian liberalism. Too often Underhill's writings have been judged only in terms of their critical nature. Yet the numerous essays and articles together add up to the most extensive and penetrating analysis of Canadian liberal thought available. It is regrettable that Underhill failed to pull his divergent ideas together to write a full-length and comprehensive study of Canadian liberalism. But rather than dwell on the negative, it would be more rewarding to celebrate the tremendous understanding that he gave Canadians of the nature and evolution of liberalism. A biography of Frank Underhill is at the same time an intellectual study of Canadian liberalism, for his thinking over time embodied the evolution and essence of that liberalism.

The irony is that Underhill, who never produced a major work of history, offered no new pedagogy, never stuck to a particular ideology, and shifted in his viewpoint while remaining highly principled about the position he advocated, did, nevertheless, acquire a position of importance and distinction that he undoubtedly would not have achieved as a traditional scholarly academic. 'The only way I know how to make myself useful is to be constantly critical,' he once told J.S. Woodsworth. He succeeded in being 'useful' through his qualities as a critic and provocateur and made an important contribution to Canadian intellectual life.

Bibliographical Note

The major source of information on F.H. Underhill is the extensive Underhill Papers in the Public Archives of Canada. There is an almost exhaustive bibliography of Underhill's writings in the festschrift *On Canada: Essays in Honour of Frank H. Underhill* (Toronto 1971), 131–92. I have been able to add a few items to this list, and, if they are of importance, they appear in the notes. Other primary and secondary sources used are indicated in the notes. For convenience, I have listed at the end of this chapter the manuscript collections consulted and people with whom I have been in contact concerning Underhill.

Information on Underhill's life up to 1927 (chapters 1–6) is based on his own autobiographical recollections (unless otherwise indicated) from two sources. One source is two extensive interviews conducted by W.D. Meikle and entitled 'F.H. Underhill Interviews,' 1967 and 1968. The originals of these interviews are in volume 95 of the Underhill Papers. The second source is rough notes of Underhill's 'Eightieth Birthday Speech' given 26 November 1969 and located in volume 26, Speech file Nov. 26, 1969.

MANUSCRIPT SOURCES

Public Archives of Canada
A.L. Burt Papers
Co-operative Commonwealth Federation
 Papers
D.G. Creighton Papers
J.W. Dafoe Papers
Eugene Forsey Papers
R.B. Hanson Papers
W.L. Mackenzie King Papers
W. Kaye Lamb Papers
Grace MacInnis Papers
Arthur Meighen Papers
George Parkin Papers

L.B. Pearson Papers
N. Penlington Papers
Norma Robertson Papers
C.B. Sissons Papers
Graham Spry Papers
Frank H. Underhill Papers
J.S. Woodsworth Papers

Public Archives of Ontario
Attorney General's Records
H.J. Cody Papers
G. Howard Ferguson Papers
Mitchell Hepburn Papers

Canadian Broadcasting Corporation
  Archives
Public addresses, Couchiching Conference speeches, and CBC interviews on
  tape

Dalhousie University Archives
Carleton Stanley Papers

McMaster University Archives
CCF (Ontario Section) Papers
Woodsworth Memorial Foundation Papers
  as deposited by Edith Fowke

Metropolitan Toronto Public Library
Papers of the Deeks versus Wells Case

Queen's University Archives
Co-operative Commonwealth Federation
  Papers (Ontario Section)
George Grube Papers
Norman Lambert Papers
A.R.M. Lower Papers
C.G. Power Papers

University of British Columbia Archives
Angus Family Collection
Norman Mackenzie Papers
Alan Plaunt Papers

University of Saskatchewan Archives
George Britnell Papers
A.S. Morton Papers
W.C. Murray Presidential Papers

University of Toronto Archives
Board of Governors Records
George Brown Papers
Harry M. Cassidy Papers
H.J. Cody Presidential Papers
Department of History Records
R.A. Falconer Presidential Papers

H.A. Innis Papers
J.S. Woodsworth Memorial Collection in-
  cluding the LSR Papers deposited by
  W.J. McCurdy
G.M. Wrong Papers

York University
Edgar MacInnis Papers

Private Collections
J. King Gordon Papers
Escott Reid Papers
Frank Scott Papers
Sisman of Canada Limited Records

London Royal Commonwealth Society
Sir Charles A. Lucas Papers

London Public Record Office
1st Battalion, Hertfordshire Regiment
  War Diary

Oxford University Bodleian Library
Lionel Curtis Papers
MSS English History
Oxford University Gazette
Oxford Fabian Society Records
Reports of Examiners of Modern History

Oxford University Balliol College
College Records

Oxford University Rhodes House
Ralegh Club Papers
Round Table Papers (Coupland)

Hertfordshire County Records Office
B.J. Gripper Papers

Massachusetts Williams College Library
W.W. McLaren Papers re Williamstown
  Institute of Politics

INTERVIEWS, CONVERSATIONS, AND CORRESPONDENCE

Henry Angus, 21 August 1978
Carl Berger, 3 January 1972
Claude Bissell, 8 June 1982
Andrew Brewin, 11 May 1978
Leonard and Ivy Bowman, 6 March 1982

J.M.S. Careless, 6 June 1978
M.J. Coldwell, 30 November 1972
Gerald Craig, 7 June 1978
Donald Creighton, 8 June 1978
R.E.G. Davis, 11 October 1980

Sydney Eisen, 13 October 1982
Barker Fairley, 16 November 1972
Douglas Fisher, 30 May 1978
Eugene Forsey, 1 December 1972,
    16 May 1978
Edith Fowke, 24 January 1973
King Gordon, 9 February 1972, 31 May
    1978
Roger Graham, 7 February 1972
George Grube, 28 January 1972
Elizabeth Harfenist, 6 June 1978,
    10 June 1980, 17 May 1983
Eric Havelock, 11 April 1973
H.L. Keenleyside, 28 September 1979
William Kilbourn, 18 January 1972
Kaye Lamb, 11 February 1972
David Lewis, 17 January 1975
A.R.M. Lower, 11 February 1972
Grace MacInnis, 28 November 1972
C.J. Mackenzie, 14 February 1972

Kenneth McNaught, 4 January 1972
W.L. Morton, 27 November 1980
Jean Murray, 24 August 1979
H. Blair Neatby, 30 May 1978
Hilda Neatby, 7 February 1972
Joseph Parkinson, 10 February 1972
W.W. Piepenburg, 21 January 1972
Escott Reid, 15 February 1972
Richard Saunders, 7 June 1978
Frank Scott, 17 February 1972, 15 June
    1978
Graham Spry, 10 February 1972,
    23 May 1978
Irene Spry, 18 March 1972
George Tatham, 21 January 1972
Frank Underhill, 27 October 1970
Ruth Underhill, 10 February 1972, 23
    August 1972, 15 November 1972
Elizabeth Wallace, 7 June 1978
S.F. Wise, 24 February 1982

Notes

Where no author is indicated in the notes, the article is by Frank H. Underhill.

CHAPTER I: A GIFTED CHILD

1 This event was described by the following, all of whom were present: Peter C. Newman, 'A Good Man with a Great Mind,' Toronto *Star*, 27 Nov. 1969; Christopher Young, 'Wise Man's Story,' Ottawa *Citizen*, 29 Nov. 1969; Norman Smith, 'What They Thought of Frank Underhill "Who Tried to Keep Liberalism Honest,"' Ottawa *Journal*, 5 Dec. 1969; and Douglas Fisher, 'Underhill, the Reluctant Liberal,' Toronto *Telegram*, 27 Nov. 1969.
2 Markham *Economist*, 23 Sept. 1880
3 Information on Richard Underhill from Meikle interview, 1967, 18–19; 'Shoe Merchant Here 60 Years Ago Dead,' Stouffville *Tribune*, 7 March 1946; and Public Archives of Canada [PAC], Frank H. Underhill Papers, MG 30, D 204, vol. 14, Frank Underhill to J.D. Underhill, 22 April 1959 (re family genealogy).
4 Information on Stouffville from *Stouffville: 1887–1977: A Pictorial History of a Prosperous Ontario Community*, comp. J. Barkey (Stouffville 1977); *A Planning Study: An Appendix to the Official Plan: The Town of Whitchurch-Stouffville* (1977); and 'Historical Background' for 'Historical Plaque to Commemorate "The Founding of Stouffville,"' by the Ontario Heritage Foundation (1977)
5 Information on the Monkhouses from Meikle interview, 1967, 18, 24; 'Oldest Local Businessman Retiring after 57 Years' (nd), copy in Underhill Papers, 92, Miscellaneous Clippings file; Robert Miller, *The Ontario Village of Brougham: Past! Present! Future!* (Brougham 1973); Lillian Gauslin, *From Paths to Planes: A Story of the Claremont Area* (Claremont 1974); and Michelle Greenwald, *The Historical Complexities of Pickering–Markham–Scarborough– Uxbridge* (North Pickering 1973)
6 Interview with Betty Harfenist (Underhill's daughter)
7 PAC, William Lyon Mackenzie King Papers, MC 26, J 4, vol. 35, p. 31144, J.D. Aitchison to King, 12 Nov. 1917. I am indebted to J.L. Granatstein for bringing this letter to my attention.
8 Recollections in *The Image of Confederation*, The Massey Lectures, 1963 (Toronto 1964), 38

9 Underhill papers, 26, 'Eightieth Birthday Speech'
10 *Stouffville Sentinel*, 18 July 1901, copy in Underhill Papers, 94, University of Toronto clippings file
11 *Aurora Banner*, 'Important Business Change,' 25 March 1904. Information from Sisman of Canada Papers in possession of Sisman Factory, Aurora. I am indebted to Duncan Meikle for this material.
12 Toronto *World*, 15 Aug. 1907, copy in Underhill Papers, 89, University of Toronto clippings file

CHAPTER 2: STUDENT DAYS AT THE UNIVERSITY OF TORONTO

1 Public Archives of Canada [PAC], Frank. H. Underhill Papers, MG 30, D 204, vol. 2, Universities – Toronto 1907–1927 file, Wallace to Underhill, 25 Sept. 1907
2 Information on the University of Toronto and on University College from W.S. Wallace, *A History of the University of Toronto, 1827–1927* (Toronto 1927), 172–206; Claude Bissell, *The Young Vincent Massey* (Toronto 1981), 30–49; Claude Bissell, ed., *University College: A Portrait, 1853–1953* (Toronto 1953), 10–13
3 On the honour classics program see Bissell, *University College*, 54–65; W.S. Milner, 'The Higher National Life,' in *Canada and Its Provinces*, ed. A. Shortt and A.G. Doughty (Toronto 1914), 420–6.
4 On Hutton's ideas see Alan J. Bowker, 'Truly Useful Men – Maurice Hutton, George Wrong, James Mavor and The University of Toronto 1880–1927' (PH D thesis, University of Toronto, 1975), ch. 2; and S.E.D. Shortt, *The Search for an Ideal: Six Canadian Intellectuals and Their Convictions in an Age of Transition, 1890–1930* (Toronto 1976), 77–94.
5 Carleton University Archives, Convocation Address by F.H. Underhill, 22 May 1959, 2
6 Bissell, *University College*, 76–83, for a discussion of Alexander. See as well 'In Memoriam: Wallace John Alexander,' *University of Toronto Quarterly*, XIV, Oct. 1944, 1–33.
7 On George Wrong's ideas and his contribution to the history department at the University of Toronto see Bowker, 'Truly Useful Men,' ch. 3; Carl Berger, *The Writings of Canadian History: Aspects of English-Canadian Historical Writing: 1900–1970* (Toronto 1976), 8–21; Bissell, *The Young Vincent Massey*, 36–40; W.S. Wallace, 'The Life and Work of George M. Wrong,' *Canadian Historical Review*, XXIX, Sept. 1948, 229–37; W.D. Meikle, 'And Gladly Teach: G.M. Wrong and the Department of History at the University of Toronto' (PH D thesis, Michigan State University, 1977).
8 PAC, George Parkin Papers, MG 30, D 44, vol. 34, Wrong to Parkin, 12 Oct. 1911
9 University of Toronto Records Office, Official Transcript 1907–11
10 Meikle interview, 1967, 80; 1968, 20– 2
11 *Torontonensis: The Annual Yearbook of the Students of the University of Toronto Published by the Undergraduates' Parliament*, XIII, 1911, 371
12 See Bissell, *The Young Vincent Massey*, 43–7; Meikle interview, 1967, 63.
13 Underhill Papers, 1, Calvert to Underhill (postcard), 1910
14 Bissell, *University College*, 79
15 'Eightieth Birthday Speech'; Meikle interview, 1968, 56–7
16 The undergraduate essays discussed in the remainder of the chapter, 'Hobbes' Leviathan,' 'Hobbes and Milton,' 'John Stuart Mill,' 'Burke and Hobbes as Guides to

Modern Democracy,' and 'The Philosophy of Thackeray' are found in vol. 17, University of Toronto file, of the Underhill Papers.

17 Underhill Papers, 1, Hanna to Underhill, 20 June 1911
18 See University of Toronto Archives, G.M. Wrong Papers, Underhill to Wrong, 2 Feb. 1912; also 'The Revival of Conservatism in North America,' Royal Society of Canada, *Transactions*, LII, Series III, June 1958, Section II, 1.
19 Underhill Papers, 89, Class List File, 'University of Toronto Class and Prize Lists for Faculty of Arts, 1911'; 89, University of Toronto 1907–11 file, 'Four Toronto Men to Attend Oxford,' Toronto *Star*, 8 June 1911. Carleton Stanley would go on to become president of Dalhousie University; Charles Cochrane remained a classics professor at Toronto and wrote a major study entitled *Christianity and Classical Culture* (London 1940).
20 Underhill Papers, 8, Sissons to McInnis (copy), 13 Jan. 1953. See also C.B. Sissons, *A History of Victoria University* (Toronto 1952), 264 n13
21 Underhill Papers, 1, Bell to Underhill, 4 Aug. 1911

CHAPTER 3: A SCHOLARLY GENTLEMAN: OXFORD

1 See Jan Morris, *Oxford* (Oxford 1965), and Christopher Hollis, *Oxford in the Twenties: Recollections of Five Friends* (London 1976). On Balliol College see H.W. Carless Davis, *A History of Balliol College* (Oxford 1963). An excellent account of political and intellectual developments in the Edwardian Age is Samuel Hynes, *The Edwardian Turn of Mind* (Princeton 1968). See also J.B. Priestley, *The Edwardians* (London 1970). On the Fabians see A.M. McBriar, *Fabian Socialism and English Politics, 1884–1918* (Cambridge 1966); and Willard Wolfe, *From Radicalism to Socialism: Men and Ideas in the Formation of Fabian Socialist Doctrines, 1881–1889* (New Haven 1975).
2 Oxford, Balliol College Library, *Oxford University Handbook of 1914–1915* (Oxford 1915), 135
3 Oxford Public Library, City Directory for 1911
4 Public Archives of Canada [PAC], Frank. H. Underhill Papers, MG 30, D 204, vol. 1, Calvert to Underhill, 15 Nov. 1911
5 Ibid., 89, Balliol College file. Underhill's timetable is on the front and back covers of his notebook.
6 Davis, *A History of Balliol College*, 261. Also see Drusvilla Scott, *A.D. Lindsay: A Biography* (Oxford 1971).
7 Oxford, Bodleian Library, Oxford University Fabian Society. Description of the society written in 1905. Minute Book of The Oxford University Branch of The Fabian Society, 1895–1916
8 Introduction to *In Search of Canadian Liberalism* (Toronto 1960), x
9 University of Toronto Archives, Wrong Papers, Bell to Wrong, 25 Nov. [1911]
10 Oxford, Balliol College Records, Information and Statistics of Balliol College, 1908
11 Wrong Papers, Underhill to Wrong, 2 Feb. 1912. I have quoted extensively from this letter in the next few paragraphs.
12 Ibid., Bell to Wrong, 17 Dec. [1911]
13 The Oxford *Varsity* reported: 'F. Underhill argued ably for the privileges of Oxford to all classes, but spoke little above a whisper. To be effective he should raise his voice a tone and yell.' *Varsity*, XI, 23 May 1912; Underhill's Canadian colleagues at Oxford would all teach for a time at Canadian universities – Stanley, Cochrane,

Wrong, and Massey at the University of Toronto and Sage and Angus at the University of British Columbia.

14 Underhill Papers, 1, Kylie to Underhill, 10 Feb. [1912]; 2, Wrong to Underhill, 14 March 1912

15 Ibid., 17, Lectures and Papers – Balliol and Saskatchewan file, 'History of English Trade Unionism'

16 Ibid., 1, Calvert to Underhill, 2 March 1913

17 'Eightieth Birthday Speech'

18 Oxford, Bodleian Library, *Oxford University Gazette*, 1911–15; Underhill Papers, 89, Balliol file, 'University List,' *The Times*, 31 July 1913; Toronto *Mail*, 1 Aug. 1913

19 Underhill Papers, 2, Wrong to Underhill, 3 Aug. 1913; Curtis to Underhill, 1 Aug. 1913

20 Ibid., 2, Tait to Underhill, 29 Aug. 1913; Meikle interview, 1968, 25–6

21 Ibid., 1, Kylie to Underhill, 27 Jan. [1913]. Kylie wrote: 'I have a letter from Lindsay in which he speaks of you and your work in the highest possible terms. It is the opinion of the President, Mr Milner, and myself that you should stay and take two shots if necessary at the All Souls [Fellowship]. Something may open up here should you wish to return then.'

22 Interview with Henry Angus. Angus's recollections of Oxford are available in his autobiography (unpublished) in the University of British Columbia Archives, Angus Family Papers, box 1. Angus was a member of the Royal Commission on Dominion-Provincial Relations established in 1937, and from 1941 to 1945 was special assistant to the undersecretary of state for external affairs. He was also the first dean of graduate studies at UBC.

23 For a description of the approach of the School of Modern History see Oxford, Bodleian Library, Reports of Examiners of Modern History: 1905–12. Also, School of Modern History Exam Papers, 1912–14; Miscellaneous Scrapbook – R. Muir's Views of the School of Modern History at Oxford, 1913

24 University of Saskatchewan Archives, W.C. Murray Presidential Papers, Series 1, Applications and Appointments, Underhill to Murray, 16 Feb. 1914. In this letter in which he agrees to let his name stand for a position at the University of Saskatchewan, he outlines his studies at Toronto and Oxford.

25 Oxford, Balliol College Records, *Oxford University Handbook for 1914–1915*, 157–8. It notes: 'Such a candidate will as a rule only have a year for the work, but his superior training often enables him to grapple successfully with the task. He has already acquired an acquaintance with Political Science and possibly with Political Economy, as well as with the general methods of historical study, which will prove invaluable to him; and the only real difficulties which he will encounter are the technicalities of English Constitutional History. Of late years it has been a not uncommon practice to take Modern History after Literae Humaniores, and the man who does this probably gets the best literary education which is offered by the Oxford system.'

26 Underhill Papers, 1, Curtis to Underhill, 1 Aug. [1913]; Lindsay to Underhill, 14 Sept. 1913

27 Oxford, Rhodes House Library, Ralegh Club, Minute Book, 'Historical Note on the Club'

28 Claude Bissell, *The Young Vincent Massey* (Toronto 1981), 100

29 Oxford, Bodleian Library, Round Table Papers (Coupland), Lionel Curtis to A.J.

Glazebrook, 1914. Also Lionel Curtis Papers, Round Table Corrrespondence, 1909–21, Patterson to Horsfall, 14 March 1913. For a good description and analysis of Lionel Curtis and the Round Table Movement see John Kendle, *The Round Table Movement and Imperial Union* (Toronto 1975).

30 Underhill Papers, 17, Lectures and Papers – Balliol and Saskatchewan files, 'Doctrinaire Imperialism,' 1

31 See Carl Berger, *The Sense of Power: Studies in the Ideas of Canadian Imperialism, 1867–1914* (Toronto 1970).

32 Underhill Papers, 17, Lectures and Papers – Balliol and Saskatchewan files, 'Imperialism,' 2

33 For a good description of the attitude of Oxford graduates in the pre-World War I era see Colin R. Coote, *Editorial: The Memoirs of Colin R. Coote* (London 1965), and L.P. Carpenter, *G.D.H. Cole: An Intellectual Biography* (Cambridge 1973).

34 See Hollis, *Oxford in the Twenties*, 13–15.

35 Mciklc interview, 1968, 31

CHAPTER 4: ACADEMIC APPRENTICE AND SOLDIER

1 Public Archives of Canada [PAC], Frank. H. Underhill Papers, MG 30, D 204, vol. 1, Milner to Underhill, 9 July 1913

2 Ibid., 20 Dec. 1913

3 University of Saskatchewan Archives [USA], W.C. Murray Presidential Papers, Series I: Applications and Appointments, Murray to Underhill (copy), 20 April 1914

4 Underhill Papers, 2, Stanley to Underhill, 25 Jan. 1914

5 'What Then Is the Manitoban, This New Man? or This Almost Chosen People,' Canadian Historical Association, *Historical Papers*, 1970, 35

6 For Saskatoon see Bruce Peel, *The Saskatoon Story: Up the Years from the Temperance Colony, 1882– 1952* (np nd), and John Archer, *Historic Saskatoon: A Concise Illustrated History of Saskatoon* (Saskatoon nd). On the history of the University of Saskatchewan see A.S. Morton, *Saskatchewan: The Making of a University*, rev. and ed. Carlyle King (Toronto 1959), and W.P. Thompson, *The University of Saskatchewan: A Personal History* (Toronto 1970).

7 Murray Presidential Papers, Series I: Departmental Reports – History, 'E.H. Oliver's Report for History for 1912–1913'

8 For a sketch of Morton's life and an estimation of his work in western Canadian history see L.G. Thomas, Introduction to *A History of the Canadian West to 1870–71* (2nd ed., Toronto 1973).

9 Underhill Papers, 1, Eaton to Underhill, 5 Oct. 1915; USA, A.S. Morton Papers, Morton to H.A. Innis (copy), 20 Jan. 1931

10 Underhill Papers, 16, Underhill to his mother, 18 Oct. 1914

11 Ibid., 1, Coupland to Underhill, 5 March 1915

12 Ibid., 16, Underhill to his mother, 5 Nov. 1914

13 Ibid., 2, Underhill to Stanley (copy), 24 July 1925

14 'What Then Is the Manitoban,' 9

15 Underhill Papers, 16, Underhill to his mother, 23 Jan. 1915, 18 Oct. 1914, and 5 Nov. 1914

16 Murray Presidential Papers, Series I: Departmental Reports – History, 'Report on Classes of Year 1914–1915 by F.H. Underhill'

17 Underhill Papers, 16, Underhill to his mother, 5 Nov. 1914
18 Meikle interview, 1967, 169; interview with Ruth Underhill, Aug. 1972
19 Underhill Papers, 1, Coupland to Underhill, March 1915
20 Ibid., 16, Underhill to his mother, 23 Jan. 1915
21 See, for example, *Saskatoon Phoenix*, 'U. of S. Men May Form Company,' 6 Oct. 1914; 'Universities of Old Country Are Depleted,' 9 Oct. 1914; 'The Last Dollar and Last Man Are Ready for Empire,' 31 Oct. 1914; 'Good Luck to Our Boys,' editorial, 31 Oct. 1914.
22 USA, *The Sheaf*, 3, Oct. 1914, 16
23 Underhill Papers, 1, Angus to Underhill, 22 March 1915; 16, Underhill to his mother, 18 Oct. 1914
24 For a discussion of the English-Canadian attitude towards the war see R. Matthew Bray, '"Fighting as an Ally": The English-Canadian Patriotic Response to the Great War,' *Canadian Historical Review*, LXI, 1980, 141–68.
25 Meikle interview, 1967, 126
26 Murray Presidential Papers, Underhill to Murray, 1 Sept. 1915
27 *The Sheaf*, 'Our Roll of Honour,' 4, Oct. 1915, 21; see also 'Professor as Private: F.H. Underhill, Brilliant Graduate of Varsity Enlists,' Toronto *Telegram*, nd, copy in Underhill Papers, 89, University Career – Balliol College file.
28 Underhill Papers, 1, Murray to Underhill, 5 Oct. 1915; Murray Presidential Papers, Underhill to Murray, 15 Sept. 1915
29 Underhill Papers, 91, Diaries 1916 file, entries for 29 Sept.–2 Oct. [1915]. All subsequent references in this chapter, except where otherwise noted, are to the diary.
30 Underhill Papers, 16, Underhill to his mother, 6 Oct. 1915
31 Ibid., 4, Dec. 1915
32 Ibid., 2, Stanley to Underhill, 31 Dec. 1915
33 Ibid., 16, Underhill to his mother, 7 July 1916
34 Meikle interview, 1967, 148
35 Introduction to *In Search of Canadian Liberalism* (Toronto 1960), x; Meikle interview, 1967, 141– 2
36 Underhill Papers, 16, Underhill to his mother, 23 Sept. 1917
37 London, Public Record Office, 1st Battalion, Hertfordshire Regiment War Diary. Entry for 9 Oct. 1917 reads: 'Following reinforcements joined on 9th inst. 2nd Lieut. F. McN. Drury, Captain J.F. Christie, 2nd Lieuts F.H. Underhill, C.F. Nicholls and 40 O.R.'
38 John Terraine, *The Great War, 1914–1918* (London 1967), 187
39 Meikle interview, 1967, 150
40 Terraine, *The Great War*, 204–5
41 There is a reference to Underhill's wounding along with the records of other casualties in his battalion in Hertford County Record Office, B.J. Gripper Papers, War Diary, ch. 17, March 1918, 3. Details of the battle also from Underhill Papers, 16, Underhill to his mother, 23 March 1918; Meikle interview, 1967, 136ff; 'Sask. Professor Wounded,' Toronto *Telegram*, 30 March 1918
42 Murray Presidential Papers, Series I: General Correspondence, Underhill to Murray, 18 Jan. 1919
43 Underhill Papers, 2, Wrong to Underhill, 26 Jan. 1919; diary entry for 24 Feb. 1919; 8, Application for Transfer to FHU file, Notice from Headquarters of Overseas Military Forces of Canada re transfer of Underhill to Canadian Army (copy), 5 March 1919

44 Underhill Papers, 16, Underhill to his mother, 28 Feb. and 6 March 1919; Underhill to Mrs Angus, 30 March 1919

CHAPTER 5: THE SASKATCHEWAN YEARS

1 Meikle interview, 1967, 154
2 London, Royal Commonwealth Society, C.A. Lucas Papers, Lucas to Underhill (copy), 10 July 1919
3 Ibid., Underhill to Lucas, 19 April, 1 Oct., and 20 Dec., 1920
4 Public Archives of Canada [PAC], Frank H. Underhill Papers, MG 30, D 204, vol. 1, Lightbody to Underhill, 20 June 1924 Lightbody inquired why Underhill had not mentioned the chapter that he had discovered only by chance.
5 'The Canadian Forces in the War,' in C.A. Lucas, ed., *The Empire at War* (London 1923), II, 285–6
6 University of Saskatchewan Archives [USA], Murray Presidential Papers, Series I; General Correspondence, Underhill to Murray, 16 April 1919; ibid., Morton Papers, Underhill to Morton, 26 July 1919
7 USA, Murray Presidential Papers, Series I: Departmental Reports – History, 'Report on History for 1919–1920'
8 Underhill Papers, 17, Writings, Lectures – University of Saskatchewan file, 'French Revolution'
9 Outline of lecture in ibid., 'The New Europe'
10 Underhill Papers, 51, Research – Canada file, 'Canada 1791–1837,' 'Canada in 1839,' 'Durham's Report,' and 'Canada 1839–1854'
11 Ibid., 'C' General File, J. Ethel Gennant, Ida Lewis, and Annie Clark to Underhill, 25 April 1921
12 Interviews with Hilda Neatby, Jean Murray, and Roger Graham
13 Underhill Papers, 1, David Cowan to Underhill, 15 Oct. 1923
14 Quoted in 'What They Thought of Frank Underhill "Who Tried to Keep Liberalism Honest,"' Ottawa *Journal*, 5 Dec. 1969
15 University of Sasktchewan, *Calendar*, 1920–1. Shirley Spafford is completing a study of the Saskatchewan Department of Economics and Political Science. I am indebted to her for a draft copy of her chapter on Frank Underhill.
16 Underhill Papers, 2, Underhill to Carl (Stanley) (copy), 24 July 1925; Morton Papers, 1, Subject Files, University of Saskatchewan History Department, Morton to Jean (Murray) (copy), 10 Feb. 1925; Murray Presidential Papers, Series I: Departmental Reports – Political Science, 'Underhill's Report,' 19 May 1924; Underhill Papers, 1, Underhill to Cochrane (copy), 22 July 1925
17 Underhill Papers, 2, Underhill to Thiessen (copy), 24 May 1926
18 Interview with Leonard and Ivy Bowman; *Prince Albert: 100 Years – 1866–1966* (np nd); Underhill Papers, 92, Miscellaneous Clippings file, 'Figure "90" Significant in Life of George Carr' (nd)
19 *The Sheaf*, 'Ruth Mary Carr,' 6, April 1918, 307; Interview with Ruth Underhill, Aug. 1972
20 'The Liberal Arts and Public Affairs,' address at official opening of Arts Building, University of Saskatchewan, 16 Jan. 1961, 2
21 Prince Albert *Daily Herald*, 'Prof. Underhill and Miss Carr Married Today,' 21 June 1922; *The Sheaf*, 'Underhill Carr,' 11, 2 Nov. 1922, 5
22 Underhill Papers, 89, University Career: Balliol file (misfiled), Financial Statement as of 1 July 1920

23 Ibid., 1, Underhill to Charles (Cochrane) (copy), 22 July 1925
24 Ibid., 2, 'Report of Committee of United Order of Canadians,' 28 Aug. 1923; Morton Papers, C.A. Lightbody to Morton, 15 Aug. (no year given)
25 'The League of Nations,' *Modern Education*, II, Oct. 1925, 10–11, and Nov. 1925, 10–12. These appear to be the first two of a six-part series on the League. There are typescripts for articles on 'Disarmament,' 'Mandates,' 'The Court of Justice,' and 'Some Odd Jobs in Europe,' in Underhill Papers, 17, Writings 1925: League of Nations file.
26 University of Alberta Archives, *The Gateway* (student newspaper), 'Canada's Status Little Changes,' XIV, 14 March 1924, 1, 6; Underhill Papers, 17, Writings and Public Speeches in the 1920s file, 'Canada's National Status,' 22
27 *The Gateway*, 'Faculty Dinner,' XIV, 4 March 1924, 1; Underhill Papers, 17, 'On Political Education'
28 Williams College Library, W.W. McLaren Papers, Correspondence re Institute of Politics Conference, Underhill to McLaren, 19 Feb. 1924; McLaren to Underhill (copy), 26 Feb. 1924
29 *Round-Table Conferences of the Institute of Politics at Its First Session, 1921* (Williamstown 1923), 'Introduction,' ix–xii; McLaren Papers, *Institute of Politics, Fourth Announcement, July 31–August 29, 1924*; Underhill Papers, 27, Sir Paul Vinogradoff file, 'Round Table Conference on Problems of Political Theory'; Notes on Vinogradoff's speech
30 *Manitoba Free Press*, 'The Institute of Politics,' 3 Sept. 1924; 'Problems of Europe,' 24 Sept. 1924; 'Co-operation or Ruin,' 25 Sept. 1924
31 Underhill Papers, 76, Charles Beard file, 'Notes on an Economic Interpretation of the Constitution,' dated May 1923
32 See, for example, William Irvine, *The Farmers in Politics* (Toronto 1920), and W.C. Good, *Production and Taxation in Canada* (Toronto 1919).
33 Underhill Papers, 1, Mrs J.F. Bryant, president of the Saskatchewan Women's Canadian Club, to Underhill, 22 Sept. 1924; 17, Writings and Speeches in the 1920s file, Speech – No title (nd), 6
34 Saskatoon *Daily Star*, 'Progressive,' 22 and 23 Oct. 1925. A copy of the speech entitled 'Some Aspects of the History of Parties in Canada' in Underhill Papers, 17, Writings and Speeches in the 1920s file; Saskatoon *Daily Star*, 'Tweedledum King and Tweedledee Meighen,' 22 Oct. 1925; 'The Sad Case of Tweedledum and Tweedledee Again,' 28 Oct. 1925
35 'Some Aspects of the History of Parties,' 4
36 Underhill Papers, 2, Underhill to his father, 29 Sept. 1925

CHAPTER 6: THE MAKING OF A CANADIAN HISTORIAN

1 Public Archives of Canada [PAC], Frank H. Underhill Papers, MG 30, D 204, vol. 1, Underhill to Bell (copy), 29 Jan. 1926
2 Ibid., 2, Underhill to Stanley (copy), 24 July 1925
3 Ibid., Underhill to Bell (copy), 29 Jan. 1926
4 Ibid., Underhill to Morton (copy), 2 April 1926
5 Ibid., Underhill to George (Simpson) (copy), 17 March 1926
6 Ibid., Underhill to Bell (copy), 29 Jan. 1926; 2, Underhill to Stanley (copy), 2 April 1926; Underhill to Woodsworth (copy), 31 March 1926
7 Ibid., 2, Underhill to Simpson (copy), 17 March 1926
8 Ibid., 1, Underhill to Brown (copy), 24 May 1926

9 Ibid., Underhill to Lothian (copy), 26 March 1926; Underhill to Allen (copy), 2 April 1926
10 University of Saskatchewan Archives, Murray Presidential Papers, Series 1: Professor's Reports – Research, Underhill's Report re his Sabbatical Leave, 27 Oct. 1926
11 Underhill Papers, 1, Underhill to McQueen (copy), 27 June 1926; 2, Underhill to Riches (copy), 1 Aug. 1926
12 See Lewis H. Thomas, *The Renaissance of Canadian History: A Biography of A.L. Burt* (Toronto 1975), ch. 8.
13 Mrray Presidential Papers, Series 1: General Correspondence, Underhill to Murray 26 Aug. 1926; Underhill Papers, 1, Underhill to Cochrane (copy), 3 June 1926
14 Underhill Papers, 17, Writings 1927 file, 'Canadian Confederation after 60 Yars,' nd, 2
15 'Some Aspects of Upper Canadian Radical Opinion in the Decade before Confederation,' Canadian Historical Association, *Report*, 1927, 46–61
16 Underhill Papers, 1, Lightbody to Underhill, nd
17 'Canada's Relations with the Empire as seen by the Toronto *Globe*, 1857–1867,' *Canadian Historical Review*, x, June 1929, 106–29
18 See Carl Berger, *The Sense of Power: Studies in the Ideas of Canadian Imperialism 1867–1914* (Toronto 1970).
19 Underhill Papers, 17, Writings 1927 file, 'Canadian Confederation, July 1, 1927,' 2–3. Saskatoon *Daily Star*, 'Prof. Underhill Speaks on Confederation at Banquet,' 2 July 1927
20 The opinion of the two senior professors, Ralph Flenley and George Smith, of Underhill was expressed in a letter from Smith to President Falconer: 'The department would be most strengthened by the appointment of Principal Grant, as head. Failing him, the appointment of Underhill, as a colleague, would be satisfactory. The criticisms of Underhill are these: (a) he is said to be over-reticent as a teacher, (b) he is said to be more interested in Political Theory than in History proper. We have gaps which can be filled by a man of his interests but the graduate work on the side of Canadian History could not be strengthened as speedily with Underhill as with Grant.' Later Smith wrote: 'I was not confident that he [Underhill] would give us much prestige in the field of research in Canadian History but if this gap can be filled by Stewart Wallace, the prospect for a strong department will be much brighter.' University of Toronto Archives, R. Falconer Presidential Papers, box 111, Smith to Falconer, 16 March and 3 May 1927
21 Underhill Papers, 1, Falconer to Underhill, 3 May 1927; Falconer Papers, 104, Underhill to Falconer, 7 May 1927; Underhill Papers, 2, Underhill to Wrong (draft letter), 20 Feb. 1927; Higginbottom to Underhill (re official appointment of the Board of Governors), 16 May 1927
22 Underhill Papers, 1, Burt to Underhill, 13 May 1927
23 Murray Presidential Papers, Wrong to Murray, 7 Jan. 1927

CHAPTER 7: CLIMBING DOWN FROM THE IVORY TOWER

1 University of Toronto, *The Presidential Report* (1927), 2; *Canadian Annual Review*, 1927–8, 384–5
2 See C. Berger, *The Writing of Canadian History* (Toronto 1976), 8–21, and Alan J. Bowker, 'Truly Useful Men – Maurice Hutton, George Wrong, James Mavor and The University of Toronto 1880–1927' (PH D thesis, University of Toronto, 1975).
3 Public Archives of Canada [PAC], Frank. H. Underhill Papers, MG 30, D 204, vol. 2, Smith to Underhill, 23 May 1927

4 *Honour Classics in the University of Toronto* by a Group of Classical Graduates (Toronto 1929)

5 Underhill Papers, 17, Writings and Public Speeches 1920s file, 'Advocatus Diaboli Loquitur'

6 Within the department Underhill became a one-man committee asked to prepare an ideal curriculum for the department without considering practical difficulties. The secretary of the department meeting noted: 'Mr. Underhill, in his introduction, described the present course as having been apparently drafted in the Colonial period. The history of the continent seemed to have been regarded as beneath the notice of a gentleman. And the result was a lack of Canadian and American History throughout the course – a defect which became more noticeable in the third and fourth years. The motivation in the last two years bore, therefore, little relation to the life which students naturally entered after graduation ... Also constitutional history in the abstract was given a place of too great importance in the course; and the political and constitutional development was insufficiently related to the economic and social background.' PAC, Donald Creighton Papers, MG 31, D 77, vol. 24, University of Toronto – History Department 1928–38 File, 'Minutes of Departmental Meeting'

7 'The First Generation,' *Canadian Forum*, L, April 1970, 32; 'Art,' *Canadian Art*, xx, May–June 1963, 194

8 See Margaret Prang, 'F.H.U. of *The Canadian Forum*,' in *On Canada: Essays in Honour of Frank H. Underhill*, ed. N. Penlington (Toronto 1971), 3–23; see also M. Prang, 'Some Opinions of Political Radicalism in Canada between the Two World Wars' (MA thesis, University of Toronto, 1953).

9 *Canadian Forum*, VIII, Dec. 1927, 465–6

10 Interview with Barker Fairley

11 Introduction to *In Search of Canadian Liberalism* (Toronto 1960), xi

12 Quoted in Peter Oliver, *G. Howard Ferguson: Ontario Tory* (Toronto 1977), 327

13 Underhill Papers, 8, Universities – Toronto file, Underhill to Falconer (draft letter), 22 Oct. 1928

14 PAC, H.J. Cody Papers, Ferguson to Cody, 6 April 1929

15 For a discussion of this incident see M. Horn, ' "Free Speech within the Law": The Letter of the Sixty-Eight Toronto Professors, 1931,' *Ontario History*, LXXII, March 1980, 27–48.

16 Underhill Papers, 16, Underhill to Dafoe (copy), 30 Nov. 1930

17 The original letter, consisting of five copies, each signed by from five to twenty-nine people, may be found in the Underhill Papers, 49, Free Speech file, 'Letter to the Editor.'

18 'The Intellectual Capital of Canada,' *Canadian Forum*, xi, March 1931, 211; *Globe*, 'Professors and Governors,' editorial, 22 Jan. 1931

19 'Canada in the Great Depression,' *New Statesman and Nation*, ns 1, 13 June 1931, 570–1

20 *The Mail and Empire*, 'An Amiable Thrust from Academic Cloister,' 27 June 1931; *Globe*, 'Professors and Politics,' 2 July 1931

21 Underhill Papers, 16, Falconer to Underhill, 28 Sept. 1931. For a fuller discussion of Falconer's views see Robert Falconer, *Academic Freedom* (Toronto 1922).

22 Underhill Papers, 16, Underhill to President (Falconer), 24 Sept. 1931

23 Metropolitan Toronto Library, Deeks versus Wells Papers, evidence submitted by the Prosecution, 73; also see Underhill's recollections of the case in Canadian Broadcasting Corporation Archives, 'Deeks vs. Wells,' Oct. 1964; George Brett was a classics scholar and taught in the Department of Philosophy; William Irwin was a

professor of English; Lawrence Burpee was a prolific writer and a founder of the Canadian Historical Association.

24 Hector Charlesworth, *I'm Telling You: Being the Further Candid Chronicles* (Toronto 1937), 332–3. For Charlesworth's views of the case see ch. XVII, 'The Amazing Case of Deeks vs. Wells.' Underhill Papers, 6, McLaughlin (lawyer) to Underhill, 18 June 1930

25 Interview with Betty Harfenist, 6 June 1978

CHAPTER 8: SOCIALIST COLLEAGUE

1 Carleton University Library, 'The Angry Thirties,' in series 'Political Radicalism in the Thirties' (unpublished manuscript, 1959), 5

2 'O Canada,' *Canadian Forum* [CF], X, Feb. 1930, 156

3 'The Effect of Large Commerce and Applied Science Schools on the Ideals and Purposes of the Arts Faculty,' Canadian Universities Conference, Toronto, 26 May 1930. Reprinted as 'Commerce Courses and the Arts Faculty' in *University of Toronto Monthly*, XXXI, Oct. 1930

4 Public Archives of Canada [PAC], Frank H. Underhill Papers, MG 30, D 204, vol. 18, Writings: 1930 file, copy of two replies to Underhill's article in a supplement to *University of Toronto Monthly*: Gilbert E. Jackson, 'Commerce Courses, the Machine Age, and a Liberal Education,' XXXI, Oct. 1930, 83–7; W.L. Grant, 'Commerce Courses and the Humanities,' XXXI, Oct. 1930, 188–90; Fifteenth National Conference of Canadian Universities, *Report*, 1932

5 Fourteenth National Conference of Canadian Universities, *Report*, 1930, 18

6 Underhill Papers, 4, Underhill to Elliott (copy), 30 Nov. 1930

7 'O Canada,' CF, XI, Feb. 1931, 169

8 Underhill Papers, 8, Woodsworth to Underhill, 26 April 1929

9 Williams College Library, W.W. McLaren Papers, Underhill to McLaren, 28 April 1932; PAC, J.W. Dafoe Papers, MG 30, D 45, reel 75, Underhill to Dafoe, 14 June 1931

10 See Underhill's reporting of the sessions in the *Manitoba Free Press*, 'World Issues in Review,' 22–25 Sept. 1931 (four-part series).

11 Frank Scott, 'FHU and the Manifesto,' CF, LI, Nov. 1971, 8–9; 'Eightieth Birthday Speech'; 'The Angry Thirties,' speech (unpublished manuscript), 5–6

12 Underhill Papers, 16, Scott to Underhill, 6 Nov. 1931; 7, Underhill to Rogers, 18 Jan. 1932. For a comprehensive treatment of the League for Social Reconstruction see Michiel Horn, *The League for Social Reconstruction: Intellectual Origins of the Democratic Left in Canada, 1930–1942* (Toronto 1980).

13 Underhill Papers, 8, Scott to Underhill, nd [1931]; F.R. Scott Papers, Underhill to Scott, 18 Dec. 1931

14 Underhill Papers, 16, Scott to Underhill, 9 Jan. 1932

15 Scott Papers, Underhill to Scott, 10 March 1932; 29 March 1932

16 For a copy of the LSR Manifesto see 'The League for Social Reconstruction,' CF, XII, April 1932, 249–50. Also in Horn, *League for Social Reconstruction*, 219–20

17 See Horn, *League for Social Reconstruction*, ch. 11

18 This view of Underhill's version of the LSR was suggested to me by Blair Neatby of Carleton University.

19 Meikle interview, 1967, 172

20 Scott Papers, Underhill to Scott, 9 April 1932. Also see Horn, *League for Social Reconstruction*, ch. 2.

21 'The Party System in Canada,' *Papers and Proceedings of the Canadian Political*

Science Association, IV, 1932, 201–12. Reprinted in *In Search of Canadian Liberalism*, 164–71

22 See 'O Canada,' CF, XII, Oct. 1931, 14–15; 'The Liberal Programme,' CF, XIII, Nov. 1932, 45–6; 'King vs. Massey,' editorial, CF, XIV, Oct. 1933; 'Liberal Yellow Book?' review of *Recovery by Control* by F. Hankin and T.W.L. MacDermott, CF, XIV, Dec. 1933, 94.

23 Underhill Papers, 5, Hankin to Underhill, 11 Jan. 1932; 7, Underhill to Rogers, 14 Jan. 1932

24 Scott Papers, Underhill to Scott, 29 Sept. 1932; Underhill Papers, 8, Scott to Underhill, 30 Sept. 1932; 16, Woodsworth to Underhill, 7 Oct. 1932

25 University of Toronto Archives, LSR Papers, Minutes, Toronto branch executive meeting, 14 April 1933

26 Scott Papers, Underhill to Scott, 29 Sept. 1932; also 'The Angry Thirties' speech, 12–13

27 'Mr. Good's Political Philosophy,' CF, XIII, Aug. 1933, 413

28 Scott Papers, Underhill to Scott, 1 Dec. 1932. See Horn, *League for Social Reconstruction*, 38; Underhill Papers, 5, McLaren to Underhill, 22 Dec. 1932.

29 'The Angry Thirties' speech, 9–10

30 Underhill Papers, 16, Woodsworth to Underhill, 17 Oct. 1932 and 4 Jan. 1933; Scott Papers, Underhill to Scott, 1 Dec. 1932

31 For a discussion of the evolution of the draft of the Regina Manifesto and a comparison to the LSR Manifesto see M. Horn, 'Frank Underhill's Early Drafts of the Regina Manifesto 1933,' *Canadian Historical Review*, LIV, Dec. 1973, 393–418. See also Horn, *League for Social Reconstruction*, 42–6. In a letter to Frank Scott, Underhill claimed he did not go to the Regina meeting because 'I am too poor to go by train and I can't afford the time to drive.' Scott Papers, Underhill to Scott, 10 July 1933

32 See Horn, *League for Social Reconstruction*, 67–70; Underhill Papers, 18, Writings: 1933 file, 'F.H.U.'s comments [on SPC]'; '"Comments on Professor Underhill's Political Section" by H.M. Cassidy.'

33 See Horn, *League for Social Reconstruction*, 3–4, 42.

34 Underhill Papers, 16, Underhill to Mrs Somerset, 30 April 1933

35 G.V.F., 'C.C.F. "Brain Trust,"' *Winnipeg Free Press*, 25 July 1933; F.H.U., 'The C.C.F. Convention and After,' CF, XIV, Sept. 1934, 463

36 Underhill Papers, 6, Underhill to Massey (copy), 25 July 1934; 8, Underhill to Atkinson (copy), 25 July 1934; *Winnipeg Free Press*, 'Academic Freedom in Regina,' letter to editor, 1 Aug. 1934. Reprinted in *In Search of Canadian Liberalism*, 110–13

CHAPTER 9: SOCIALIST INTELLECTUAL AND CRITIC

1 For a discussion of Underhill's liberal-socialism in the 1930s see R. Douglas Francis, 'Frank H. Underhill – Canadian Intellectual' PH D thesis, York University, 1976), chs. 4 and 5.

2 'Bentham and Benthamism,' *Queen's Quarterly*, XXXIX, Nov. 1932, 666

3 'Liberalism and Socialism,' editorial, *Canadian Forum* [CF], XIII, Sept. 1933, 443

4 University of Toronto Archives [UTA], Woodsworth Memorial Collection, box 10, 'The Present Crisis,' an address by Frank Underhill in an LSR radio series 'The Depression and the Way Out,' 5 Nov. 1933

5 'O Canada,' CF, XI, Jan. 1931, 131; X, March 1930, 202

6 'Correspondence,' CF, X, April 1930, 263

7 'What Should Canada Do about the Next War?' *New Commonwealth*, I, 11 Aug. 1934, 5
8 Orillia *Packet and Times*, 'Suggests Canadian Judges Are out of Date,' 1933. Copy in Underhill Papers, 18, Writings: 1933 file
9 Ibid., 'Note and Comment,' editorial, 9 Nov. 1933; Toronto *Mail and Empire*, 'Toronto Professor Rebuked,' 20 Nov. 1933
10 Public Archives of Canada [PAC], Frank H. Underhill Papers, MG 30, D 204, vol. 3, Underhill to Claxton (copy), 15 April 1931; interview with Ruth Underhill
11 Underhill Papers, 18, Writings: 1933 file, copies of newspaper articles, 'Professor and Politics,' *Star*, 28 Oct. 1933; 'Another Editorial Professor-Chase,' *Star*, 22 Nov. 1933
12 Underhill Papers, 7, Underhill to Rogers (copy), 21 Sept. 1932; 18, Writings: 1934 file, clipping from *Varsity*, 'Sexton Today,' 28 Feb. 1934
13 Ibid., 4, Dingman to Underhill, 1 Dec. 1933; 9, Wrong to Underhill, 7 and 11 Dec. 1933
14 Underhill Papers, 18, Writings 1934 file, newspaper clipping from Orillia *Packet and Times*, 16 Aug. 1934; *Saturday Night*, 'The Course of Politics Moves Leftward,' 22 Sept. 1934
15 Ibid., newspaper clipping from Montreal *Star*, 'Strength of Empire Is Dependent on Empire' (nd)
16 UTA, H.J. Cody Presidential Papers, Ross to Cody, 13 Aug. 1934
17 Ibid., Cody to Colonel Ponton (copy), 23 Oct. 1934; Toronto *Star*, 'Underhill to Make No More Addresses,' 1 Nov. 1934
18 Cody Papers, MacBrien file, Cody to MacBrien (copy), 6 April 1935
19 'Mr. Good's Political Philosophy,' CF, XIII, Aug. 1933, 413; W.C. Good, 'My Political Philosophy,' ibid., 413–16
20 Underhill Papers, 16, Underhill to Woodsworth (copy), 2 May 1933
21 Ibid., 9, Underhill to Woodsworth, 24 July 1934; Woodsworth to Underhill, 2 Aug. 1934
22 'The CCF in Canadian Politics,' *Winnipeg Free Press*, 17 July 1934; 'A New Deal in the Party System,' Notes and Comments, CF, XV, Aug. 1935, 329–30; 'Discussion' of R.A. McKay, 'The Nature of Canadian Politics,' in W.W. McLaren et al., *Proceedings, Conference on Canadian-American Affairs, 1935* (Boston 1936), 203–6
23 'Spade-Work for a New Social Order: The League for Social Reconstruction – What It Is and What It Plans to Do,' *Saturday Night*, 10 March 1934, 2; 'Democracy and Leadership in Canada,' CF, XIV, April 1934, 247
24 Underhill Papers, 16, Underhill to Keenleyside (copy), 3 Nov. 1935; Underhill to Ferguson (copy), 2 Nov. 1935
25 Ibid., 6, Underhill to McLean (copy), 23 Sept. 1935; McLean to Underhill, 23 Sept. 1935
26 'The Conception of a National Interest,' *Canadian Journal of Economics and Political Science*, I, Aug. 1935, 404
27 H.A. Innis, '"For the People,"' *University of Toronto Quarterly*, V, Jan. 1936, 282ff. See D.G. Creighton, *Harold Adams Innis: Portrait of a Scholar* (Toronto 1957), 92–3.
28 'Betty and the University Reds,' CF, XV, Dec. 1935, 385; Underhill Papers, 4, Forsey to Underhill, 19 Oct. 1937
29 'Freedom of the Press,' first broadcast by G.V. Ferguson and F.H. Underhill in CBC series, *Our Heritage of Freedom* (Toronto 1937), 9
30 *Globe and Mail*, 'Professor Underhill "Educates,"' 1 June 1937

31 *Globe and Mail*, 'Socialism Not Taught in Victoria,' reply by the chairman of the Board of Regents for Victoria College, 7 June 1937; 'Professors and the Public,' editorial, 7 June 1937

32 Underhill Papers, 16, Writings – Various Dates file, 'The Honorary President,' 2 Dec. 1936; 7, Underhill to Rankin (copy), 3 March 1938

33 Ibid., 4, Dent to Underhill, 14 Oct. 1932; Underhill to Dent (copy), 5 Nov. 1932

34 Ibid., 4, Dent to Underhill, 11 Jan. 1934; editorial, CF, XIV, April 1934, 243; Underhill to Aitchison (copy), 5 March 1934; Underhill to Dent (copy), 2 April 1934

35 See Michiel Horn, *The League for Social Reconstruction: Intellectual Origins of the Democratic Left in Canada, 1930–1942* (Toronto 1980), 130; Underhill Papers, 2, Underhill to Brailsford (copy), 5 Feb. 1937; 5, Underhill to Laski (copy), 5 Feb. 1937.

36 Underhill Papers, 16, Scott to Underhill, 6 Dec. 1935; Underhill to Scott (copy), 24 Jan. 1936

37 Ibid., 16, Scott to Underhill, 26 Feb. 1937; Underhill to Scott, 20 Sept. 1937

38 Quoted in Horn, *League for Social Reconstruction*, 131

39 Underhill Papers, 16, Underhill to Scott (copy), 30 Oct. 1937

40 Canadian Institute of International Affairs Library, F.H. Underhill, 'Canadian Foreign Policy in the 1930's,' in *Canadian Opinion on Collective Security*, a mimeographed memorandum prepared for the Eighth International Studies Conference on Collective Security, 1935, Feb. 1935, 27. See also 'What Should Canada Do about the Next War?' *The New Commonwealth*, I, 11 Aug. 1934, 5; and 'C.C.F. and Foreign Policy,' *Winnipeg Free Press*, 18 July 1934.

41 Underhill Papers, 7, Underhill to Reid (copy), 27 Feb. 1935

42 LSR, *Social Planning for Canada*, Social History Series Reprint (Toronto 1975), ch. XXII

43 'That Clear Moral Issue: Or St. George against the Dragon,' CF, XVI, April 1936, 5–6; Marvin Gelber, 'That Liberal Façade,' CF, XVI, May 1936, 18; reply by Underhill, ibid., 4

44 'Canada and Post-League Europe,' ibid., Oct. 1936, 11–12

45 Underhill Papers, 75, World Organizations file, Notes on Brailsford, *Towards a New League*, and Vigilantes, *Why the League Has Failed*, dated July 1936

46 Ibid., 5, Foreign Policy 1938 file, 'Isolationism,' address given in a debate with the League of Nations Society on '1938! Canada Looks Abroad: Which Way Should We Go?' 12 Jan. 1938. The other debators were J.M. Macdonnell, N. Ignatieff, and A. Brewin.

47 Ibid., 7, Plaunt to Underhill, 16 Aug. 1939; 'The Angry Thirties' speech (unpublished manuscript), 15

CHAPTER 10: THE UNIVERSITY CRISIS

1 *Globe and Mail*, 'Toronto Professor Censured in Legislature: Hepburn Demands Curbs,' 14 April 1939; *Toronto Daily Star*, 'University Announces Probe; Hepburn Flays Professors,' 14 April 1939; Humphrey Carver, 'Premier Hepburn and the Professors,' *Canadian Forum* [CF], XIX, May 1939, 40–1. The Underhill controversy is also discussed in C. Berger, *The Writing of Canadian History: Aspects of English-Canadian Historical Writing, 1900 to 1970* (Toronto 1976), 79–84; D. Creighton, 'The Ogdensburg Agreement and F.H. Underhill,' in C. Berger and R. Cook, eds., *The West and the Nation: Essays in Honour of W.L. Morton* (Toronto 1976), 300–20; and Douglas Francis, 'The Threatened Dismissal of Frank H. Underhill from the University of Toronto – 1939–1941,' Canadian Association of University Teachers [CAUT] *Bulletin*, XXIV, Dec. 1975, 16–21.

2 For a discussion of the Underhill controversy in the context of the role of the professor in public issues see Michiel Horn, 'Professor in the Public Eye: Canadian Universities, Academic Freedom, and the League for Social Reconstruction,' *History of Education Quarterly*, xx, winter 1980, 425–7; and Michiel Horn, 'Academic Freedom and the Canadian Professor,' CAUT *Bulletin*, Dec. 1982, 19–22, 26.

3 Underhill Papers, 4, Underhill to Keenleyside (copy), 21 April 1939

4 On the Hepburn–Mackenzie King feud see Neil McKenty, *Mitch Hepburn* (Toronto 1967), ch. 10; Public Archives of Canada [PAC], Frank H. Underhill Papers, MG 30, D 204, vol. 4, Underhill to Ferguson (copy), 21 April 1939. McKenty writes: 'His [Hepburn's] real targets, perhaps, were not the two professors so much as the University's President, H.J. Cody, and its Chancellor, Sir William Mulock.'

5 University of Toronto Archives [UTA], Cody Presidential Papers, Beatty and Innis to Cody, 19 April 1939

6 Ibid., Cody to Underhill (copy), 14 April 1939

7 Underhill Papers, 4, Underhill to Ferguson (copy), 21 April 1939

8 Cody Presidential Papers, Martin to Cody, 19 April 1939

9 Underhill Papers, 4, Underhill to Ferguson (copy), 21 April 1939

10 Cody Presidential Papers, Underhill to Cody, 18 and 19 April 1939; MacKay to Cody (telegram), 17 April 1939

11 University of British Columbia Archives [UBCA], Alan Plaunt Papers, Plaunt to Drew (copy), 17 April 1939; Drew to Plaunt, 18 April 1939. For a discussion of the attitude of governmental officials concerning professorial involvement in public controversies see Peter Oliver, *G. Howard Ferguson: Ontario Tory* (Toronto 1977), ch. 12.

12 Cody Presidential Papers, Beatty and Innis to Cody, 19 April 1939; Underhill Papers, 4, Underhill to Ferguson (copy), 21 April 1939

13 Cody Presidential Papers, H.J. Beveridge, chairman of an 'ad hoc' committee re student petition, to Cody, 19 April 1939

14 UTA, Board of Governors Papers, Minute Book no 15, 'Minutes of a special meeting of the Board of Governors, April 19, 1939,' 360

15 Underhill Papers, 4, Underhill to Ferguson (copy), 21 April 1939

16 Ibid.; *Globe and Mail*, 'Won't Press to Dismiss Professor for Remarks,' 28 April 1939

17 Cody Presidential Papers, 'Statement Regarding Professor Frank Underhill,' nd

18 'Professor Underhill Corrects,' letter to the editor, *Saturday Night*, 6 May 1939, 7; Cody Presidential Papers, Neilly to Higginbottom, secretary of the Board of Governors, 8 May 1939

19 Underhill Papers, 8, Underhill to Department of Immigration (copy), 10 June 1940

20 For a discussion of the Ogdensburg Agreement see J.L. Granatstein, *Canada's War: The Politics of the Mackenzie King Government, 1939–1945* (Toronto 1975), 128ff.

21 Underhill Papers, 19, Writings 1941 file, 'Y.M.C.A. Institute on Politics and Economics, August 1940.' Underhill listed the names of the chairman and members of the panel; Cody Presidential Papers, Silcox to Cody, 15 Sept. 1940

22 Underhill Papers, 19, 'Y.M.C.A. Institute, Speech of F.H. Underhill,' 2ff

23 Public Archives of Ontario, Ontario Attorney General's Records, 1940, no 470, OPP File re F.H. Underhill, p.2. I am indebted to Christopher Armstrong for this material. Underhill believed that 'my real crime was in welcoming the Ogdensburg agreement. The Toronto Tories dislike it immensely but don't find it expedient to say so, and so I become a convenient victim.' PAC, D.G. Creighton Papers, Underhill to Creighton, 24 Sept. 1940.

24 Ontario Attorney General's Record, 1940, no 470, OPP File re F.H. Underhill, p. 2

25 Cody Presidential Papers, Cody to Underhill (telegram), 24 Aug. 1940; Underhill to
   Cody, 4 Sept. 1940; Ontario Attorney General's Records, 1940, no 470, OPP File
   re F.H. Underhill, p. 2
26 PAC, Arthur Meighen Papers, MG 26 I, vol. 231, series 6, Meighen to Lapointe, 28
   Aug. 1940; Cody Presidential Papers, Addy to Cody (copy), nd
27 Underhill Papers, 19, Writings 1940 file, Underhill to Cody (copy), 1 Sept. 1940;
   Toronto *Star*, 'An Ill-Timed Address,' 31 Aug. 1940; *Star*, Letter from Underhill,
   4 Sept. 1940; Underhill Papers, 19, Cody to Underhill, 3 Sept. 1940; Cody
   Presidential Papers, Underhill to Cody, 4 Sept. 1940
28 Ontario Attorney General's Records, 1940, no 470, 'Memorandum from W.M.
   Martin, Solicitor to AG, to Attorney General Gordon Conant, Sept. 16, 1940';
   'Memorandum from Conant to Education Minister Dr. Duncan McArthur, Sept. 18,
   1940'; and 'Alex Wilson's Report'
29 Plaunt Papers, box 4, file 26, Underhill to Plaunt, 13 Sept. 1940
30 Board of Governors Papers, Agenda Book no 31, Board Meeting of 12 Sept. 1940;
   Minute Book no 1, 'Professor Underhill's Case,' 12 Sept. 1940, 92
31 Plaunt Papers, 4, Underhill to Plaunt, 13 Sept. 1940; Cody Presidential Papers,
   McLean to Cody, 14 Sept. 1940; Wallace to Cody, 15 Sept. 1940; Silcox to Cody, 15
   Sept. 1940; Sandwell to Cody, 16 Sept. 1940; and Brebner to Cody (telegram), 16
   Sept. 1940
32 Dalhousie University Archives, Carleton Stanley Papers, Underhill to Stanley, 18
   Sept. 1940; University of British Columbia Archives, Norman Mackenzie Papers,
   Underhill to Mackenzie, 18 Sept. 1940
33 Cody Presidential Papers, Cassels to the chairman of the Board of Governors (copy),
   16 Sept. 1940
34 Board of Governors Papers, Minute Book no 1, 'Professor Underhill's Case,' 16 Sept.
   1940, 290; Toronto *Star*, 'Won't Take Action in Underhill's Case,' 17 Sept. 1940
35 Toronto *Telegram*, editorials, 18, 20, 21, 23, 24, and 25 Sept. 1940; Cody Papers,
   Underhill to Cody, 24 Sept. 1940
36 Toronto *Telegram*, 'Letters to the Editor,' 24 Sept. 1940; Underhill Papers, 3, Creighton to Underhill, 29 Sept. 1940; 6, McNaught to Sandwell (copy), 6 Oct. 1940; 5,
   Lower to Underhill, 6 Oct. 1940; MacKay to Underhill, 25 Oct. 1940
37 Board of Governors Papers, Minute Book no 1, 'Notice of Motion from Mr. Neilly re
   Professor Underhill,' 26 Sept. 1940, 298; Cody Presidential Papers, Statement
   made by Neilly to the board, 11 Oct. 1940; Board of Governors Papers, Minute Book
   no 2, 'Withdrawal of Notice of Motion re Professor Underhill,' 10 Oct. 1940, 1
38 Cody Presidential Papers, Neilly to Cody, 13 Dec. 1940; Dalhousie University
   Archives, Carleton Stanley Papers, Stanley to Underhill (copy), 23 Sept. 1940; Plaunt
   Papers, 2, file 22, MacDermott to Plaunt, 2 Oct. 1940
39 Cody Presidential Papers, 'Confidential Report,' nd; Board of Governors Papers,
   Minute Book no 2, 'Minutes of a Special Meeting of the Board of Governors,' 19
   Dec. 1940, 59
40 Board of Governors Papers, Agenda Book no 31, 'Agenda for Special Board Meeting,
   Dec. 19, 1940,' 166–7
41 Ibid., 'Agenda for Adjoined Meeting of Board of Governors, Dec. 27, 1940,' 168–9
42 Underhill Papers, 19, Writings 1941 file, 'Statement by Professor F.H. Underhill as to
   an interview between him and a committee of the Board of Governors on January
   2, 1941'
43 Plaunt Papers, 4, file 26, Underhill to Plaunt, 13 Sept. 1940; Underhill Papers, 6,
   Macaulay to Underhill, 6 Jan. 1941

44 Underhill Papers, 19, Writings 1941 file, 'Some Account of Recent Strange Happenings in the University of Toronto,' confidential statement by Underhill, 14 Jan. 1941

45 Cody Presidential Papers, Martin to Cody, 3 Jan. 1941; Underhill Papers, 19, 'Some Account ... '

46 Cody Presidential Papers [list of professors who met Cody, 7 Jan. 1941]; Underhill Papers, 19, 'Some Account ... '; C.B. Sissons recalls mistakenly that there were ten professors who met Cody; see *Nil Alienum: The Memoirs of C.B. Sissons* (Toronto 1964), 163.

47 Underhill Papers, 'Some Account ... '; Cody Papers, Innis to Cody, 8 Jan. 1941

48 Cody Presidential Papers, petition signed by third- and fourth-year modern history students, 9 Jan. 1941; 'Graduate Student Petition,' delivered by K. Bryden, 17 Jan. 1940 [sic] [41]; for detail on the incentive behind the petition see Sissons, *Nil Alienum*, 162; information on telephone campaign from interview with Ruth Underhill; see the numerous letters from students and alumni in Cody Papers.

49 Underhill Papers, 5, Underhill to Keenleyside (copy), 6 Jan. 1941

50 PAC, W.L. Mackenzie King Papers, MG 26, J 13, vol. 336, F.H. Underhill file, C231880, 'Memorandum for the Prime Minister,' 7 Jan. 1941; Underhill Papers, 5, Keenleyside to Cody, 8 Jan. 1940. The people contacted by Keenleyside – Norman Lambert, Leslie Thompson, and O.D. Biggar in turn sent letters or telegrams to Cody. Keenleyside's own account of the Underhill case can be found in his memoirs, *The Memoirs of Hugh L. Keenleyside*, II: *On the Bridge of Time* (Toronto 1982), 105–10.

51 J.W. Pickersgill, 'The Last Challenge to the late Frank Underhill's Position at the University of Toronto: A Footnote to Carl Berger's Account in "The Writing of Canadian History."' A personal recollection of the Underhill case. Copy of statement in author's possession. I am indebted to Carl Berger for bringing this material to my attention.

52 Report by Carlton McNaught of telephone conversation with Premier Hepburn, 10 Jan. 1941 (copy); Board of Governors Papers, Agenda Book no 31, 'Agenda for Board Meeting Jan. 9, 1941,' 171; Plaunt Papers, 4, file 26, Underhill to Plaunt, 12 Jan. 1941; Underhill Papers, 19, copy of Cody's telegram to Keenleyside, 13 Jan. 1941

53 Underhill Papers, 19, "Some Account ... '

54 Cody Presidential Papers, Underhill to Macdonald (copy), 8 Jan 1941

55 Board of Governors Papers, Agenda Book no 31, 171; Minute Book no 2, 'Professor Underhill's Case,' 9 Jan. 1941, 64

56 Cody Presidential Papers, Cody to Mackenzie King (draft telegram), 10 Jan. 1941

57 *Toronto Star*, 'Sees "One Political Source" Trying to Oust Underhill,' 10 Jan. 1941; Underhill Papers, 19, Writings 1941 file. Report by Carlton McNaught of telephone conversation with Premier M. Hepburn, 10 Jan. 1941 (copy). PAC, J.W. Dafoe Papers, MG 30, D 45, vol. 12, Sifton to Dafoe, 22 Jan. 1941

58 *Globe and Mail*, 'Ontario Aloof in U. of T. Case, Nixon States,' 11 Jan. 1941; Cody Presidential Papers, Cody to Gray, 14 Jan. 1941; Underhill Papers, Dingman to Underhill, 11 Jan. 1941

59 Underhill Papers, 19, 'Some Account ... '; 8, Underhill to Davis (copy), 4 Jan. 1941; 5, Underhill to Keenleyside (copy), 31 Jan 1941

60 Board of Governors Papers, Minute Book no 2, 'Professor Underhill Case,' 23 Jan. 1941, 75; 12 June 1941, 181; 26 June 1941, 191–2

61 Plaunt Papers, 4, file 26, Underhill to Plaunt, 13 June 1941; interview with Ruth Underhill, 30 Nov. 1972; Board of Governors Papers, Agenda Book no 32, Agenda for Meeting of 25 Sept. 1941, 116

62 Underhill Papers, 5, Underhill to Lawson (copy), 20 Aug. 1941

CHAPTER II: REVISIONISM IN THE WAR YEARS

1 Public Archives of Canada [PAC], Frank H. Underhill Papers, MG 30, D 204, vol. 19, Writings 1939 file, 'L.S.R. 10 Nov., 39'
2 PAC, CCF Papers, 1, Minutes, CCF National Council Meeting, 6–8 Sept. 1939, 22–3. See also Walter Young, *Anatomy of a Party: The National CCF* (Toronto 1969), 91ff.
3 *Canadian Forum* [CF], XIX, Jan. 1940, 318–19
4 'Peace Aims,' CF, XIX, Oct. 1939, 208
5 Woodsworth Memorial Collection, box 12, Havelock to Parkin, 24 Sept. 1939; see Michiel Horn, *The League for Social Reconstruction: Intellectual Origins of the Democratic Left in Canada, 1930–1942* (Toronto 1980), 159ff.
6 Scott Papers, Louise Parkin to W.L.M. King (copy), 6 Sept. 1939
7 Meikle interview, 1968, 170–1
8 Woodsworth Memorial Collection, box 12, Grube to Parkin, nd [Sept. 1939]; 8 Oct. 1939
9 F.H. Underhill, 'Canada and the Last War,' in C. Martin, ed., *Canada in Peace and War* (Toronto 1940), 120–49
10 'What Next?' editorial, CF, XX, July 1940, 99; 'Can Britain Be Invaded?' editorial, ibid.; Meikle interview, 1968, 157
11 'What Are We Fighting For?' CF, XX, July 1940, 102; 'Canada's Problem,' CF, XX, Aug. 1940, 134–5; Underhill's reaction to the defeat of France was typical of the time. In *Total War: Causes and Courses of the Second World War* (London 1972), Peter Calvocoressi and Guy Wint write: 'The defeat of France was the high-water mark of the Germany army – and something more. The Germans had beaten the French as easily as they had beaten the Poles. From one angle these were two separate examples of the superiority of German arms. But the two events did not strike contemporaries that way. The defeat of Poland was no surprise. Nobody expected the Poles to hold the German army for long. Theirs was a much smaller, much less up to date and much less skilful force. But the French army was one of the great armies of the world and France itself stood – if any single country could be said so to stand – as the embodiment of western civilization. The fall of France was much more than a military decision. It was a portentous distortion of history ... Whereas the defeat of Poland had been a tragedy which further shifted the balance of power in Europe Hitler's way, the fall of France opened an abyss of uncertainty for the whole continent and shook the imagination as perhaps nothing had shaken it since the victory of the Turks at Mohacs in 1526' (130–1).
12 'War by Revolution,' CF, XX, Jan. 1941, 301
13 'Reading and Listening,' CF, XX, July 1940, 101
14 'A New Balance of Power,' editorial, CF, XX, Sept. 1940, 163
15 Underhill Papers, 5, 'Notes on Hankin Manuscript,' 2, with accompanying letter dated 30 Dec. 1940
16 'The Next Ruling Class,' CF, XXI, July 1941, 101–3
17 Quoted in M. Horn, 'The League for Social Reconstruction: Socialism and Nationalism in Canada, 1931–1945' (PH D thesis, University of Toronto, 1969), 117
18 Underhill Papers, 8, Scott to Underhill, 26 April 1941; Forsey to Underhill, 2 May 1941
19 University of Toronto Archives [UTA], Department of History Papers, box 7, Canadian Historical Association 1941–2 file, Underhill to Fieldhouse, 22 July 1941; Queen's

University Archives [QUA], A.R.M. Lower Papers, series C, section 11 C 47, Underhill to Lower, 10 Oct. 1941. See Canadian Historical Association, *Report*, 1942, for copies of Fieldhouse's and Underhill's papers.

20 On the York South by-election see J.L. Granatstein, *Conscription in the Second World War, 1935–1945* (Toronto 1969), 38ff; and R. Graham, *Arthur Meighen: A Biography*, III: *No Surrender* (Toronto 1965), ch. IV.

21 Interviews with Ruth Underhill and Betty Harfenist; Underhill Papers, 54, Meighen file, drafts of election speeches 'What Are We Fighting For?' 'The Plebiscite Issue,' 'Appeals to Liberals and Conservatives,' 'About Conscription,' and 'The Meighen versus the Churchill Type of Toryism'

22 CF, XXI, Jan. 1942, 295; 'Correspondence,' Forsey to the *Forum* editor, ibid., March 1942, 370–1; April 1942, 23–4, and Underhill's reply, 24; Underhill Papers, 4, Underhill to Forsey (copy), 12 May 1942

23 'J.S. Woodsworth,' CF, XX, Dec. 1940, 259, and XXII, April 1942, 4

24 Underhill had to trace out illegible words on a carbon paper and then use a mirror to decipher them. Meikle interview, 1967, 174–5; interview with Betty Harfenist

25 'Edward Blake, the Supreme Court Act, and the Appeal to the Privy Council, 1875–6,' *Canadian Historical Review* [CHR], XIX, Sept. 1938, 245–62; 'Edward Blake, the Liberal Party, and Unrestricted Reciprocity,' Canadian Historical Association, *Report*, 1939, 133–41; 'Laurier and Blake, 1882–1891,' CHR, XX, Dec. 1939, 392–408; and 'Edward Blake and Canadian Liberal Nationalism,' in *Essays in Canadian History: Presented to George M. Wrong*, ed. R. Flenley (Toronto 1939), 132–53

26 Review of *Western Ontario and the American Frontier* by Fred Landon in CHR, XXIII, March 1942, 77–8

27 Underhill Papers, 4, J.S. Guggenheim Foundation file, Underhill to Moe (copy), 22 Oct. 1941; application for Guggenheim; Underhill to Moe (copy), 3 Nov. 1941, 17 Feb. 1942

28 UTA, Harold Innis Papers, box 1, file 1941–2, Moe to Innis, 7 Feb. 1942; Innis to Steinhuser (copy), 14 April 1942

29 Underhill Papers, 4, Underhill to Moe (copy), 27 Feb. 1942; Moe to Underhill, 20 March 1942; 2, Brebner to Underhill, 6 April 1942

30 Ibid., 4, Flenley to Underhill, 30 Oct. 1942; 5, Underhill to Lankes (copy), 9 Nov. 1942; Underhill to Havelock (copy), 29 March 1943

31 'The Canadian Party System in Transition,' *Canadian Journal of Economics and Political Science*, IX, Aug. 1943, 301

32 'Discussion,' ibid., 313–16

33 See 'Canada – One or None?' CF, XX, June 1940, 17. Underhill wrote: 'Its [the Rowell-Sirois Report] analysis of how the Dominion since 1867 has altered between periods of constructive nationalism and periods of reaction into sectional bitterness, and its conclusions as to why national disintegration developed after 1918, needs to be studied by anyone who is going to understand the difficulties of the present wartime.'

34 Underhill Papers, 5, Underhill to Joyce (copy), 12 April 1943; interview with Betty Harfenist

35 'The Radical Tradition in Canadian History,' interview with Paul Fox (Toronto CBC 1960), 7, 12

36 Underhill Papers, 5, Underhill to de Kiewiet (copy), 23 Oct. 1943

37 Ibid., 7, Underhill to Rugg (copy), 28 July 1943

38 Ibid., 4, Underhill to Moe (copy), 13 Nov. 1943; PAC, Eugene Forsey Papers, MG 30, A 25, Underhill to Forsey, 9 June 1942
39 Review of *Sir Francis Hincks: A Study of Canadian Politics, Railways, and Finance in the Nineteenth Century* by Ronald Longley in CHR, XXVI, March 1945, 68; see also Underhill Papers, 2, Underhill to Buckingham (copy), 4 Aug. 1943
40 For a fuller discussion of Underhill's historical writings see C. Berger, *The Writing of Canadian History* (Toronto 1976), 54–84, 195–201; and my chapter 'Underhill the Historian' in 'Frank H. Underhill, Canadian Intellectual' (PH D thesis, York University, 1976), 308–43.
41 Underhill Papers, 6, Underhill to McNaught (copy), 7 May 1943
42 Meikle interview, 1968, 100
43 Underhill Papers, 3, Lewis to Godfrey (copy), 9 June 1944; QUA, George Grube Papers, Lewis to Grube, 14 June 1944 (two different letters on the same day)
44 Underhill Papers, 5, Underhill to de Kiewiet (copy), 7 Feb. 1945; Meikle interview (1968), 147ff; interview with Betty Harfenist
45 Underhill Papers, 3, Underhill to secretary of CIIA (copy), 18 Aug. 1944; Lazarus to Underhill, 1 Sept. 1944; interviews with J.M.S. Careless and Richard Saunders
46 'J.S. Woodsworth.' Speech reproduced in pamphlet form by the Ontario Woodsworth Memorial Foundation of Toronto (nd). Reprinted in *In Search of Canadian Liberalism* (Toronto 1960), 148–63
47 Underhill Papers, 5, Kohns to Underhill, 10 Oct. 1945 and 8 Jan. 1946; 19, Writings 1945 file, Lecture on John Morley at University of Toronto, 1945

CHAPTER 12: LIBERALISM IN THE POSTWAR ERA

1 The discussion of Underhill's teaching is taken from personal interviews with J.M.S. Careless, G.M. Craig, Douglas Fisher, Syd Wise, and Sydney Eisen. See also William Kilbourn, 'The Writings of Canadian History,' in Carl Klinck, ed., *Literary History of Canada: Canadian Literature in English*, vol. II (Toronto 1965), 22–42.
2 Public Archives of Canada [PAC], Frank H. Underhill Papers, MG 30, D 204, vol. 15, Wise to Underhill, 1 Dec. 1969
3 Underhill Papers, 16, Letters of Condolences file, A.O.C. Cole to Mrs F.H. Underhill, 19 Sept. 1971
4 Interview with Douglas Fisher; Meikle interview, 1968, 115ff
5 Underhill Papers, 21, Writings 1956 file, 'Valedictory.' Farewell address on leaving the University of Toronto (rough draft), Jan. 1956
6 'Some Reflections on the Liberal Tradition in Canada,' Canadian Historical Association, *Report*, 1946, 6. Reprinted in *In Search of Canadian Liberalism* (Toronto 1960)
7 Meikle interview, 1968, 113
8 'The Politics of Freedom,' *Canadian Forum* [CF], XXIX, Dec. 1949, 198
9 Much of the information on the early history of Woodsworth House is taken from Ontario Woodsworth Memorial Foundation, *Toward the Future: Shaping an Ideal at Woodsworth House* (Toronto 1944).
10 For a discussion of the CCF's position in the Ontario election of 1945 see Gerald Caplan, *The Dilemma of Canadian Socialism: The CCF in Ontario* (Toronto 1973), 155ff; on the federal election see M. Beck, *Pendulum of Power* (Toronto 1968), 241ff.
11 Queen's University Archives, George Grube Papers, Minutes of the Ontario CCF Steering Committee, 28 July 1945
12 Underhill Papers, 19, Writings 1946 file, 'Socialism and Liberty,' 25 Nov. 1946
13 Underhill Papers, 19, Writings 1947 file. Copies of 'Socialist Professor Turns Turtle.'

Reprinted from *Canadian Statesman*, Bowmanville, Ontario [np nd]; editorial in *Canadian Register* of the Catholic church, 23 Aug. 1947

14 Ibid., 23, Writings 1965 [sic] file. Copy of article 'Socialist Professor Turns Turtle,' with note from F.R. S[cott]: 'You see what use is made of your article. A little more careful wording would surely have made this impossible'; G.M.A. Grube, 'Socialism and Freedom,' CF, XXVII, Sept. 1947, 128–30

15 Ibid., 16, General Correspondence file, newspaper clipping 'Can See "Little Real Difference" between UK Tory-Labour Policies' (np nd); 25, Fabians and Fabianism file, 'Fabianism 60 Years Later,' 25 Oct. 1948

16 Ibid., 12, Loeb to Underhill, 19 Oct. 1948. George Brown of the Department of History at the University of Toronto expressed a similar criticism of Underhill in a letter to Pearson. Brown wrote: 'Our "realists" have made me just as mad as our romantics. I came away from your second lecture with Frank Underhill. We understand each other and I like and admire him – but he is one of my prize examples of a "realist." He has an instinctive distrust of what he feels are idealistic generalizations and he said he didn't realize that you had so much of the idealist in you – that wasn't the word, but I forget exactly how he put it. Then he went on with an amusing bit of self-revelation to say that he had always felt he must curb himself when he had any impulses in the direction of such verbal idealism. You see Frank is a kind of inverted Methodist (!) – a crusader who doesn't want to admit it even to himself. He does a lot of crusading for the unattainable – but distrusts anybody who openly espouses some faith in the same sort of thing.' PAC, L.B. Pearson Papers, Brown to Pearson, 28 Jan. 1942; I am indebted to Robert Bothwell for drawing my attention to this letter.

17 Underhill Papers, 20, Writings 1951 file, 'News Letter' re beginning of *CCF Newsletter*; 'Notes on Current Events,' 1 Oct. 1951; also 'Comments on the First News Letter'

18 For a discussion of the controversy see my article, 'The Ontario Woodsworth House Controversy, 1944–1954,' *Ontario History*, LXXI, March 1979, 17–39.

19 McMaster University Archives, CCF Papers, Woodsworth Memorial Foundation Material, Board of Directors meeting file, 'Minutes of Special Board Meeting of Woodsworth Foundation, Feb. 25, 1952'; 'List of Members – Not Renewing, New Members'

20 Underhill Papers, 9, Woodsworth Foundation file, 'Annual Meeting Reports'

21 Interview with George Tatham

22 'Power Politics in the Ontario C.C.F.,' CF, XXXII, April 1952, 7–8; Andrew Brewin responded to Underhill's article 'Corrrespondence: Woodsworth Foundation.' A. Brewin to editor of the *Canadian Forum*, and Underhill replied, ibid., May 1952, 34–5, 37

23 Interview with Frank Underhill, Feb. 1970; David Lewis wrote: 'In February 1952 I became involved in a conflict which concerned the provincial party and the Ontario Woodsworth Memorial Foundation. Although it was an incident of some importance, it has received much more prominence than it deserves because Frank Underhill wrote a scathing article about it in the *Canadian Forum* of April 1952. This article was full of prejudice and misrepresentation, but because of his reputation, it has been accepted by many as an accurate account.' *The Good Fight: Political Memoirs, 1909–1958* (Toronto 1981), 419

24 Underhill Papers, 13, Underhill to Rothney (copy), 12 July 1961; 12, Bryden to Knowles (copy to Underhill), 23 June 1963; interview with George Tatham. It was

for Underhill a rare personal vindictive comment that revealed the bitter legacy of the Woodsworth House controversy. A year after making this comment, memory of the unpleasant event surfaced again when Underhill received via Stanley Knowles a copy of a letter from Marion Bryden appealing for funds for the Woodsworth House Foundation to offset money stolen by the ex-president of the foundation while acting as solicitor in the sale of the property. 'Definitely not,' Underhill replied. In later life, he remarked in reference to the stolen money: 'It almost made me believe in God.'

25 Meikle interview, 1968, 102ff; Underhill Papers, 5, M. Hicks file, 'List of Blood Donors Who Gave Blood for Prof. Underhill'
26 See, for example, 'u.s. Foreign Policy,' CF, XXVI, Oct. 1946, 150–1.
27 'The Lights Go Out in Czechoslovakia,' CF, XXVIII, April 1948, 1
28 'Korea,' CF, XXX, Aug. 1950, 98
29 S.W. Bradford [Kenneth McNaught], 'The CCF Failure in Foreign Policy,' CF, XXX, Sept. 1950, 127–8; F.H. Underhill, 'Canadian Socialism and World Politics,' ibid., Oct. 1950, 149–51
30 The five articles are 'The Close of an Era: Twenty-five Years of Mr. Mackenzie King,' CF, Sept. 1944; 'Twenty-five Years as Prime Minister,' CF, July 1946; 'Liberalism à la King,' CF, Feb. 1948; 'The End of the King Era,' CF, Sept. 1948; and 'Concerning Mr. King,' CF, Sept. 1950.
31 Underhill Papers, 6, Underhill to McGregor, 29 Oct. 1950
32 PAC, N.A. Robertson Papers, vol. 3B, Robertson to Williams (copy), 30 Oct. 1951. I wish to thank J.L. Granatstein for drawing this letter to my attention.

CHAPTER 13: CURATOR OF THE LIBERAL TRADITION

1 Public Archives of Canada [PAC], Frank H. Underhill Papers, MG 30, D 204, vol. 5, de Kiewiet to Underhill, 3 Feb. 1953; Underhill to de Kiewiet (copy), 14 Feb. 1953
2 Ibid., 20, Writings 1953 file, 'Couchiching Conference.' See also in same file rough draft of a speech 'The Historian in Our Present Age of Anxiety' given 13 Jan. 1953.
3 His Royal Society paper was published in a revised form in the *Canadian Historical Review*, XXXII, Sept. 1951. The following quotations are taken from that article.
4 Underhill Papers, 20, Writings 1955 file, 'R. Flenley,' 3
5 Interview with Donald Creighton
6 Meikle interview, 130
7 Underhill Papers, 3, Creighton to Underhill, 22 Sept. 1955; 2, Brown to Underhill, 24 Oct. 1955; 3, Craig to Underhill, 30 Nov. 1955; 21, Writings 1956 file, 'Dinner List for Frank H. Underhill'
8 Ibid., 21, Writings 1956 file, 'Valedictory' (rough draft), Jan. 1956; 8, Jeanneret to Underhill, 13 Feb. 1956
9 'Eightieth Birthday Speech'
10 PAC, W. Kaye Lamb Papers, MG 35, B 5, vol. 2, Laurier House file, Lamb to Pickersgill (copy), 28 May 1954; Pearson to Pickersgill (copy), 5 Aug. 1955; Underhill to Pearson (copy), 7 Aug. 1955; *Prince Albert Daily Herald*, 'Historian, Laurier House Curator' (nd), copy in Underhill Papers, 20, Writings 1955 file
11 Interview with Kaye Lamb; Meikle interview, 1967, 70
12 Underhill Papers, 13, Hilda Neatby to Underhill, 25 Aug. 1957

13 Ibid., 12, Underhill to Dobbs (copy), 24 Sept. 1958; interview with Betty Harfenist
14 Kaye Lamb Papers, 2, 'Edward Blake's Family,' 30 Sept. 1957; Underhill Papers, 70, Research on Blake file 796, rough draft of chapter 1, 'A New Nationality'; chapter 2, 'Edward Blake – Early Life'; and 'Ireland' (no chapter number indicated)
15 'Edward Blake' in Claude T. Bissell, ed., *Our Living Tradition, Seven Canadians* (Toronto 1957), 18
16 Underhill Papers, 8, Gibson to Underhill, 12 April 1956
17 Ibid., 14, President A.D. Dunton to Underhill, 4 June 1964 and 6 Feb. 1969
18 Ibid., 91, Carleton University file, course outline for Political Science 535 and final examination paper, May 1966; interview with Ruth Underhill
19 'Canada and the North Atlantic Triangle,' *Centennial Review*, fall 1957, reprinted in *In Search of Canadian Liberalism*, 255–62; 'How to Defend Ourselves against the United States,' *Ontario Liberal Review*, XLI, Aug. 1956, 181–3
20 'Prof. Morton's Stern Thesis,' review of *The Canadian Identity* by W.L. Morton in *Winnipeg Free Press*, 7 Oct. 1961; 'Reality Is More American,' ibid., 9 Oct. 1961; W.L. Morton, 'An Author Replies,' ibid., 21 Oct. 1961
21 Underhill's speech, 'The Future of Canadian Political Thought,' was reproduced in the Saskatoon *Star-Phoenix* in serial form: 18, 19, 21, 22 Sept. 1964; and in the *Winnipeg Free Press* in serial form: 28, 29, 30 Sept., 1 Oct. 1964.
22 Arthur Lower, 'Sound of Battles Long Ago,' review of *In Search of Canadian Liberalism* in *Saturday Night*, 10 Dec. 1960
23 Underhill Papers, 10, Underhill to Trotter (copy), 20 Jan. 1963
24 *Images of Confederation*, 1963 Massey Lectures on CBC (1964); see *On Canada: Essays in Honour of Frank H. Underhill*, 135 n3.
25 CBC Archives, 'Conservatism, Liberalism, Socialism: What Do They Mean in Canada?' Distinguished Lecture Series, University of Western Ontario, 10 Oct. 1962. I am indebted to Ramsay Cook for providing me with a typed copy of this speech.
26 CBC Archives, 'What's Left or Right? The Sixties,' TV series, conversation between Senator Grattan O'Leary and Frank Underhill, 9 Nov. 1964
27 'Canadian Liberal Democracy in 1955,' in G.V. Ferguson and F.H. Underhill, *Press and Party in Canada* (Toronto 1955); reprinted in *In Search of Canadian Liberalism* (Toronto 1960), 228–9
28 'The Revival of Conservatism in North America,' *Transactions*, Royal Society of Canada, vol. LII, Series III, 1958, Section II, 18–19
29 'The Winnipeg Declaration of the C.C.F.,' Toronto *Globe and Mail*, 21 Aug. 1956; reprinted in *In Search of Canadian Liberalism*, 243–7
30 Underhill Papers, 12, Underhill to Dobbs of Macmillan Publishing Company (copy), 25 Nov. 1969
31 M. W[estern], 'Unrevised, If Not Quite Unrepented,' review of *In Search of Canadian Liberalism*, in *Winnipeg Free Press*, 17 Dec. 1960; Norman Smith, 'Prof. Frank Underhill's Quiver of Shimmering Arrows,' *Ottawa Journal*, 28 Feb. 1961
32 Underhill Papers, 13, Underhill to Pearson (copy), 22 Nov. 1964
33 Ibid., 20 Jan. 1958; Pearson to Underhill, 11 Feb. 1958
34 L.B. Pearson, *Mike: The Memoirs of the Rt Hon. Lester B. Pearson*, vol. 3 (Toronto 1975), 52; Underhill Papers, 13, Underhill to Sharp (copy), 22 May 1960
35 Underhill Papers, 21, Writings 1960 file, 'After-Luncheon Speech of Frank H. Underhill, Liberal Conference, Kingston,' 10 Sept. 1960, 14

CHAPTER 14: THE APOTHEOSIS OF THE CRITIC

1 'New Canadian Frontier?' review of *Social Purpose for Canada*, ed. by Michael Oliver in *Queen's Quarterly* [QQ], LXIX, summer 1962, 295–6
2 'Politics as a Pilgrim's Progress,' review of *The Anatomy of a Party: The National CCF 1932–61* by Walter Young in *Globe Magazine*, 7 Feb. 1970
3 Public Archives of Canada [PAC], Frank H. Underhill Papers, MG 30, D 204, vol. 24, Writings 1967 file, 'Canadian Intellectuals and Politics' (typed draft of speech), 9
4 'The University and Politics,' QQ, LXVI, summer 1959, 218; reprinted in *In Search of Canadian Liberalism* (Toronto 1960), 263–79
5 Royal Society of Canada, *Proceedings and Transactions*, Series IV, I, 1963, Section II, 64–5
6 Underhill Papers, 24, Writings 1970 file, 'What Then Is the Manitoban, This New Man or This Almost Chosen People' (typed copy of speech); reprinted in serial form in *Toronto Star*, 27 and 28 Oct. 1970; Underhill Papers, 11, Ivo Lambi to Underhill, nd [1971]
7 Ibid., 13, Penlington to Underhill, 14 and 23 Jan. 1970; reviews by Carlyle King in *Saskatchewan History*, XXIV, spring 1971, 76–7; P.B. Waite in *Dalhousie Review*, LI, spring 1971, 113–14; N. Ward, 'Apples for the Teacher,' *Globe Magazine*, 13 March 1971; B. Neatby, *Canadian Historical Review* [CHR], LII, Dec. 1971, 424–5
8 PAC, Sound Archives, F.H. Underhill Collection, interview of F.H. Underhill by Douglas Collins on CBC program, 'Something Else'; CBC 1980 Birthday Tribute
9 Underhill Papers, 24, 26 Nov. 1969 Speech file, 'Report on the Frank Underhill Dinner,' 12 Dec. 1969; rough drafts of his speech; interview with Blair Neatby
10 See note 1, Ch. 1.
11 Underhill Papers, 14, Slater to Underhill, 27 Oct. 1970; 55, Miscellaneous file, 'York,' nd; interview with George Tatham
12 'Obituary for Frank Underhill,' *Globe and Mail*, 17 Sept. 1971
13 King Gordon's 'Eulogy on FHU 1889–1971: Sept. 18, 1971.' I am indebted to King Gordon for a typed copy of his remarks.
14 See Underhill Papers, 16, Letters of Condolences file; Toronto *Star*, 16 Sept. 1971; *Winnipeg Free Press*, 17 Sept. 1971; Blair Neatby, 'Frank Hawkins Underhill,' CHR, LII, Dec. 1971, 480–1; Douglas Fisher, 'The Legacy of Frank Underhill,' Toronto *Telegram*, 20 Sept. 1971
15 *Canadian Forum*, LI, Nov. 1971, 9. In the same commemorative issue are articles by J.F. Parkinson, 'Frank Underhill,' 7–8; F.R. Scott, 'F.H.U. and the Manifesto,' 8–9; and Carl Berger, 'F.H. Underhill and the Tenacity of Liberalism,' 10–13.

Index